PLAYBOY'S
GUIDE TO
ULTIMATE SKIING

(Photo: Vail Associates/Peter Runyon)

PLAYBOY'S GUIDE TO ULTIMATE SKIING

TOM PASSAVANT
and
JAMES R. PETERSEN

PLAYBOY PRESS

NEW YORK

Manufactured in the United States of America.

FIRST EDITION.

Playboy Press / A Division of PEI Books, Inc.

Library of Congress Cataloging in Publication Data

Passavant, Tom.
       Playboy's guide to ultimate skiing.
          1. Ski resorts—United States—Guide-books.
  2. Skis and skiing—United States—Guide-books.
  I. Petersen, James R. II. Playboy. III. Title.
  IV. Title: Guide to ultimate skiing.
  GV854.4.P37   796.93'025'73   81-80399
  ISBN 0-87223-700-1   AACR2

Designed by Tere LoPrete

This book is dedicated to Barbara,
who still thinks that moguls are
fat guys with cigars.

CONTENTS

THE EXPERIENCES

ACKNOWLEDGMENTS

It was a dirty job, but somebody had to do it. We would like to thank our unindicted co-conspirators: Charlie Sopkin at Playboy Press for thinking this was a good idea and Tere LoPrete for helping to make it look that way; Arthur "What Brings You Guys to Town?" Kretchmer and Barry Golson at *Playboy* magazine for letting two of their serfs disappear for weeks on end; Neil Stebbins at *Powder* magazine for guidance above and beyond; Doug Benson for reading this manuscript and for not skiing in the Rockies at the same time we did; John Berg for getting us started on the right foot; Kip Stacy for advice and dissent; Paul Webb and Peggy Ricketts at Alta for being there; Stu Campbell at Heavenly Valley for two days of instruction that allowed us to survive this project; Gloria Reeves and Regina Martin for virtuoso keyboard performances; all of the photographers who were enthusiastic about this book and generous with their files; the manufacturers of Salomon bindings and boots, Rossignol and Dynamic skis, and I.B.M. Selectrics; Mother Nature for two schizophrenic but generally white winters; and a final word of thanks to all the people at all of the resorts who, wittingly or unawares, provided the good times we've tried to recount in these pages.

We thank Rossignol for their help in the distribution of this book.

Fourplay: Jeff Packard plunders a private powder preserve at Park City. (Photos: Pat McDowell)

INTRODUCTION

We envisioned this book as the skier's equivalent to a wine tasting—a gourmet guide to the top twenty-five mountain resorts and the ten ultimate ski experiences. As with a wine tasting, we would provide history and statistics wherever necessary, but we would concentrate on the experience of the event. We wanted to produce a book that would compare favorably with those Sierra Club celebrations of the wilderness, only ours would show the kind of mountains you experience with skis instead of backpacks. The photographs in the book were selected with the same goal in mind. We realized that we had seldom seen photos that showed what a ski area actually looked like. We wanted Ansel Adams on skis.

This book is a consumer guide, a road test of resorts. We don't bury the reader with details—the names of every lodge and pizza parlor or the prices of every conceivable lesson package. Instead, we concentrate on the best each resort has to offer and how the different personalities and flavors of twenty-five ski resorts will affect a skier's vacation. In trying to capture the experience of each place, we interviewed tourists, locals, local legends, marketing people—trying to get an insider's view of the mountain and the resort. We sought out the secret runs, the best days, the best restaurants. The reader should come away feeling like a local, an intimate—someone who has a season's ticket to the best mountains in America. Our favorite question was "What was the best day you ever had on this mountain?" In one sense, we've tried to be like music critics. The book is an anthology of good runs, melodies, and harmonies.

The first part of the book tells you *where* to ski; the second part is a celebration of the different kinds of skiing that are possible, the ultimate experiences. Skiing is a unique sport. Each skier sets his or her own dial, moves at his or her own pace. It's a sport in which even novices can feel like Phil Mahre. There are people doing snowplow turns who are having the best day of their lives. As they learn more about skiing, they encounter new challenges, new ways of having fun: cruising, bumps, trees, skiing the steeps, diving into deep powder, getting air off a gentle mogul or full-blown cliff edge, skiing by helicopter. We have tried to present the entire curriculum and a description of the top places to attend school.

On the other hand, this book has been described as "Abbott and Costello Go Skiing." It was written on chair lifts as we observed behavior we didn't believe existed. It was written at the Formica tables of more chili and cheeseburger cafeterias than our stomachs care to remember, and it was written as we dined elegantly amid white tablecloths and fine china. When people heard that we were being paid to go around the country and sample the mountains they had only heard about, they were respectful, envious. When we set out on this project, our friends told us that the resorts would all start looking alike very quickly. They were wrong. Our travels have left us with clear and distinct images of the most exciting winter vacation destinations in America.

The research for this project took two years. We have skied, tasted, and inspected every single resort of the twenty-five, and a few more that didn't make the cut. In all that time we never had a bad day. Just being alive in such beautiful surroundings, being able to ski at all, no matter what the conditions, was always enough.

Visually, this book is a Sear's catalogue of those ultimate experiences. We contacted the hottest ski photographers in North America and asked them for their best work. Not the commercial, ski-magazine cover photos, but the trophy shots. The great days, brought back alive. A few of the photos have appeared elsewhere, but we thought they deserved an encore. Most are debut discovery photos. We hope they will live for a long time. We know we aren't tired of looking at them, and we can't imagine that ever happening. They are shots to peruse, to dream about, to enter into. Use them to psych yourself up for next year's ski trip. If you have as much fun looking at this book and reading it as we have had putting it together, we've done our jobs.

J.P.

A SKIER'S SURVIVAL GUIDE

NOTES ON LODGING

As mentioned, we have made no attempt to give a complete rundown of available housing. Instead, we've tried to single out lodgings that provide consistent, outstanding quality. We were particularly interested in those special, romantic retreats that can make a ski vacation truly memorable. Although some of these places are very expensive, the vast majority cost about the same as far less desirable lodgings. Information about current rates is easily and quickly available from any travel agent and from the phone numbers listed in each chapter. Better to call and get up-to-date figures rather than have us mislead you with rates that are obsolete before this book is published.

In general, the quality of the housing at most ski areas, particularly in the West, is not very high. Condominiums that cost half a million dollars can have paper-thin walls and closet-sized bedrooms. Even so, there are only a few good alternatives to condos out West (which we have tried to identify), and if there are three or more people in your group, a condominium is practically inevitable. Also, there are far more spectacular three-bedroom and two-bedroom condos than studios or one-bedrooms. If there are just two of you, consider renting the studio end of a multibedroom condo. You'll usually get a kitchen, dining, and living area (you'll have to sleep on the sofa bed, but at least you can curl up in front of the fireplace) for about the same price as a standard hotel room. More and more housing, particularly in the West, is being built on this so-called lockout principle, so that a single condo can be rented as a studio or a one-, two-, or even three-bedroom unit, and the unoccupied bedrooms rented out as standard hotel rooms that open out onto the main hallway. These studio lockouts often represent terrific values. For example, at Vail, you can rent a beautiful, spacious studio in a new wing of the Vail Lodge, complete with a fireplace and wide decks overlooking the lifts, for less money than what a double room costs at the Holiday Inn (about $90 per night at Vail).

Back East, an entirely different attraction exists that is just about nonexistent in the Rockies. New England maintains the tradition of the gracious, old, country inn or ski lodge, and although very few of them are right on the lifts, they offer a unique, sensuous, and almost magical vacation experience. Even the most luxurious Aspen condo somehow pales in the shadow of an old, classic inn, complete with Saint Bernards snoozing in front of the fireplace. The sense of warmth and well-being these inns offer is something no Rocky Mountain resort can match, and the prices at most of the inns we've described are extremely reasonable, especially when you consider that breakfast and dinner are almost always included. For a final bit of advice, we can't urge you too strongly to take the time and the few dollars necessary to call the Central Reservations office of the ski area you're thinking of visiting. Nearly every area has an office staffed by knowledgeable and helpful people. It's just smart tactics to take a minute to write down your needs and preferences in lodging and tell them exactly what you'd like and then listen to their advice. Their goal, after all, is to get you to come back to their area year after year, and if they mislead you about the quality or facilities of a lodge or condo, they've probably lost you and everyone within earshot when you return home.

NOTES ON FOOD

We've tried to list restaurants in this book that have proven themselves over the years, but new places keep popping up every season. Rather than depend on Chamber of Commerce reviews or blurbs in the local Yellow Pages for dining ideas, try asking the saleswoman in the local ski shop where she likes to go for dinner on her birthday. Or ask the shuttle bus driver where he goes on a hot date (it was this method that first tipped us off to Irwin Lodge at Crested Butte and Roget's at Mammoth). The folks who drive the grooming machines usually have ideas about where to catch a few beers and lots of local color after work. Take notes and cross reference them with your companions.

As with lodging, the differences between East and West couldn't be more dramatic. Out in the Rockies, it seems that every ski area has the same two places to eat: a Mexican restaurant, usually called Tres Amigos or La Cantina de Margarita, and the other standard-issue ski-town dining room, which is usually the Steak Pit, except when it's the Mine Shaft. The restaurants never take reservations. This is not to say the food at these places is bad or overpriced. Often they are among the best places in town for dinner. (The Steak Pit at Snowbird and Mi Casa in Breckenridge are two delicious examples.)

If the clichés out West are Mexican and Steakhouse Moderne, the New England byword is "Continental" cuisine. Roast duck and veal in cream sauce are inevitable. For-

tunately, the quality of cooking at the better country inns and top restaurants is truly superb (breakfasts are usually a knockout), and it is our opinion that the skiers who are as dedicated to their palates as they are to their skiing will fare a lot better in Vermont and New Hampshire and Maine than in Colorado or Utah.

No matter where you go to ski, keep in mind the general rule that all smart travelers follow: Eat what the locals eat. For example, you wouldn't journey to the Rocky Mountains to eat fresh fish, unless you're planning to pull trout out of a stream yourself. So stick with what they grow locally, like lamb and beef. If you go to Vermont, don't expect barbecued brisket or grits like Mom makes. Instead, head for the muffins and maple syrup at the breakfast table. Non-meat-eaters obviously should plan a ski vacation very carefully, since Wyoming and Colorado and New Hampshire are not known for their crops of fresh vegetables in February. As for drinking, a ski trip to California obviously will yield a bountiful selection of hard-to-find California wines at very reasonable prices. A choice bottle or two carried back on the plane isn't a bad idea, either.

NOTES ON TRAVEL

Getting to most of the western ski areas mentioned in this book is no piece of cake. Except for Alta, Snowbird, and Park City, all of which are within an hour of the Salt Lake City airport, you can figure on using an entire day to get where you are going. Some areas, like Telluride and Taos, are more accessible from the West Coast than from the Midwest or the East. If there is any single piece of advice we can offer, it is to avoid the Saturday departures-and-arrivals routine that most ski trips are built around, especially if you have to go through Denver's Stapleton Airport, where the Saturday mob scene resembles a Japanese subway car with ski luggage. If you are catching a connecting flight to Aspen or Steamboat or Gunnison or anywhere that requires a change of aircraft, do yourself a favor and claim your bags in Denver and recheck them yourself through to your destination. Arriving in Aspen or Crested Butte while your ski equipment sits in Denver for another day or gets sent to the wrong town is no fun at all. For some reason, the local airlines never seem to have much trouble getting your bags to the right place when you're heading home, but arriving passengers who are connecting up to the ski areas should personally give their bags (yes, we know they're heavy) to the local airline.

Sometimes we have not suggested the fastest way to get somewhere, but rather the most sensible or convenient, or even the most scenic. Our recommendations are based on personal experience and the thoughts of locals at each area who have made the journey hundreds of times. If you have some other route or method in mind, check carefully with the people at the ski area when you call Central Reservations, and do not take anyone's word unless he or she has personally tried and succeeded with that route. Winter weather in the Rockies can be ferocious, and trying to drive over, say, Teton Pass in Wyoming without chains can be suicidal. Along the same lines, pay close attention to the equipment that comes with your rental car. Ski racks are standard out West, but chains are impossible to obtain (even snow tires have to be requested in some places) unless you buy or bring your own.

At some ski areas in the West, a car is necessary, even if management insists it's not. At other ski areas, the local shuttle bus system isn't very helpful, even though management insists it is. We strongly urge you to get a second opinion, based on your own needs, from someone who knows the area well. We have tried to identify each area where a car is truly not needed and have said so in the Transportation sections of the chapters.

The eastern ski areas present less of a problem, since nearly everyone drives to them and, with the possible exceptions of Sugarbush, Sugarloaf, and Waterville Valley, everyone would want a car to drive during a week's stay at any of them. The problem here is that rental cars in New York or Boston seldom come equipped even with snow tires, much less chains. If possible, try to rent a car locally in Vermont or New Hampshire, where snow tires are not considered an unreasonable request.

This book is as accurate as we could make it at publication time, but services are constantly changing at ski areas. It never ceases to amaze us how many people eagerly lay out hundreds of dollars for a ski trip and yet balk at spending five dollars to make a long-distance call to the people at the ski area who can make all the difference between a great vacation and a frustrating week out in the cold. We hope this book helps you with the information and especially the inspiration for the most memorable ski trip of your life.

T.P.

A NOTE ABOUT THE STATISTICS

We have tried to provide a set of uniform figures so that readers can compare some of the most important features of the twenty-five resorts listed in this book. In some instances, however, it was just not possible to obtain every single number we wanted. We have marked those instances with the notation "NA" (not available). We believe that you can gain many interesting and revealing insights by making a chapter-by-chapter comparison of the information. Start with an area that you are familiar with and go to one you'd like to know more about.

The paws that refreshes: This laid-back Telluride pooch knows long skis are in. (Photo: Neil Stebbins)

The powder and the glory: Jon Bezzola dives deep in the Bobbie Burns mountains.
(Photo: Peter Wingle)

THE SKI AREAS

*It's powder time on Westward Ho! as Paul Webb hits a drift head-on at Alta.
(Photo: James R. Petersen)*

1

ALTA, UTAH

ALTA: Best Days

"One day, shortly after I moved to the canyon, I went skiing with Paul Webb and one of the guests at the Rustler Lodge. Paul was showing us some of the secrets of the mountain. We came down the ridge from the Sugarloaf chair. Paul told me to wait below a stand of trees and to watch what happened to the snowdrift between them. He climbed back above the trees, pushed off, and dove into the drift. The snow just exploded—into large chunks of white that disintegrated into flakes, which danced in the sun like diamonds. In the middle of this explosion you could see Paul, grinning. And then his friend did the same thing. You had to be there."

PEGGY RICKETTS

It is an accident of the alphabet that this book begins with the two resorts that define the alpha and omega of the sport for many skiers. Alta offers a total mountain experience; Aspen, a complete resort experience. Everyone knows about Aspen, but a lot of skiers have never heard of Alta. A small but devoted group would like to keep it that way.

Alta's statistics give no real sense of the place. There are five small lodges, about six hundred beds, six chair lifts, a parking lot, and a mountain. The trail map only lists twenty-nine trails. The vertical drop is smaller than most major New England areas. But there is a lot more here than meets the eye. The mountain consists of two wide-open bowls, Albion and Germania, divided by a frighteningly steep central ridge that wanders down from the heights of Mount Baldy. The resort is nestled at the end of a box canyon; the peaks are close in, almost devoid of trees; so white they hurt the eyes. The effect is not claustrophobic, but comforting.

Alta is a ski monastery. There is nothing to do there except ski, eat, and sleep. One of the authors learned to ski at Alta and has been going back every winter for eight years. In all that time he thought *après ski* was French for "Go to sleep." He is one of that small, devoted group mentioned above. When asked about Alta by strangers, he claims the place is a shriveled hunk of rock only rarely covered by snow, inhabited by clumsy skiers with no fashion sense, and run by Mormons who make life miserable for anyone looking for a party. On the other hand, if someone offered him a plot of land at Alta, even one located smack in the middle of an avalanche slide path, he would mortgage his motorcycle and sell the cat to raise the down payment.

Alta has attracted skiers for more than forty years for one reason. Snow. This shriveled hunk of rock up at the top of Little Cottonwood Canyon is actually covered by up to 500 inches of the lightest, driest snow on earth. Storms cross the salt flats of Utah before reaching the Wasatch Range: The moisture is sucked out of each flake of snow. The peaks catch the storms for days at a time and wring them dry. The mountain is different every day. Each snowfall creates a new canvas, a new set of challenges.

Skiers have been coming to this canyon for years, even before the first chair was installed in 1938. The old guard is still around. You can spot them by their twenty-five-year-old skis, leather boots, and long poles. It is equipment that has worked fine for a quarter century. There's no reason to change. If something works, don't fix it. There are skiers who know this mountain in their sleep. They can find their way down Westward Ho in a blizzard, a not uncommon condition. Skiers learn to ski by feel, because half the time they aren't really on a trail anyway. They are floating through powder, dropping down cotton-filled elevator shafts. They are skiing clouds.

Skiers at Alta study the mountain. They take reconnaissance runs in good weather, looking for runs that will work in a blinding snowstorm. They stake out private powder preserves. The mountain rewards curiosity and energy. You have to work for the best parts of the mountain. Skiers who get off the Germania chair can climb a ridge to the Yellow Trail, or hurtle down the high traverse, past the jagged edges of a landscape that seems more at ease with eagles, rams, or angels, for a variety of steep slopes. Alta is raw, ungroomed mountain real estate.

The management does maintain some trails for beginners and intermediates. Albion Basin has one of the best novice trails in the West, comparable to Snowshed at Killington. The Sugarloaf chair and the Germania chair both feed gentle, meandering ego alleys for the cruisers and kamikazes. The upper reaches of the bowls and the ridge dividing them are steeply angled stages where experts can put on a show. The prow of the ridge is the famous High Rustler—1,250 vertical feet of ultimate exposure. Skiers stop at the top, by a dead tree, catch their breath, then launch, while the whole world watches from the Alta Lodge. It is one of the benchmark runs in the West.

If you don't want to go all the way to High Rustler, you can drop off the high traverse

into the equally precipitous runs on the western side of the ridge: Sunspot, Stone Crusher, Race Course, Lone Pine. You can take off your skis and climb through the notch for a crack at Eddie's High Nowhere and Gunsight. When the patrol opens the Yellow Trail, skiers have access to the supersteep runs on the eastern side of the ridge and, after that ordeal, the more gentle meadows of Greeley Bowl. When the obvious slopes are cut with powder eights, the experienced skiers head into Westward Ho for tree skiing. When the patrol opens Devil's Castle, there's a land rush for what may be the best powder on the mountain.

There are bumps on Wildcat, and tree-lined alleys on Westward Ho—the ridge that separates Alta from Snowbird. Something for everyone.

If the mountain always changes, the lodges (and lots of the guests) are constant. The two best places, the Alta Lodge and the Rustler, are full of the same people year after year. Guests are on a first-name basis with the staff. They ski with them. On our second trip to the Rustler we went into the bar and the bartender started mixing our drinks without asking. How did he remember? "Well," he said, "you gave me a lot of reminders last year. About a hundred times a week, I think. You don't forget that kind of thing." Neither do we.

The night life at Alta doesn't change either. There has never been any and there never will be. A night on the town at Alta has all the drama and planning of a prison break. A few desperadoes ricochet down the road a mile to the Tram Bar at Snowbird to pillage, plunder, and burn. If you have anything more in mind than skiing and eating, bypass Alta completely. If you stay awake through dinner, the staff will just figure that you didn't ski enough that day.

Actually, there are times when life at Alta is exciting. Little Cottonwood Canyon is so steep and narrow that avalanches are a constant threat. The five lodges are built on the only five sites that aren't periodically obliterated by thundering walls of snow. Sometimes guests are forbidden to leave their room until the danger passes. Interlodge travel, to say nothing of skiing, is banned. Just before our arrival one year, an avalanche deposited a pickup truck into the kitchen of one of the lodges. The bright side of this threat is that when the road up the canyon is closed, you have Alta all to yourself with 600 other peo-ple and powder so deep you have to pole your way down even the steepest parts of the mountain. Even the richest man cannot pass through a road closed by avalanche signs to enter this kingdom of heaven.

There are one or two anecdotes that might give you some sense of the dedication Alta skiers have. We sat one day at a table at the

Spring snow: Phil Davis cuts tracks in East Greeley Bowl at Alta. (Photo: © 1980 Robert Chamberlain)

midstation restaurant, above the Sugarloaf lift. There were five skiers at the table, each one wearing a knee brace of one sort or another. They were comparing notes, trying to design something that would allow them to ski another season or so. Crazy? Not really.

One of the authors once spent a week at Alta, a few months after his own knee injury. He decided to take it easy. He spotted four senior citizens who were playing follow-the-leader on Mambo, an intermediate trail that runs partway down the middle of Germania bowl under Baldy peak. They had impeccable style, so he tucked in behind them for a free lesson. Before he knew what was happening, his flight leader cut across the Collins face into the trees under the Wildcat chair. They all got on a chair and did the trees again, this time in deep powder through a hidden preserve they knew. Then they found some crud and cut it up, too. At that point his legs gave out and he peeled off. The next day he figured he'd follow a little old lady with silver hair. He introduced himself, and she told him she was just recovering from major surgery. He told her he was relieved to hear that, since he'd skied the day before with some Gray Panther refugees from the 101st Airborne. "Oh," she replied, "you must mean my husband, Gunther, and his friends. They're in training for the Bugaboos." The first trail she took him to was Sunspot, a run off the face of West Rustler that relates to level ground the same way the Washington Monument does. Moral of story: Don't mess with the old guard at Alta. Above all else, experience counts here.

Skiing this mountain is like watching a lover turn in her sleep, covered by a white blanket. It's not always a continuous event but a series of connected discoveries. Chapter and verse. Haiku, seventeen turns long. We could go on with our own choruses about the getting of wisdom at Alta, but that's not the point. We could tell you about skiing in a blinding snowstorm behind a guy in a Hefty garbage bag who led us down through the trees on Westward Ho. We could tell you about the spectacular touring terrain, of the cloudless night when we put on cross-country skis and climbed into Albion Basin, to a cabin chosen for the occasion. We drank some wine, ate cheese, and howled at the full moon. We could tell you eight years of stories, but then, you might tell someone else, and they would tell someone else . . . and really. Enough is enough.

BEST BETS

LODGING

Of the five lodges at Alta—the *Rustler*, the *Alta Lodge*, the *Peruvian*, the *Goldminer's Daughter*, and the *Snowpine Lodge*—the first two are by far the choicest. The Lodge attracts a slightly more sedate crowd than the Rustler, but the accommodations are very nice at both. All the lodges at Alta, especially the Rustler and the Alta Lodge, are booked far in advance, and guests often sign up for the next year when they end their current stay. Alta also has two condominiums, *Hellgate* and *Blackjack*, located on an access road between the resort and Snowbird. Both are fairly modern and are a good bet for larger parties or folks who prefer to cook their own meals. The ultimate in lodging is the Hans Bemer house: It sleeps ten and comes with its own Jacuzzi, sauna, heated driveway, and chef—for about $600 a night. Reservations at 801-742-2040.

DINING

All five lodges operate on plans that include breakfast and dinner in the cost of your room. Again, the *Alta Lodge* and the *Rustler* have the best food, and while it isn't quite the gastronomic extravaganza it's sometimes

Two Alta ski patrolmen autograph a blank canvas below Eddie's High Nowhere. (Photo: Bill Hoffman)

touted as being, the food is hearty and very tasty. Breakfasts, in fact, are tremendous, and include virtually anything you can persuade the kitchen to whip up for you. The only alternatives to dining at your lodge are a steak place, the *Shallow Shaft*, which is across the street from the Alta Lodge, and a trip down the road to Snowbird, with its half-dozen or so dining places. If you have a car (it's hard to imagine why you'd want one), there are several interesting restaurants down in Salt Lake City itself, although the drive back up the canyon at night can be hairy.

TRANSPORTATION

Alta and its neighbor Snowbird are the most accessible major ski areas in America. Alta is exactly 32 miles from the parking lot of the Salt Lake City airport, and shuttle buses and taxis make the run frequently. If you insist on driving, you can rent a car at the airport, and if you really can't wait, there is a helicopter service available from the airport at about $40 a head.

RANDOM NOTES

Most of the discos and cowboy bars that line the canyon road between Alta and Snowbird open when the lifts close, but the casinos and brothels usually don't get going until around 11 P.M. (although they keep going until the lifts open). As if all this weren't enough, there are also bingo games that take place on the lifts, with the numbers being called out over loudspeakers, and nude mud-wrestling contests (ski boots optional) that are weekend highlights . . . just kidding, folks. Après ski is pretty much limited to talking, staring out the window at the snow, and wondering if the road will be open tomorrow. Although some single females have been spotted at Alta, the last one was back in '55, so if you gentlemen have any desire for nighttime action, we'd suggest you plan a vacation in Colorado or the Virgin Islands instead of in Little Cottonwood Canyon. More intrepid skiers can sign up for the Ski the Other Side program, which shows you those hidden places you might not come across on your own or truck just down the road to Snowbird for a day of powder-feeding frenzy courtesy of Wasatch Powderbird Guides, the granddaddy of heli-skiing outfits.

Base elevation	8,550 ft.
Vertical drop	2,000 ft.
Number of lifts	8
Skiable acres	1,300
Average skiers per day	NA
Average snowfall	500 in.
Number of trails	29
Trail breakdown	24% beginner
	46% intermediate
	30% expert

2
ASPEN, COLORADO

BEST DAYS: Aspen

"There's an unofficial rating system for days at Aspen, from 1 to 100. Good snow and a clear day is an 80 or so. Ten inches of new snow and a day warm enough to ski without a jacket is in the mid-90s. Add good friends and some good wine and smoke and you hit 97. Ten inches of new snow, good friends, drink and smoke plus a woman on the chair with you performing carnal acts on your body is 98. If the woman on the chair is Cheryl Tiegs, you have a 99. My average day here is about a 95. That's why I like Aspen."

NAME WITHHELD BY REQUEST

Our Father, who art in Aspen, Hollywood be thy name. . . .

Aspen is where you confront the difference between myth and reality. After all, skiers who have never even heard of Taos, who think of Whistler only as a guy who painted his mother, know all about Aspen: You get there by going to Hollywood and turning left. Once you've arrived, you ski the bumps on Ruthie's all day under warm, clear skies—the famous Colorado "blue fronts." When the lifts close, you meet Mr. or Ms. Right at Little Nell's, head off to the Crystal Palace for dinner and a cabaret show, and end the night with drugs, sex, and rock 'n' roll in somebody's hot tub up in the hills near John Denver's house. After all, isn't Aspen supposed to be a free-fire zone for counterculture types, eco-freaks, and rock stars? Aspen invented drop-dead chic: Credit is given for cash, cocaine, and caviar. Conspicuous consumption has been elevated to an art form. Is this the myth or the reality? We went to Aspen to separate the two and came back confused.

On the one hand we found a real, honest-to-goodness, expensive and very charming town with a permanent population of about 13,000 citizens. People actually live here who do not ski or take drugs. They are shopkeepers, concerned about schools, zoning, and traffic problems. They have come here for the mountains, the characters, the setting. What other skiers sample for seven days and six nights, they inhabit all year round, and they work for it. Gone from this scene is the legendary ski bum who could open his wallet and tell you his life story by the changes in his photos on ten years of accumulated season's passes for the ski lifts. All these earnest entrepreneurs make Aspen a wonderful place to visit even if you never get near a chair lift and just spend your time eating, browsing, and people-watching. We ran into a doctor from Atlanta who comes to Aspen for two weeks every December just to do his Christmas shopping. If you do ski, there are four separate mountains (Ajax, the town slope, plus Aspen Highlands, Buttermilk, and Snowmass, all of which are a short bus ride away) with a total of over 113 miles of ski trails that are covered by 250 inches of dry, light powder

each year. The average daytime temperature here in winter is 32 degrees Fahrenheit. These attractions are real, not myths. We are certain of them.

We are also certain that two of the first sights we saw when we arrived in Aspen, aside from the line of Lear Jets double-parked at the airport, were a pair of heartbreakingly beautiful women climbing out of a jeep in front of our lodge. Each one wore an endangered species on her back, with two extras over each arm. They looked like they had been fur trapping for six months. Our host explained, "Oh, that's my first wife and my soon-to-be ex-wife number two." Current live-in number three, maybe the most appealing of the lot, frowned but did not complain.

Later that day we spied a sparkling green Bentley parked in the local Husky gas station, which is not unusual in Aspen except that this Bentley had white-sidewall snow tires. It was very late by the time we had dinner that night, but we are pretty sure that the silver-haired matron seated at the next table turned to her dinner companion and complained, "You know, our maid stole the best dope we ever had." And so to bed.

The next day we walked over to the lifts on Ajax, the big ski mountain that spills right down into the streets of town, and rode up into the cold air above a mountain that has been described as shaped like a giant molar tooth—two ridges with a gully running down the middle. These ridges are where you find the trails that made Aspen famous, runs with power, elegance, continuity, and exposure (the gullies tend to be overcrowded demolition derbies with names like Grand Junction and Kleenex Corner—where you wipe out, get it?). Ajax has wonderful expert skiing up on these ridges, down the bumps and trees and steeps, but it has little of interest for intermediates except for the vastly overrated Ruthie's Run. Ruthie's wanders down some 2,500 vertical feet over its 1½-mile length. The average grade is 17 degrees. This is the

stuff of legends? There is nothing at all for beginners here. Nonexperts are much better off at Highlands, which has some spectacular intermediate terrain, or Buttermilk, which is an entire mountain ideal for beginners, and especially at Snowmass, which we discuss in its own chapter. Experts back on Ajax still have to cope with a lift system that occasionally takes you sideways or in some other peculiar direction besides up. Ajax skis a lot shorter than its 3,300 vertical feet would indicate, but when the snow is light and fresh it is a very challenging mountain. For the toughest run, try International to Silver Queen to Elevator Shaft (with its 42-degree pitch). Sometimes you get the elevator and sometimes you get the shaft.

On perfect days, or whenever the spirit moves them, a local, unofficial ski club gathers at the top of the ridge of Bell, the east side of the molar, and, like fighter planes peeling off of formation, the club members sweep through the bumps playing follow-the-leader. They hit the smoother runs in the gully and synchronize Astraltunes and cruise, skiing in each other's tracks like ice skaters doing school figures. Riding the last chair of the day, they can make out their groove— it catches in the setting sun and glistens, brighter than the random tracks of the crowd. When we asked one member how you join this club, he said, "The only requirement is keeping up." If there is a motto for Aspen, this is it.

On another day we took the shuttle over to Aspen Highlands. Highlands is the only area of the four that is not owned by Twentieth-Century-Fox, the film company that bought Aspen Ski Corp. with the profits from *Star Wars*. Highlands has its own lift ticket and a separate and justly famous ski school plus its own loyal crowd (but just a couple of lodges and no night life). A week spent learning to ski here may be a better investment than Krugerrands. The instructors make a point of taking beginners up to the top to enjoy the

Stairway to Heaven: Sitting pretty at Aspen Highlands; beyond are the Maroon Bells. (Photo: © 1979 David Brownell. All rights reserved.)

spectacular view back into the Maroon Bells. The school also presents noontime lectures at the midstation cafeteria for everyone taking lessons. On Fridays there is a freestyle contest on Floradora, open to anyone who wants to entertain the skiers lounging on the sundeck below. When conditions permit, the ski patrol members jump 50 feet over the deck of the Cloud Nine picnic cabin patio trailing a toboggan that may or may not contain an injured skier. "Fly the friendly skies at Highlands" is the message. The area works hard to keep its crowd, and it succeeds. Highlands also has the steepest skiing in Aspen, over in the Steeplechase section, which features 50-degree slopes and lots of trees. After a couple of sudden-death descents you may need a week in intensive care or an evening at the Jerome bar.

It used to be that after a day of skiing in Aspen people would sit around and talk about drugs, sex, and the carved turn. Now they talk about drugs, sex, and real estate deals. Escrow. Mortgage rates. Aspen is like a poker game where someone has just raised the table stakes to an astronomical sum in order to drive out the amateurs. The game is the same, only it costs a lot more. There are still a lot of good skiers here, but now they are probably good rich skiers. You're never sure if you are dealing with a vacationer from back East who has saved up all year for this trip or with a trust-fund refugee who lives here because he or she likes the company of other rich folks. You'd best play it safe and always assume the latter. Don't, for example, be surprised when the woman who works as a hostess at the airport tells you that she just sold her house for $350,000 or that her friend, who is *really* rich, just landed a job flipping hamburgers at the Highlands cafeteria. As we've noted, most of the locals must work for a living, and they are generally competent and industrious. They have to be. The fast town of legend belongs to the

eighteen-year-old waitress away from home for the first time, and to the superrich, who drop in for two months before moving on to the islands (any islands). The locals are left to deal with the rich Texan who, when he found out he couldn't rent a four-wheel drive vehicle in town, muttered darkly about turning around and going home, except that he'd already send his pilot back to Lubbock with the plane. The story goes that he then went out and bought his own jeep on the spot and found someone in town willing to drive it back to the ranch when he was finished with it. As we were saying, we kept trying to separate the myths from the realities of Aspen, but every time we stood alone in a lift line and yelled out "Single," someone took it as a proposition. After a week or so in Aspen, we stopped worrying about these distinctions and finished our Christmas shopping.

BEST BETS

LODGING

Aspen lodgings run from small inns where personality is the most important product to fabulously expensive private homes and condos that can cost as much as $1,200 a night (plus lift tickets). The vast majority, however, are industrial-strength condominiums, undistinguished $500,000 accommodations that give less value for your money than at many other ski areas, so you must pick and choose carefully.

At the very top are the private homes that dot the nearby hills, and include extras like Jacuzzi tubs, exercise rooms, and private security guards at the gates of the subdivision. Back down closer to earth are several very fine lodges and condos in Aspen proper, of which our absolute top choice is the brand new *Aspen Ski Lodge*, maybe the most sen-

Run silent, run steep: Peter Hutter approaches free fall above Dipsy Bowl. (Photo: © 1980 Grafton M. Smith)

suous and most tasteful snuggery in all ski country. Every room here is gorgeous, but we are especially partial to the suite with the oversize Jacuzzi that nestles under a bronze skylight in the middle of the living room. The *Molly Gibson Lodge* has tasteful rooms and a very pleasant but not overbearing communal atmosphere. Among the many condos in town we prefer the elegant *Mountain Queen*, which is right by Lift 1A; the *Gant*, with its small outdoor pools; and the *Aspen Alps*, a spacious, ideally located spot that nurtures a slightly older, more affluent crowd. Aspen Central Reservations (303-925-9000) has a very helpful brochure that includes ratings of many local places done by the Rand McNally Travel Research Center. ACR can answer questions about most of the local accommodations and usually book you into one of their member lodges with one phone call.

DINING

Most lodges in Aspen have the local restaurant guide—a wooden box filled with menus from some of the one hundred or so eating establishments in town. You could spend a week here doing nothing but eating and making dinner reservations. Perhaps the most appealing places to spend an evening are the *Crystal Palace* and the *Parlour Car*. The former offers a full-length musical revue with your dinner. The waiters and waitresses who serve you take to the stage to present one of the best cabaret shows west of Broadway. The Parlour Car is an elegant old railroad car serving delicious food in a very private, very romantic setting. Other long-time favorites that deliver consistently good food are the *Golden Horn* and *Guido's* for Continental and Swiss dishes, *Galena Street East* and the *Charthouse* for beef, and *Arthur's* for Chinese food (even Barbra Streisand has to wait for a table at Arthur's). Lunch and dinner at the *Ute City Banque* are deservedly very popular, and the *Copper Street Pier* is a local favorite and best buy. Carboholics should also be aware of the fresh pastries and doughnuts at *Little Cliff's* bakery

Rocky Mountain Mass Transit: At night, the Drunk Run bus collects revelers. (Photo: David Brownell)

and should not miss the fresh, hot croissants at the Aspen airport every morning.

TRANSPORTATION

Most skiers fly to Aspen on either Rocky Mountain or Aspen Airways from Denver. In the old days, partygoers would take short hops over the mountains on these flights just so they could suck on the oxygen tubes and clear up their hangovers. Nowadays things are different, and unless you love mob scenes, you should avoid flying up to Aspen on Saturdays. You can get to Aspen by bus or car, but cars aren't really necessary in town unless you are staying in some remote location. The local free shuttle during the day gets you to the outlying ski areas, and the Pitkin County bus is effective at night.

RANDOM NOTES

Those legendary Aspen hangouts really do exist, except for the Red Onion, which is a shuttered dead onion at present. The *Paragon* and *Andre's* are still four-alarm discos packed to the rafters every night, and *Little Nell's* and the bar of the *Hotel Jerome* are quieter but still lively. The basement lounge in the Jerome, *Richard's*, has been booking some solid acts. The *Tippler* has recently become a star attraction with its fresh oyster bar. For even more local cowboy color, try the *Public House*, a subterranean hangout known as the Pub. Aspen has seen a marked decline in live entertainment lately because of the high cost of importing bands. The famous Gretl's restaurant up on Ajax is now *Bonnie's*, and both Gretl and her famous strudel are gone. Powder tours of the proposed Little Annie's ski area on the back side of Ajax are available if you get tired of the other hundred miles of Aspen trails. The Ashcroft Touring Center has exquisite cross-country skiing around an old ghost town and night excursions to Pine Creek Cookhouse, but the skiing is better than the food at the latter. You should also know about the network of six ski-touring huts operated by Fred Braun of Aspen, which are wonderful for longer excursions into the back country. You can write him (send S.A.S.E.) at 702 West Main St., Aspen, CO 81611, or call 303-925-7162. We really can't tell you if Aspen is as mellow as everyone says, but the solar-heated airport and the ubiquitous Mellow Yellow taxis certainly make it seem that way.

	Aspen Mountain	Buttermilk/Tiehack	Aspen Highlands
Base elevation	7,912 ft.	7,840 ft.	8,000 ft.
Vertical drop	3,300 ft.	2,000 ft.	3,800 ft.
Number of lifts	7	5	8
Skiable acres	620	422	425
Average skiers per day	2,000	2,000	1,675
Average snowfall	300 in.	200 in.	250 in.
Number of trails	57	43	60
Trail breakdown	25% intermediate	50% beginner	25% beginner
	75% expert	31% intermediate	50% intermediate
		19% expert	25% expert

3
BANFF, ALBERTA, CANADA

BEST DAYS : Banff

"It was a Monday at Norquay. I was the first down Lone Pine, a steep, steep bump run with two feet of new snow and plenty of sunshine on it. I was with a ski patrolman and wanted to get some photos. I told Peter I'd go first and almost didn't stop. Snow in the face on every turn! From that one roll of film I got two brochure covers, one poster, one magazine cover, and one shot that hangs in the Mount Norquay Lodge. That was memorable run number one for me."

RON ADLINGTON

When we first read Stephen King's *The Shining*—a book about a haunted turn-of-the-century hotel in the mountains—we immediately thought of the Banff Springs Hotel. Most ads for Banff show a picture of this remarkable stone fortress of turrets and towers rising out of a carpet of evergreens. There are no skiers in the picture, no lifts or trails—only the hotel. Just the notion of old-world elegance and romance inspired by this Scottish-baronial castle set in the middle of a virgin forest is enough to draw visitors all year round. Everyone should stay in a place like the Banff Springs Hotel at least once just to wander through the endless hallways lined with tapestries and antique furnishings and suits of armor. Banff was originally a stopping point along the Canadian Pacific Railroad. Wealthy people pulled their private railroad cars off on a siding and indulged in the sparkling air. It wasn't until the 1930s that people began coming here in the winter to ski. Nowadays the down-suited vacationers in the lobby of the Banff Springs Hotel look a bit out of place, seemingly at odds with the ghosts of the past, the robber barons and railroad magnates who strolled these corridors.

No matter how jarring ski boots look in the hotel lobby, skiers belong in Banff. In the 38-mile stretch of Trans-Canada Highway between Lake Louise and the town of Banff proper are three eminently skiable mountains with more variety, more challenge, than any single resort in the Rockies.

In a sprawling way, Banff is Canada's answer to Aspen. Mount Norquay, which is located right on the edge of the town of Banff, is a single-ridge mountain like Aspen Highlands, only steeper. It features a narrow wall of bump runs that seem to tumble directly into downtown Banff. Mind you, Norquay does have a patch of beginner terrain off to one side of the steep stuff, but hardly anyone seems to notice. The locals love Norquay. They have the mountain to themselves much of the time. Somehow, most out-of-towners do not consider assault and battery in a mogul field to be a jolly way to spend their holidays. Every year there is a contest on Norquay to see who can make the most runs down Lone Pine in a day—a 1,300-foot

Ricochet romance: Stu Campbell lifts off from a ridge at Lake Louise. (Photo: Ron Adlington)

demolition derby for iron-legged youths. The winner, assuming he or she lives, gets a free week of helicopter skiing. Losers get a set of kneecaps that vibrate like cymbals for a month.

Sunshine Village is akin to Buttermilk: a wide-open expanse of novice and intermediate terrain with a touch of expert stuff. The resort is perched on the edge of a broad plateau. There are no real trails, just rolling hills and a few steep, heart-stopping dropoffs. The steeps come in handy when it snows. Sunshine is a natural snow pocket that traps storms and collects ransoms of powder. Sunshine, which is located 11 miles west of Banff, is the only resort we know of where you have to take a gondola (a sixteen-minute ride at that) from the parking lot up to the base lodge. It's a great time to catch a few extra winks of sleep in the morning. At the bar in the base lodge, the band stops its afternoon set to announce the last gondola down to the parking lot for those who aren't staying up at the inn (the only place to bed down at the lifts) and who are in no condition to ski down to the parking lot.

The third area, Lake Louise, is 35 miles west of Banff. It would be comparable to Ajax Mountain at Aspen if Ajax were as massive and complex as, say, Taos. It is among the largest, most varied mountains in North America—offering a stunning array of steeps, bowls, trees, cruises, bumps, and climbs scattered over three separate peaks. Getting lost here is no problem. The chair lifts shoot off in all directions, like random freeways to the sky. The area has a group of volunteer guides called "Friends of Louise" who take first-timers around the mountain, a much-needed and appreciated service. The entire south face of the mountain is a network of intermediate and expert trails. One trail over here, with the unambiguous name of Men's Downhill, is the spawning ground of the Canadian National Ski Team—a group known affectionately as the Kamikaze Kids. Non-

kamikazes can still take the T-bar up to the summit and drop over the back side to a couple of steep chutes not unlike the Stauffenberg Chutes at Taos. When the surf's up, there are also some superb powder shots back here as well. The only drawback is that to get back to the top one has to circle all the way around the mountain. If Sunshine is for families and Norquay for hot-doggers, Lake Louise seems to be favored by lone-wolf ski instructor types whose idea of a good time is to climb to the top of a nearly vertical chute, step into a pair of 223s, and take the thing in a tuck, while Terrible Ted, the local fed, sits at the bottom with a radar gun and calls out terminal velocities. Lake Louise is also a base for back-country skiers who take the lift, then climb and traverse to the adjacent ridges. There are no enforced boundaries. The only limits seem to be guts and energy.

When it comes to night life, a skier would never mistake Banff for Aspen, but there are a lot more bars and restaurants than you might expect for a town that seems as downright healthy as this one. At night and on weekends the town jumps, at least to the extent that the provincial liquor laws will allow. Banff is considered a suburb of Calgary, 77 miles away, and on weekends the town's population doubles. Even so, things are always informal and friendly. On St. Domini Day (named after a locally popular jug wine) everyone on the mountain indulges. Skiers hold impromptu kissing slaloms and stage races at the drop of a snowflake. Canada hasn't encountered the legal and insurance hassles that have sanitized American ski resorts. The Canadians have a very relaxed attitude about the dangers of the sport and role of the government in protecting you from yourself. Risking your life is considered a legitimate use of park land. Freestyle skiing is encouraged. You'll find madmen doing inverted aerials in plain sight of impressionable tourists. At Sunshine we climbed to something called Delirium Dive. We lowered our-

Cross-country skiers kick and glide in the shadow of Victoria Glacier near Banff.
(Photo: Ron Adlington)

selves down a cliff face holding on to a rope, put on our skis, and made a few supremely critical turns down a face as steep as the Sears Tower. At the bottom of this face was a cliff, the sort of place where you confront the true definition of extreme skiing: If you fall, you die.

Sometimes as you are skimming down a slope in the Banff area it occurs to you that there is no reason to be on one particular mountain when all those other peaks are beckoning in the distance. The Continental Divide cuts through Banff National Park like the upturned blade of a ripsaw. As far as the eye can see in any direction is ridge after ridge of primal rock. An ocean of mountains and glaciers topped by whitecaps of snow. The view from the top of Norquay or Louise or Sunshine is so intimidating, so ancient, and at the same time so raw and youthful, that the visitor begins to wonder how this place got to be this way. The local bookstore in Banff offers the complete mountain library for advanced study of the landscape. There are books on avalanches, glaciers, and mountain formation. They are filled with words like *syncline* and *anticline* and *fault blocks*— just the thing for those who think that words can tame the wilderness. When words fail, the mountains still bristle with an energy that is visceral. It flows from your eyes to your thighs by way of your heart.

The early skiers who came to Banff on the railroad toured these mountains on cross-country skis. Today, their descendants take full advantage of the 2,500 square miles of parkland. Banff is not a destination but a starting point, a trailhead. From here the whole world opens up. Canadian Mountain Holidays offers one-day jaunts into the Bugaboos via helicopter, and the Club Ski program will get you ready for this ultimate ski adventure with a one-day special seminar called Powder, Bumps, and Bushes. We recommend it. For cross-country explorers there is the trek to Skoki Lodge 11 kilometers beyond the lifts of Lake Louise. This is skiing the way it used to be, another shining adventure at Banff.

BEST BETS

LODGING

The *Banff Springs Hotel* is not quite centrally located, being one mile from the center of town, but it is a center of activity all to itself, with every imaginable amenity and facility. Just remember that while it is a truly grand hotel, the individual rooms are not the last word in luxury, although they are comfortable and clean. If you want to stay right in Banff near the bars and nightspots, the *Banff Park Lodge* will do nicely. About one mile from the town center is the brand-new *Inns of the Park*, a large hotel like the Lodge that has a shuttle bus stop for both day and night getting around. Up at Sunshine is the *Sunshine Village Inn*, a modern, ninety-room lodge right on the slopes. The gondola does run a few times at night for guests who want to rumble down into Banff. Also, check to see if the well-known *Chateau Lake Louise* is open for winter business. This popular spot in Lake Louise Village has been undergoing renovation and should be open for the 1982 season. There is no one central reservation number to call in Banff, and we suggest you either contact the airline that is flying you into Calgary (most likely Air Canada, CP Air, or Western) or call Club Ski (403-762-4561) to book any package plans. Club Ski is an intelligently designed weekly package of ski activities: a sort of Club Med without bead necklaces or pretension, and is recommended. Banff Reservation Service (403-762-4722) will book hotels for a fee, and for plenty of info about everything to see and do, call the Banff Chamber of Commerce at 403-762-3777.

Crazy Canucks: Skiers at Sunshine are known for their exuberance, if not their control. (Photo: Simon)

DINING

Banff is not exactly a hotbed of gastronomy, but you can eat fairly well in the three dozen or so restaurants and cafés in the area. The nicest part is that dinners are very reasonably priced, especially for Americans, who enjoy a favorable exchange rate. The *Banff Springs Hotel* has a number of dining rooms, and you should make a point to attend when they are serving one of their popular buffets. *Ticino's* is a good Swiss/Italian place in town, and the *Post Hotel* is even better, serving excellent Swiss fare. *Melissa's Missteak* is a good bet for beef, as is *Bumpers*, which specializes in prime rib, and the *Caboose*, which, not surprisingly, is located right in the Banff train depo. *El Toro's* has Greek food. Finally, *Le Beaujolais* is the one delicious exception to the reasonable-prices rule in Banff. It is French, expensive, and generally regarded as the best in town.

Transportation

Calgary is the gateway to Banff, 77 miles away down the Trans-Canada Highway. From there, rent a car or take a bus from Brewster Bus Service. Be sure to ask for a "winterized" car with ski rack and chains. In town, a shuttle bus runs between the major hotels and the ski areas during the day. At night, however, the Happy Bus runs only around the town of Banff, so if you are staying in the boonies you'll need a car to get around. The car will come in handy for one special treat: the stunning drive from Banff to Jasper. This day-long trip winds through some of the most spectacular real estate in North America, and in the winter you have it all to yourself.

Random Notes

Banff is definitely not a boogie town, but they don't roll up the sidewalks at 6:30 either. If you have to have loud noise, try the *Great Divide* in the Cascade Hotel downtown. *Silver City* has a country-and-western band, and in the evening *Melissa's Missteak* has a lively bar with lots of singles action. *Bumpers* shows ski movies between the entertainers' sets. If you're wondering where the springs are, they're right up at the edge of town. Upper Hot Springs' warm sulfur pool is great for soaking, and the steam room will stew some life back into your tired bones. Helicopter skiing by the day is available out of Radium or Golden. The neatest thing to do at night is to sign up for an outdoor western barbecue that you reach via an old horse-drawn wagon. The menu is roast beef and beans and the music is C&W brought to you by some locals in snowmobile suits. You can sign up at the Banff Springs Hotel. If you're dying to know about how those mountains got there, pick up a copy of *Banff National Park* by D. M. Baird at a local bookstore. Finally, there are nearly unlimited amounts of cross-country skiing available in the Banff area, and you should always sign in with the park warden before heading out of town.

	Mt. Norquay	Sunshine	Lake Louise
Average skiers per day	10,000 (weekends) 4,500 (weekdays)		
Base elevation	5,700 ft.	7,200 ft.	5,400 ft.
Vertical drop	1,300 ft.	1,820 ft.	3,250 ft.
Number of lifts	6	9	8
Skiable acres	300	8,160	10,880
Average snowfall	130 in.	400 in.	185 in.
Number of trails	15	22	33
Trail breakdown	25% beginner 45% intermediate 30% expert	40% beginner 33% intermediate 27% expert	24% beginner 32% intermediate 44% expert

4
CRESTED BUTTE, COLORADO

BEST DAYS : Crested Butte

I spent my last day at Crested Butte skiing with an Astraltune, listening to the Doobie Brothers and Earth, Wind, and Fire. It was like having rockets on my feet. My last run was to Pablo Cruise's "A Place in the Sun." It all hit me: what skiing gave me, what Crested Butte gave me. It filled me up so much I cried."

JOHN BERG

Crested Butte is a ski resort with multiple personalities, but its overall impact is to give schizophrenia a good name. Consider the differences between the ski area at the base of Crested Butte mountain and the town, three miles down the road, that took the mountain's name. Crested Butte, Colorado, population 1,200, is a Victorian gem, an old silver mining town that has been designated a National Historic District. In contrast, the ski village at the base of the slopes is a cluster of modern condominiums, shops, and restaurants. The town and the village are linked by a shuttle bus that is closer to a time machine, ferrying visitors from the twentieth-century resort to the nineteenth-century stage set of a town. Both sites are nestled in a broad valley surrounded by jagged, 12,000-foot peaks. Crested Butte mountain dominates this splendid view no matter where you stand, and lives up to its name: It's a tilted butte with a distinctive crest that resembles a Tastee-Freeze vanilla cone with a lick curling off its top.

While the ski village is shiny and bustling, there is not a single neon sign anywhere in town. Gas streetlights line the main thoroughfare. The local version of air pollution is caused by too much wood smoke lingering above the valley floor. On Sunday mornings in town no one makes loud noises or honks a horn or engages in a domestic dispute. A minor disagreement with your lover could rouse half the citizenry. It's a kind of gentlemen's agreement—on Saturday night the whole town pulls the pin and goes out of control. On Sundays it recovers slowly. Up the road the lifts may start moving by 9 A.M., but hardly anyone is astir at that hour along Elk Avenue.

The townsfolk are largely professional eccentrics, bull goose loonies, and refugees from Aspen. After being there three days you can walk into the Wooden Nickel or the Grubstake Saloon and recognize most of them. Crested Butte is the home of the Ski to Die Club, of roller racquetball, and the Miss Grubstake Pageant. The accepted way to order another drink in a bar is to yell out "Nurse!"

One night we found ourselves surrounded by locals at one of the several splendid restaurants in town. Crisp table linen, candles,

Crested Butte at sunrise. This is as quiet as it gets along Elk Avenue. (Photo: John Berg)

crystal, the works. At the end of the meal a woman asked the waitress for a clean white plate. While the waitress poured coffee the woman chopped up a gram of coke on the plate and passed it around the table. We thought we had died and gone to Hollywood. The next day we found ourselves sharing the Silver Queen chair with two of the many cross-country skiers who zoom along Crested Butte's downhill trails. The chair lift broke. We were 100 feet above the ground. The cross-country skiers shouted to each other, "You want to get out here?" Turns out that they didn't trust modern machinery, and carried complete evacuation kits in their back-

packs. They decided to be good hosts and stay with us. One guy filled a pipe with mari-juana, then asked his partner in the lead chair for a match. "I have a match. Why don't you pass the pipe up here?" came the reply. "No, I have the pipe, why don't you pass the matches back here?" the first in-sisted. A voice interrupted from the chair be-hind us: "I have a pipe and a match. Why don't you come back here?" We asked who the guy in back was. Our two guides looked over their shoulders and calmly remarked, "The town sheriff." We asked if we could borrow the evacuation kits.

Crested Butte is a frontier town. It is also

quite possibly our favorite ski area, the most entertaining place we have visited. This opinion is shared by the 80 percent of skiers who return to Crested Butte after their first visit. The place builds loyalty, even fanaticism, especially among the Atlantans and Texans who flock here.

The ski mountain that inspires these feelings is a 2,100-foot layer cake. The totals seem ordinary enough: eight lifts and forty trails covering 350 acres of groomed skiing. This is hardly larger than most New England ski areas, and about one tenth the size of places like Whistler and Jackson Hole. What makes the area a bonanza is not quantity but quality. Crested Butte is buried beneath 30 feet of superb, light Colorado powder every year and the snow covers trails that are perfect for all levels of skiing. Beginners, for example, ski the wide, rolling bottom layer of the cake, on runs like the gentle Houston or the broad stairsteps of Roller Coaster. Intermediates have the entire north side of the mountain to frolic on, a playground of bumps, glades and powder, all in manageable bites in the middle layer of the cake. From the top of the Paradise chair intermediates can dive into Paradise Bowl, a wide-open amphitheater of powder that has some easy glade skiing through tall pines near the bottom. It's all a cruiser's paradise, where Astraltunes and Sony Walkmans are considered essential accessories. One day we watched a lone skier pause at the top of Floresta, humming off-key accompaniment to the music in his earphones. We tried to play "Name That Tune." As he pushed off and started carving turns through the moguls to the beat of the music, we decided that he was listening to either "Surfin' Safari" or "Little Deuce Coupe."

The uppermost reaches of Crested Butte mountain, the parts beyond Paradise Bowl, are an expert's delight. Forest, Peel, North Face, and Glades are steep, gladed powder pockets marked with chutes and natural hazards (like rocks and cliffs). There are at least another 300 acres of prime-time powder up here. Other sections, such as Headwall,

Phoenix Bowl, Spellbound, and the notorious Banana Chute, are part of the Outer Limits program and accessible only with a guide, so check with the ski patrol before heading above and beyond.

Another side of Crested Butte's split personality becomes obvious when you see how many people here are sliding along the downhill trails on cross-country ski equipment. The locals here have reinvented and popularized the telemark turn, an old and previously forgotten maneuver for controlling speed and direction on steeper terrain. We tried to learn Telemark turns and decided they should be renamed prayer turns. You go down on one knee and implore the Lord to please make these skis turn.

These born-again Nordic skiers believe that the person, not the equipment, makes the difference. They think that paying attention, learning to listen to the mountain yourself without using your equipment as a chauffeur, is the way skiing is supposed to be done. (The joke we heard in Crested Butte was about the alpine skier who was so dependent on his equipment that he always skied with a caddy. At the top of each slope they would consult: "I think I should try the Olin Mark VIs with the bindings set loose." "Well, are you sure you don't want the K2-710s?") These intrepid skiers have managed to carry their notion to its logical conclusion by instituting an annual race at Crested Butte, the Al Johnson Memorial for Nordic No-Minds. Contestants climb up into the steep headwall of North Face and throw themselves off down through the trees. What starts out as a slightly twisted cross-country race quickly becomes a full-tilt, ass-over-teacup crash down the most serious terrain on the mountain. First one across the finish line—airborne, head over heels, or however—wins the race. Last year, out of forty-five starters, only four finished without crashing.

Crested Butte made us reconsider our standards for judging a destination resort. What are the minimum daily requirements for a good time? There are certainly larger, more accessible ski areas than Crested Butte, but hardly any resort exists where you'll have more fun.

BEST BETS

LODGING

The best accommodations are concentrated up at the mountain, while the town of Crested Butte, three miles down the valley, has a lock on the top spots to eat. There is a lot of construction going on here, and some very nice new condos are within walking distance of the slopes. Our top choice for comfort and location is *Crested Mountain Condos*, a luxurious installation with Jacuzzi tubs right on the slope. Right behind it is the *Buttes*, and *Wood Creek* and *Evergreen* condos are slightly farther away but still within walking distance. *Outrun* and the *Three Seasons* are both at the far end of the parking lot, about 300 yards from the lifts. The former features some units with beautiful stone fireplaces, and the latter functions as both a condo and a hotel. The *Crested Butte Lodge* is the best straight hotel, being freshly renovated and located right in the center of all the action. Central Reservations at Crested Butte (303-349-6601) handles all of the above listings.

DINING

Crested Butte probably has more fine restaurants per capita than any town in the country. Proof of this comes in the form of a series of dinners at *Le Bosquet, Soupçon,* and *Slogar's,* and the fastest way to start an argument in town is to ask locals which one is best. Book far in advance for all three, and for the weekend brunch at *Penelope's,* which is pleasant almost to the point of sensory overload, especially when it takes place in the glass-roofed back room amid a riot of

hanging plants and bougainvillaea. Our last meal there began with fresh peach daiquiris, warm homemade blueberry coffee cake, and then some elaborate egg dishes and more daiquiris. At 9,600 feet the whole thing was intoxicating. Other good bets include the *Stargazer Café,* the *Vineyard,* and, back up at the mountain, *Jeremiah's* and the *Alpenhof.*

TRANSPORTATION

Crested Butte is 230 miles west of Denver, 30 miles north of Gunnison, and just 18 miles (as the crow flies) over Pearl Pass from Aspen. It is not exactly on the beaten path, so the best plan here is to call Central Reservations and discuss the best routing when you book your room. Your best bet is a flight into either Grand Junction or Gunnison, and then a bus trip to town. There are a few direct flights from Denver daily on tiny Colorado Air, a spectacular ride that is not for the faint-hearted. They also fly over from Aspen. Driving is probably more trouble than it is worth, since the roads are tricky and cars are not needed to get around town. The local shuttle bus is punctual and free. Also, check with Central Reservations about charter flights from a town near you, especially if you live in Texas, California, or the Deep South.

RANDOM NOTES

Perhaps the best-kept secret at Crested Butte is *Irwin Lodge,* a rustic, twenty-five-room inn perched at 10,700 feet on an isolated mountainside 15 miles from Crested Butte. Irwin Lodge sits in the middle of an eight-million-acre National Forest. The view goes on forever, stretching out over the Ruby Range all the way to the San Juan Mountains over 70 miles away. The only access to the lodge in winter is by Snow-Cat or snowmobile, and the minimum stay is three nights. You can powder ski—up to 10,000 vertical

At Crested Butte telemark turns bring the best skiers to their knees. (Photo: Russell/Kelly)

feet a day—up in the beautiful forest behind the lodge, hauled up by a Sno-Cat. You can go snowmobiling, ski touring, or ice fishing or just sit on the front porch and enjoy the incredible view. You can't watch TV, read the newspaper, or listen to the radio because they don't have any. It is a most thrilling escape. Back in Crested Butte, the liveliest bars are the *Wooden Nickel* and the *Grubstake*, while après-ski action up at the lifts centers on the *Artichoke* and *Jeremiah's*. What used to be the Red Lady bar is now called *Rafters* and it features a dinner theater revue like Aspen's Crystal Palace. Crested Butte's mellowest music comes from "Earth Station," a cable radio outlet that is piped into lodges and comes in on TV, too. *Sunshine's Paradise Bathhouse* is a funky place to steam and sauna away your aches and pains, but don't expect to find the Osmond family or many bathing suits on the premises. Crested Butte has an abundance of truly spectacular cross-country skiing that doesn't take place on the downhill slopes, too. There are moonlight tours, back-country trips, and even two-day excursions over Pearl Pass to Aspen. And don't forget that Crested Butte has one of the highest base elevations of any ski area. Take it easy the first few days, and watch out for those daiquiris.

Base elevation	9,100 ft.
Vertical drop	2,150 ft.
Number of lifts	8
Skiable acres	650
Average skiers per day	NA
Average snowfall	360 in.
Number of trails	40
Trail breakdown	35% beginner
	38% intermediate
	27% expert

5

HEAVENLY VALLEY, CALIFORNIA

BEST DAYS : Heavenly Valley

"The mountain doesn't really have a boundary. The patrol keeps its eyes out for tracks cutting into the trees, and if someone is reported missing, they'll go back and explore. My best day? Well, let me put it this way. This is not a run you do wearing your ski school jacket. We changed into civilian clothes and skied down Fireline, a straight cut down the Nevada side of the mountain, in two feet of fresh powder. I ended up in someone's backyard next to Harrah's."

NAME WITHHELD BY REQUEST

Heavenly Valley challenges our notion of what a ski area is supposed to be. The confusion has nothing to do with the skiing. Any resort with twenty-six lifts and up to 500 inches of snow a year blanketing a 4,000-foot ski mountain is, at the very least, worth considering, and Heavenly is one of the most underrated ski mountains in America. The confusion comes from the gambling casinos, bright lights, and big-city glitter/tackiness arrayed along the south rim of Lake Tahoe a few miles from the ski lifts. The juxtapositions are just too jarring. Skiers work out all day on supersteep runs like Gunbarrel and Waterfall, then go back to a motel room with waterbeds and X-rated movies on closed-circuit TV. Cruisers wail away on an unbelievable 7-mile-long intermediate trail and then indulge in après ski that ranges from Willie Nelson and Ol' Blue Eyes to a tits-and-ass revue complete with feather boas. Those who don't care to go out order drinks from a computer-controlled dispenser built into the wall of their hotel room.

After a few uneasy days, the subtle comforts of room service in a first-rate hotel like Harrah's began to soften us up. Finally one morning we wandered through the casino in our ski boots at about 8 A.M. on our way to the slopes. Outside, the sun was rising over the crest of the Sierra Nevada, illuminating the deep blue oval of Lake Tahoe. The gamblers at the tables were oblivious to the beauty. All they wanted was some action, something that would tell them if they are hot or if they're not today. It occurred to us that we were heading outdoors with the deliberate desire to launch ourselves down a ski slope looking for that same action, the same self-assurance, the same feeling that today was our day. The dissonance and confusion began to subside.

Heavenly has more groomed skiable acres than any other area in the United States, with the possible exception of Vail (there is a fight over exactly which is bigger). The view of Lake Tahoe from the chairs on the California side of the mountain is absolutely stunning. Tahoe is the largest alpine lake in America (no dispute here that we know of), so deep that it never freezes. It is completely encircled by snow-capped mountains. The view sucks your lungs out and leaves a hollow ache in your heart. The view underneath the tram breeds butterflies in the stomach. Gunbarrel is 4,000 feet of bumps diabolically arranged over 1,700 vertical feet. Along with Telluride's famous Plunge and Spiral Stairs and the face of KT-22 over at Squaw Valley, Gunbarrel offers the most unrelenting bump skiing in America. Its neighbors, East Bowl and West Bowl, are no bargains either.

The tram dropped us off at a large building halfway up the California side of the ski area. Adjoining a standard-issue cheeseburger cafeteria up here is a comfortable, gracious restaurant with wall-to-wall views. It's the ideal panorama for instant romance or marriage proposals along with your avocado-and-sprouts sandwich.

Three more chairs rise above a forest to the very top of the California side. Heavenly is famous for its tree skiing, and from the top you can drop off into the pines at any point along Sky Line trail. The ponderosas are fat and their branches heavy with snow, but they are thoughtfully spaced far enough apart so that wandering down through them is like being inside a tall evergreen cathedral. Skiers have time to sightsee; it's not unlike driving through a national park. The only thing missing is a tree with a tunnel cut through it in the shape of a skier. One word of warning from a Heavenly hostess: "Those branches may look like fat white feathers, but believe me, they feel like fat white baseball bats."

It is difficult to convey the vastness of the mountain. You can easily ski here for a week and never repeat yourself. The day *after* a storm there are still powder preserves—at 3:30 in the afternoon. Peter Duke, who heads the Heavenly Valley Ski School, likes to go up in a helicopter to scout possible runs. We asked how, after a particularly good run, does he ever find his way back to the same shot. "By the grace of God," he replied.

The marked trails on the California side are a collection of cruising's greatest hits. They can hold their own against such favorites as Porcupine at Taos, Flying Squirrel at Sun Valley, or Naked Lady at Snowmass.

Ridge Run curves down the southern edge of the ski area and has corners on it where the world abruptly falls away and skiers seem to soar over Lake Tahoe a half mile below.

For the skier who winds up lost, there are ski hostesses who will help find an easy way down. The trail signs are as big as freeway exit markers. This is only appropriate on a mountain that draws weekend throngs of 10,000 people. The lift attendants are polite masters of crowd control, a handy skill to have when the lift lines resemble small towns. But this is California and people are used to heavy traffic. Everybody is invariably friendly and patient and, yes, beautiful. They remind us of the crowds we've seen filing into a Grateful Dead concert: expectant but quiet. Waiting for the drugs to come on, or, in this case, the impending rush from the top of the chair.

One way to avoid the crowds is to hire an instructor for a private lesson. You get to cut lines and, on top of that, learn to ski. The Heavenly Valley Ski School has developed something called Natural Easy Carve. They get you onto your edges early and teach the feel of optimal ski performance. No matter what your level, there's something to learn. We skied for two days with Stu Campbell and Carol West, Zen masters of the carved turn. They untangled our skiing, teaching one fundamental per run, until all of the strings were in tune. They showed us how to ski moguls intelligently—if that's not a contradiction in terms—on Waterfall, a short, vicious, supersteep classroom. The insights lasted the rest of the winter. The ski school offers ratings, like belts in the martial arts. We rather like the notion of skiing as a path to higher awareness in the face of greater knee problems.

From the top of Sky Line, skiers pitch over to the less crowded Nevada side of the mountain. You've heard the phrase "out of sight"? Well, at Tahoe they say "out of state" and mean it literally. Since the Nevada side faces northeast, most skiers think it has better, drier snow. Sierra cement is much maligned, but we kept asking ourselves:

Wasn't there a mountain here a minute ago? Heavenly Valley, and the ever-present Lake Tahoe.

Compared with what? New England chowder? True, the stuff is not light, and Utah gourmets may be a little uncomfortable with it, but it isn't the enemy, either. Skiers just have to assert themselves. Catch a wave of snow. Bank and rebound.

There are some who claim that the snow on the Nevada side of Heavenly is as light as Colorado powder. The Nevada side definitely has a totally different look and feel from California. The trails drop down through a couple of fairly steep bowls and then branch out into seemingly endless runs. One of them, Galaxy, is a full 7 miles long. The upper part drops 1,800 vertical feet with a 37-degree pitch. Taking it nonstop will burn your muscles and bones and brain—this is no cream-puff country road. It just keeps dropping and dropping all the way to the dusty

plains of the Nevada desert, leaving you standing in sagebrush country, staring eastward across a thousand miles of brown wilderness. *This is Kirk to Enterprise. Beam me up, Scotty.* You feel like you might become the first skier ever to be hit by tumbleweed out here. There are other, even longer runs out of bounds in places like Mott Canyon and the Palisades. For all we know, they end up in Carson City or the Mustang Ranch.

After the relative isolation of the Nevada side, it felt good to return to the bar at the base lodge in California. The ski school was there in full force, eying the passing parade. "There is a girl with a simply awesome overhang on her cornice," someone said. We sit and listen to the band and the come-ons. There was talk of heading for the hot tubs, a Heavenly institution where you can rent a private cauldron and steam and soak under the stars. Drinks are ordered by telephone. With all the action in town, the mountain seemed to close down fairly quickly. Skiers head down to Carlos Murphy's or one of the bars on Route 44 for a drink. If you don't find a companion here, you can always try Lady Luck down the street in Nevada.

BEST BETS

Heavenly offers something no other ski area has: hotels that come complete with gambling casinos, Vegas-type showrooms, and lavish dining facilities. The new *Caesars Tahoe*, *Harrah's Tahoe Hotel Casino* and the *Sahara Tahoe* are all modern, comfortable high rises set in the middle of the gaudy strip of entertainment that straddles the California/Nevada state line in South Lake Tahoe. Many of the rooms at Caesars have

built-in hot tubs, a feature that we think gives this hotel a slight edge, with Harrah's a close second. These hotels are excellent choices as long as you don't crave isolation and rustic charm. The nicest condos in the area are the *Lakeland Village* units, which have Jacuzzis and fireplaces and wonderful views from the lakeshore. If you insist on staying right by the lifts, *Heavenly Valley Townhouses* are adequate, but you should be aware that all of the nighttime action is elsewhere. Call 702-588-4584 for reservations at any of the above.

DINING

Choices range from the sixteenth-floor *Summit* dining room at Harrah's, which requires a jacket for men, to *Cantina Los Tres Hombres*, a Mexican restaurant that merely requires solvency. In between there are the

Bright lights, big city: Heavenly's slopes tower over the neon casinos of South Lake Tahoe.

very popular and low-priced buffets at the big casinos, plus assorted other dining rooms in all of them. The *Chart House* and the *Greenhouse* both feature steaks and seafood, and *Chez Villaret* is the south-shore French restaurant said to rival *Le Petit Pier* up at the other end of the lake.

TRANSPORTATION

Skiers arriving by air from the east normally fly to Reno, 55 miles from Heavenly Valley. Rental cars are your best bet for getting around the area, although a skier shuttle stops at all the major hotels during the day. Aspen and Golden West Airlines fly directly into South Lake Tahoe from Los Angeles, with Aspen also coming in from San Francisco. Coast-to-coast promotional fares can sometimes make it cheaper to fly into L.A. or San Francisco and then connect up to Tahoe. Buses are available from Reno or Tahoe to the hotels, although, again, a car seems like a more logical choice. If you are driving from San Francisco, the trip takes about three and a half hours over U.S. Highway 50.

RANDOM NOTES

Night life around Tahoe is, to put it mildly, full of variety. The major casino/hotels have big-name entertainment, cabaret acts, discos, and, of course, gambling. There are other, smaller casinos in town as well. More traditional après-ski entertainment can be found in the *Red Chimney Room* bar at the base of the California side of the mountain, where there is usually live music, and at *Nephele's*, which is a combination bar, restaurant, and hot-tub complex just down the road from the lifts. Across the street is *Shingle Creek*, another bar and hot-tub combo, and the new *Carlos Murphy's* is very popular. For a day of variety, head over to Kirkwood, a ski area which some folks believe belongs in our top 25 all by itself.

Base elevation	6,550 ft. (Calif.)
	6,100 ft. (Nevada)
Vertical drop	3,600 ft. (Calif.)
	4,000 ft. (Nevada)
Number of lifts	26
Skiable acres	14,080
Average skiers per day	10,000 (weekends)
Average snowfall	300–500 in.
Number of trails	NA
Trail breakdown	25% beginner
	50% intermediate
	25% expert

6
JACKSON HOLE, WYOMING

BEST DAYS : Jackson Hole

"It was spring. I put on my cross-country skis and headed out to the back country. I found myself in a place so beautiful I was speechless. I felt awe for the first time in my life. I had never felt that small before. To think that most people only come to Jackson in the summer. They never leave their cars or their camper palaces. Just a mile from the road, a few minutes on skis, are lakes that only a few people have ever seen. In the winter, the whole world is yours out here."

LARRY RIESER

Our first morning at Jackson Hole was a day full of the promise of fresh, deep powder. We stumbled out of bed and headed for the gondola station in the center of Teton Village to catch the first tram of the day at about 8:15 A.M. Already in line ahead of us were the owner of the ski area, the general manager, the marketing director, half the ski school, and most of the ski patrol. We'd heard of testing the product but this was ridiculous.

The tram slipped out of its berth, ascending from the long, flat valley floor (a "hole" in frontier language) into the leading edge, the breaking wave of the Tetons. The slopes of Jackson are crowned by huge monoliths of rock, discarded on the premises by a retreating glacier millions of years ago. Stretching into the distance to the left of the tram was a seemingly endless series of enormous bowls, ridges, and gullies. Looking the other way, we could see gentler slopes covered with gladed forests sprawling all the way to Apres Vous Mountain over a mile to the north. Towering over it all was Rendezvous Peak and its collection of headwalls, cirques, and avalanche chutes—the full vocabulary of

mountain thrills awaiting any skier with the skills to speak its language. The tram took twelve minutes to cover 4,139 vertical feet, almost too fast a trip for passage into the throne room of the mountain gods.

The combination of ruggedness, size, and isolation is what sets Jackson Hole apart from other ski areas. The ski lifts at Teton Village are twelve miles from the town of Jackson Hole itself, and neither place aspires to glamour or pretentiousness. Jackson Hole got its start when John D. Rockefeller, Jr., wanted to keep hot dog stands from marring the view of the Tetons. Rockefeller bought as much land as he could get his hands on and gave it to the federal government. Today, if Aspen is where people go to show off wealth, Jackson Hole is where they go to hide. There are over eighty millionaires in a town of 5,000 residents. Instead of wearing fur coats, they work for the volunteer fire department. The wealthy people who live here make a point of not distracting anyone or being conspicuous, although we did see a T-shirt in a shop that read "The Man Who Dies with the Most Toys Wins."

Alpenglow: A skier finds inner peace and meaningful steepness at Jackson. (Photo: © 1979 Bob Woodall)

The ski area has a marketing slogan that says, "Ski the Big One." "Ski the Empty One" would fit, too. On the busiest day of the season the crowd barely exceeds one skier per acre. Only 20 percent of the skiers buy tram tickets (the rest work out on the vast intermediate and beginner terrain between the tram and Apres Vous), so it can get mighty lonesome on some slopes. Bring a friend.

At Jackson you ski the weather, as well as the terrain. On one run we unloaded the tram into the teeth of a 70-mile-per-hour gale and blinding snow. We dropped through thick fog and more snow until finally, near the bottom, we emerged into warm, humid sunshine. On another run we got to the top and found 9 inches of fresh powder that no one at the base knew anything about. Don't like the weather at Jackson Hole? Just wait a thousand feet. Even off the mountain the weather can be interesting. We actually experienced a whiteout in the pool at the Americana Snow King.

Another way to look at it is that Jackson Hole has so much varied terrain that a skier can have a good time in any condition. For example, when we got off the tram one morning we headed down through Rendezvous Bowl, a spectacular porcelain scoop of snow. From there we could try one of the steep, wide ridges like Colter or Sublette, or the broad bowls like Laramie, Rawlings, or Cheyenne (Jackson names its ridges for mountain men of yore and its bowls for guess what). If the powder lived up to its promise we could head out to the Hobacks on the far northern edge of the ski area. We had the bad luck to catch this hefty flank of the mountain under extreme death crud conditions a few days earlier. It was a couple of miles of forced turns through ankle-scraping muck. Another time, when the powder promise wasn't broken, the Hobacks were a symphony. Three thousand linked turns on the edge of the world.

Jackson has plenty to keep skiers busy—on and off the slopes. The best-kept secret here (much to the chagrin of management) is that Jackson's intermediate and beginner terrain by itself is bigger than 90 percent of all the other ski areas in America. The traverse from Apres Vous to the delightful cruises off the Casper chair opens up acres of secret glens, powder preserves, and tree skiing. A ride on the tram or a ski technique like Pepi Steigler's isn't necessary to enjoy any of this. About the only thing Jackson doesn't have is moguls. Thunder is the only bump run on the mountain and it isn't all that long. Members of the Hot Dog Air Force may need a refresher course in the art of giant slalom to get the most out of Jackson.

This is not to say that you can't get air here. The top of the notorious Corbett's Couloir consists of 15 or 20 feet of uninterrupted vertical. Looking down into Corbett's is like looking over the wall at Hoover Dam. Our guide told us to think of the first step as reentry from outer space. "When you finally touch down," he advised, "you can either make very quick turns or hit very large rocks." He pointed out more steep trails like the Alta Chutes, Hourglass, and Once Is Enough, but, this time at least, even once was too much.

Jackson Hole offers plenty of distractions away from the main ski slopes. There are tours of Yellowstone Park on cross-country skis or by snowmobile. The absence of tourists in winter magnifies the beauty of Old Faithful a thousandfold. Horse-drawn sleds glide into the National Elk Refuge, home of 10,000 wintering elk. Cross-country excursions to a hot springs and four-mile, downhill descents from the top of Teton Pass take place daily. There is also skiing at nearby Grand Targhee, a smaller, wide-open area set amidst the grandest of Teton scenery. A billboard on the access road proclaims: "Ski Mother Nature's Highest Energy." The bus ride to Targhee is unforgettable. Our driver stopped at the top of Teton Pass to let us all get out and take pictures of the clouds nestled in the valley below. The access road itself is hair-raising, easily a black-diamond trail, but the powder skiing (Targhee gets over 500 inches a year) is worth the scare.

The supreme distraction at Jackson Hole is a day (or week) spent with High Mountains Helicopter Skiing. It's a perfect introduction to the ultimate skiing experience. The guides are patient with powder virgins, the terrain is spectacular without being intimidating, and the helicopter rides are better than anything Disneyland has come up with. We had signed up with High Mountains, and, because the weather had closed in, we were put on their waiting list. The next day, while we were standing in line at the ski area to get lift tickets, the woman behind the ticket counter said, "Oh, High Mountains called. Today you get to go helicopter skiing." We looked out at Rendezvous Peak, covered with two feet of fresh powder. The skier in line behind us said, "Life is full of tough choices, isn't it?"

Within a half hour we had joined the group at the takeoff point behind the Americana Snow King. A Hughes attack helicopter lifted us up into a valley called Cache Creek. When Averell Harriman was looking for a place to build Sun Valley, his scouts recom-

This is what they mean by vertical feet: Corbett's Couloir is a Jackson legend. (Photo: © 1979 Bob Woodall)

mended the terrain up in Cache Creek. Unfortunately, the entrance to the valley is highly susceptible to avalanches, which would have annoyed the rich socialites Harriman wanted to bring out West on his railroad no end. Sun Valley moved west to Ketchum, and we had the Meat Doctor (High Mountains names its runs in honor of its clients) to ourselves for our first run.

The helicopter had landed on a peak where mortal men would not have had room to pitch a tent. We dropped over the cornice in pairs. The snow was meaty, gorgeous, filet mignon powder. We started making turns, getting used to the consistency. The one thing no one tells you about powder is this: Learn to do one turn in it and you've got it licked. Repeat the motion a few hundred times and you're back at the copter, out of breath and ready to do it again. The first run was a bit awkward. A few of us made contributions to the beer fund (anyone who falls down antes up). One of us qualified for the hard-alcohol fund. Gradually we got the hang of it and sailed along the perfect, natural terrain, through glades, down chutes carved by avalanches, and over meadows covered with 20 feet of snow.

Later that day we met up with a friend in a bar. He had spent the day skiing the Hobacks, and was happy. We muttered something about the impossibility of going back to a lift-serviced mountain after tasting helicopter skiing. The waitress put down our drinks and said, "You've got nothing to worry about. Jackson is one of the few mountains you can come back to." She was right.

About the only attraction you can't come back to at Jackson Hole is women. Things aren't quite as bad (or as good, depending on your gender) as they are at Alta or Snowbird, but when we asked the marketing director about the ratio of men to women here, he said, "Nine." Nine percent? "No, nine women." After a day of wrestling with the big one, you'll probably be too tired to

wrestle with anything else anyway. We did see one special woman, though, up at the marketing office. She was waiting to turn in her "Ski the Big One" scorecard that records the total number of runs and vertical feet you've skied on your visit. She was holding up an entire busload of companions who were eager to return to civilization, but she had earned her 100,000-foot pin—enough skiing to get her through an equally high stack of paperwork at whatever job awaited her. Just as downhill racers try to carry the energy of the mountain through their whole run, Jackson had given her the energy to carry her through the entire year. The bus could wait.

BEST BETS

LODGING

All of the accommodations, restaurants, and other facilities for Jackson Hole are physically split between Teton Village, a small, self-contained area at the base of the ski lifts, and the cowboy/resort town of Jackson Hole, 12 miles away. Although Teton Village lacks a truly first-class place to stay, the *Alpenhof*, the *Sojourner*, and the *Inn* are all nice, modern lodges just a few yards from the lifts. The *Village Center Inn* has apartment-style units with kitchens, and there are a number of condominiums strung out along the base of Rendezvous Mountain, although some of them can be a very stiff walk from the center of the village. *Rendezvous* is especially nice, and *Nez Perce* is also good. About four miles away are the well-appointed (racquetball, tennis, swimming pool, health spa) *Jackson Hole Racquet Club* and *Aspens Condominiums*, which are served by a shuttle bus to the lifts. The very nicest place to stay, however, is in Jackson Hole proper. The *Americana Snow King* is a beautifully designed

Doing it by the numbers: Jackson Hole invented the Powder Eight contest. (Photo: Bob Woodall. All rights reserved.)

The powder is almost always grand at Targhee, even in early winter. (Photo: © 1979 Bob Woodall)

202-room hotel that has been decorated by local Wyoming artists and craftsmen. The Snow King offers amenities like a pool, sauna, Jacuzzi, its own restaurants. Buses to Teton Village and Grand Targhee. The High Mountains helicopter also departs from here. The only drawback is the stiff hike to the town center, about a half mile away. Reservations at Teton Village and information about other lodgings can be had toll free at 800-443-6931.

DINING

The center of activity at Teton Village is the *Mangy Moose*, a steak and salad bar place where, if you're too tired to stand in line for your greens, someone will bring them to you. The *Inn*, which has the best lunchtime fondue we've ever tasted, has been making a comeback at dinner lately. The *Sojourner* has nice breakfasts and lunches, but, along with the *Alpenhof*, is a bit chancy at dinner. The *Steak Pub* is another good beef house, but you'll need a car to reach it. Right in downtown Jackson Hole, the *Open Range* is a pricy French restaurant that tries hard and succeeds fairly well at bringing *haute cuisine* to Wyoming. *Anthony's* serves copious Italian dinners in a friendly, unpretentious atmosphere.

TRANSPORTATION

Jackson's biggest problem has always been getting people to the ski area. Within the last year they have begun operating their own charters from Salt Lake every Saturday. Regularly scheduled daily jet service from Denver on Frontier Airlines began last season. These are by far the easiest ways to get there. Otherwise, the best gateway is Idaho Falls, Idaho, 100 miles away, where buses from Jackson Hole meet Saturday arrivals. The drive from Salt Lake is about five hours and covers some of the most gorgeous mountain scenery in America. As always, it is best to discuss your needs with the folks at Central Reservations when you book.

RANDOM NOTES

What après-ski life there is at Teton Village takes place in *Dietrich's*, the bar at the Alpenhof Inn, at the *Sojourner*, and over at the *Mangy Moose*. The real action gets going later around the town square in Jackson Hole, at the *Rancher*, the *Silver Dollar*, and especially at the *Cowboy Bar*. The bar stools here are real saddles, complete with stirrups, and the chandelier is a merry-go-round with miniature cowboys chasing Indians. The whole place looks like John Wayne's rumpus room on bad drugs, but it definitely has that wild West atmosphere. Real drunks, real cowboys, and real cowgirls, too. On Sundays, the locals pull the pin and party at the *Stagecoach* bar in nearby Wilson.

You should take advantage of the Ski Host program at Jackson Hole. They'll give you a free (tipping permitted) tour of the mountain on request any day of the week. Also, Pepi Steigler's Ski Guides (he's head of the ski school) will, for a fee, escort you to the more remote parts of this massive area. Pepi himself, a former Olympic Gold, Silver, and Bronze Medalist, is one of the very finest skiers alive today, so take advantage of any chance you get to watch him in action. If you need more places to ski, a guide can take you to Rock Springs Bowl, Cody Bowl, and other out-of-bounds terrain, especially in the spring when they hold the famous Powder Eight contest in Cody Bowl. Also note that Jackson has a relatively early snow season. Although spring skiing here can be spectacular, January and early February are the best times for light, dry powder.

Base elevation	6,311 ft.
Vertical drop	4,139 ft.
Number of lifts	7
Skiable acres	3,000
Average skiers per day	2,000
Average snowfall	450 in.
Number of trails	NA
Trail breakdown	10% beginner
	40% intermediate
	50% expert

7
KILLINGTON, VERMONT

BEST DAYS : Killington

"It was the day they closed Boston and nobody could leave the cities to get here. A blizzard had shut everything down—the airports, the roads, everything. We had the mountain all to ourselves with four feet of powder."

SEVERAL KILLINGTON LOCALS

Killington's Bear Mountain reputedly has the steepest slope in New England. We're not sure if Bear is really more ferocious than the Starr or Goat at Stowe or Stein's Run at Sugarbush, but the debate seemed academic as we stood at the top of a trail named Outer Limits and stared down at rows of large white teeth waiting to devour our ski tips. Our guide, a Killington ski instructor, cheerfully explained, "Well, we like to say that if you can ski Killington, you can ski any place out West." We had just spent a year and a half in the Rockies. We *had* skied everywhere out West. We weren't sure if we could ski Killington.

Outer Limits, one of two trails that dive down the face of Bear Mountain, was as slick as a billiard ball. Our guide told us that in the first year the trail was open, a local ski shop owner had delaminated four pairs of skis in one day on this combination of glare ice and moguls. Neat. We pushed off over the edge. As soon as we found a workable rhythm we were thrown by a humongous mogul, a white mound called a snow whale by the locals. It seems that the snowmaking guns build up these monsters and then skiers do human trail grooming when they fall and push the snow around the trail. Unfortunately for skiers with weak knees or lungs, these whales run in very large schools, and are tilted at about the same angle as a refrigerator door. Driving up to Killington, we'd passed a store called Denture World. At the time we thought it was a theme park, like Disneyland, but it turned out to be an outlet for false teeth. After a few runs down Outer Limits we were convinced that a lot of Denture World's business comes from skiers on Bear Mountain. Last year Killington held a marathon on Outer Limits to raise money for the U.S. Olympic Team. The winner covered 72,900 vertical feet in eight hours. If that isn't a world record, that person at least deserves a Purple Heart.

The day after this bone-jarring experience, we were being shown around the vast Killington terrain by this same ski instructor. It turned out that we knew in common some former New Englanders who had moved to Heavenly Valley, California—friends who had described the difference between eastern

Sticking to their guns: A machine-made snowstorm attacks Killington Peak. (Photo: © Bob Perry)

and western skiers to us very clearly. It seems that when our friends would come to a cornice or blind curve at Heavenly, they would stop to assess the situation, decide how to ski it, and then proceed smoothly. Their California companions, on the other hand, simply rocketed along, sailing around the corner or over the lip without a second thought. The moral of this story was supposed to be that eastern skiers are cautious and depend on finely honed skills, whereas the western skier just goes for it, no guts, no glory. Our instructor listened to all of this and then said quietly, "No, it's just that the east-

ern skiers were probably the only ones in the group who knew *how* to stop." Touché.

One evening at dinner during our stay at Killington the conversation turned up the fact that Vermont got to be the way it is—underpopulated—during the Civil War. It seems that all those farm boys who served in the Union Army side by side with soldiers from the Midwest heard stories about how you could plow a straight line for hours on end without turning up a single rock. It sounded like a New England farmer's idea of heaven, and a lot of them left their hardscrabble towns for the promised land of Ohio,

Illinois, and points west. The people who stayed behind were more stoic, more accepting of what God had put on the ground.

Today, their descendants, spiritual or otherwise, still live here and ski what nature and the snowmaking wizards give them. They don't much care if out in the Rockies somewhere you can ski all day without hitting a single rock or a patch of ice. This attitude has given rise to the well-known joke about the Killington School of Powder Skiing: Instead of skiing powder up to your knees, here you ski hardpack up to your edges. Occasionally someone from Killington breaks camp and heads for Park City or Alta and sends back pornographic post cards about Utah powder, but generally the locals like what they have here. It's enough. It teaches them humility, not to mention hardass skills on an order that most western skiers don't believe exist.

But it would not be fair to assume that Killington skiers are all frostbitten, tight-lipped Yankees and that their ski resort is a Marine boot camp with bindings. Killington is an enormous, smoothly functioning ski complex that draws a very loyal crowd back to the center of Vermont week after week, and for good reason. Killington offers the most consistent—if occasionally difficult—conditions in the East. They are a terrific challenge that rewards you with a sense of your own capabilities and the satisfaction of knowing you can do it right when it really matters. Skiers keep coming back to Killington because it is the largest ski area east of the Rockies; because it has the widest choice of terrain and the longest ski season in New England; and because its snowmaking operation is second to none (they cover over 250 acres with man-made snow). Killington's trail map, which somehow manages to take in all seventy-five trails scattered over five separate mountains, resembles the battle plans for the Normandy invasion etched in a topographic drawing. Skiers come back because they know Killington is big enough to keep them busy, no matter what mood they're in, for a full week or more.

Skiers approach the ski area up a long access road off U.S. Route 4, winding past some unpretentious lodges and shops. From the lower base of the mountain, trails seem to sprawl in all directions at once. Battalions of beginners take classes on the gentle, broad Snowshed slopes right above this main base. An awesome number of skiers first learned the sport at Killington, and the ski school is a big attraction. Novice ski weekers are even shown a movie that prepares them for the real thing. It's a thoughtful little gesture, a bit of comic relief that takes the edge off the terror that may have been building for six months or so. The ski school takes reservations far in advance, puts them into their computer, and then sends out letters reminding everybody to bring extra socks, extra money, etc. They don't like to talk about their computer much here, but you can see the logic of having it: It means that they *know* how many instructors they'll need on any Monday of the season in order to hold class sizes to a maximum of eight, or how many sets of rental skis should be available.

Over across the road from the main base is the chair up Ramshead, which has a couple of long, intermediate cruises where you can meander on uncrowded weekdays. Ramshead also allows passage over to the central part of Killington—an enormous, wraparound bowl full of intermediate and expert trails, with its own base lodge and parking lot. If you ride the chairs to the top of this section you can head off in any of several directions to at least four other parts of the mountain. There is some nice glade skiing on the south ridge triple chair, wide-open cruising in the Needle's Eye section, and endless sliding down Great Eastern and the accurately named Four-Mile Run. These last two deposit you at the base of the gondola on U.S. Route 4, completely around on the other side of the mountain 10 miles from the main base. From here, it's a twenty-eight-minute ride back to the top, and, as you might imagine, people have dreamed up some very creative ways to pass the time. Our favorite story involves a naked Japanese couple, a stalled gondola car, and the mistaken impression that they should leave the car immediately, which was dangling just a few feet above the ground. If you want all the details, just ask a Killington ski patrolman some day.

There is plenty of other terrain to explore, especially on weekdays, when the mountain seems empty. Riding up a chair one day, we saw a sign that said: "These mountains are as cold and dark at night as they were 200 years ago. Don't ski alone." Good advice at an area as sprawling as Killington. We don't know about temperatures 200 years ago, but last Christmas the wind-chill reading fell off the chart, which stops at 124 degrees Fahrenheit below zero. It was so cold that the oil for the furnace at one of the lodges turned to jelly. The cold makes for an interesting form of skiing at times like that—one run and a cup of hot chocolate. If you just can't bear to go outdoors at all, the base lodge at Killington is always lively, and there is good music at the end of the day, plus fresh doughnuts that we would walk a mile in ski boots for.

Off the mountain, no one will ever mistake Killington for Sun Valley or even Sugarbush, which is just up the road. Management has poured a lot of money into sophisticated trail grooming, snowmaking, and lifts, but the lodges and restaurants on the access road remain down-home simple and purely functional. There are no trendy discos or chic ski-wear boutiques to lighten your wallet. Most skiers head down to the *Pickle Barrel* and to *Charity's* when the lifts close. With so many people around, especially on weekends, there is no lack of night life, but it is decentralized at the lodges and hotels and bars all over the area. People tend to be discreet in their excesses. One innkeeper told us about a guest who spent his entire week in his room, naked, passing suicide notes ("Tell Ray Charles I love him") under the door. The police came to cart the guy away and the owner yelled, "Dress him first!" Later the guest wrote threatening letters to the lodge owner about the sexual preferences of the lodge's two giant Saint Bernards.

There is one more way in which Killington and other eastern areas are different from Colorado, and we think it explains a lot about why people keep coming back here. The Rocky Mountain resorts are, in a way, movie sets in the middle of nowhere. Prices are high and the audiences are captives for the length of their vacation. In New England, resorts don't have to pay off all their expenses in a short, three-month winter ski season, and the steady mix of day and weekend skiers with vacationers helps keep prices in line. As a result, fewer people seem to have their hands in your pockets. The resorts develop loyal customers who drive up to the mountain from New York or Connecticut or Boston every weekend. People come to Vermont to be calmed by the barnboard, for the experience of New England as much as for the skiing. The lodges are like second homes and the inns become entertainment centers. The owners know how to keep people occupied when the snow turns to rain in the middle of January or when the temperature falls to somewhere around absolute zero. They know that if guests aren't happy they can hit the road for home any time. When you sit down for dinner, you get a choice of eight entrées instead of two. When the rains or the boreal blizzards strike, impromptu parties and open bars break out. Few people leave for home. They seem to like what they have up there.

BEST BETS

LODGING

The lodging at Killington is spread out over a very wide area along the access road and in all directions along Route 100, Route 4, and into Rutland, a twenty-minute drive away. Many of the rooms are standard-issue motels and vaguely Tyrolean lodges that would get tedious over a week's stay, but there are several places that are well above average and two that are simply outstanding. Starting at the top, there's the wonderful

Bob Elliot on Downdraft, the last trail in the East to close—usually in May. (Photo: © Bob Perry)

Summit Lodge, 3 miles down Killington road with its own shuttle bus to the mountain every morning and afternoon. The rooms at the Summit are simple and functional, but everything else, from the big indoor Jacuzzi to the superb food and warm, cozy atmosphere, is exactly what a ski lodge should be. A unique and romantic alternative to lodges and motels is renting a private home at *Hawk Mountain*. Hawk consists of five clusters of lovely modern houses tucked into the woods of central Vermont, and the closest one to Killington is called Salt Ash, 6 miles from the gondola base on Route 4. There's another cluster twenty minutes up Route 100 in Pittsfield as well. Hawk is run like a hotel, which means the homes are rented by the day and management handles everything. Also, rates are based on people, not on the

size of the home, making it a reasonable deal for couples. Some of the homes are so private that sometimes the owners can't even find them. A notch or two below these accommodations, but still very nice, are the *Mountain Inn* and the *Cascades*, two new lodges located right by the parking lot at the main base. The *Cortina* is a pleasing blend of a modern hotel and the atmosphere of a lodge, situated about fifteen minutes from the lifts. Good food, and a nice indoor pool, too. For reservations and information about the above call 802-422-3711.

DINING

The Modified American Plan, whereby your room rate includes breakfast and dinner, is wide spread up here, so a restaurant has to be pretty good to lure people away from their dining rooms in the lodges. The very best lure is *Lauren's*, a renovated old house that serves superb French and Continental dishes. Lauren's recently was awarded four stars in the *Mobil Travel Guide*, the only restaurant in Vermont with this distinction. There's a great wine cellar, too, which Lauren or Tom Rabeck will be glad to show you. Back up at the mountain, the *Summit Lodge* is the first name most people mention around the slopes, and well they should. The menu changes every night and offers at least eight choices; everything is homemade and superb without falling into one particular style. *Royal's Hearthside* is a popular choice down in Rutland, and guests at the *Cortina Inn* have high praise for the food there. *Annabelle's* at the Hawk Mountain center in Pittsfield is elegant, ambitious, and popular. Finally, don't overlook *Blanche and Bill's* down-home breakfasts, served all day in their small dining room on Route 100. Locally popular, as they say.

TRANSPORTATION

Cars. Period. Most Killington skiers drive up from New York and Connecticut, and they need their cars to get around both day and night. Killington Peak attracts and holds snowstorms, too, so snowtires or chains are a good idea.

Random Notes

The après-ski action starts at the upstairs bar in the main base area when the lifts close, then shifts down the access road to *Charity's*, a lively bar and casual restaurant that shows ski movies on one wall. Across the street is the *Wobbly Barn*, a bare-bones cavern with minimal decor that doesn't really get rolling until later at night. A bit further along are the *Pickle Barrel* and the *Orient Express*, a Chinese restaurant with a huge bar with an electric train running around the wall. The bar is very crowded after skiing. Most of the bigger inns and lodges have quiet music and some dancing, so pay attention to the signs up on the bulletin boards around the area. The Killington Ski School is offering a well-designed week-long instruction program for advanced and expert skiers called Mountain Ski Week. It features videotape sessions, ski-tuning seminars, and lots of hard skiing during the day, along with instruction as you need it. Very popular. Remember that Killington is traditionally the first ski area in the country to open and the last in the East to close. The skiing may not be terrific in October or May (although March and April are increasingly popular), but the fact that it's there at all is great fun.

Base elevation	1,160 ft.
Vertical drop	3,060 ft.
Number of lifts	13
Skiable acres	400
Average skiers per day	8,500 (weekends)
	4,000 (weekdays)
Average snowfall	300 in.
Number of trails	75
Trail breakdown	42% beginner
	24% intermediate
	34% expert

8
MAMMOTH MOUNTAIN, CALIFORNIA

BEST DAYS: Mammoth

"One day I did fifteen runs in Christmas Bowl. I had it all to myself. Most skiers stay right under Chair Three and don't cut over into the bowls. I kept making wide, giant slalom turns, with the snow flaring out behind my skis, kicking up a wake of snow, a rooster tail twenty feet long. I kept repeating it, cutting the groove deeper and deeper. I didn't stop until I got it right."

PAM MURPHY

Before we left home everyone asked if we were going to Mammoth. They pretended to be curious about the skiing, but their voices betrayed a kind of verbal tumescence. They obviously had an image of this place as a sort of Plato's Retreat on an inclined plane. When we got here we asked a shuttle bus driver how Mammoth got this kind of reputation. "On weekends we get twenty to a hundred buses in here," he replied as we headed through the parking lot of the Main Lodge. "You wouldn't believe what pours out of those buses. It is heartbreak city. There are more blond-haired eighteen-year-olds here on a weekend than there are in all of Scandinavia."

Another reason Mammoth inspired so much prurient interest on the part of uninformed easterners was the legendary natural springs about ten miles outside of the town of Mammoth Lakes. The hot springs were Mother Nature's own Jacuzzi, the site of impromptu and frequent skinny-dipping parties. It was *Bikini Beach Party*, only without the bikinis. Unfortunately, the local authorities have been forced to close the springs. Things were literally getting too hot in Hot Creek, and bathers were coming out parboiled.

Even without being able to check out the heavenly bodies at Hot Creek, we discovered that Mammoth is very much about scenery. The panorama from the summit of Mammoth Mountain at 11,053 feet is breathtaking, extending from the ragged peaks of the Minarets out to desolate Mono Lake, across the Owens Valley and sometimes all the way to Death Valley, 75 miles and 12,000 feet below. This is Ansel Adams country.

Mammoth is the local ski area for the entire population of Southern California. On an average Saturday or Sunday 14,000 people ski there, and virtually all of them arrive by car or bus. The seven-hour drive up Interstate 395 from L.A. is just like going to the beach. Mammoth is open for skiing until about the Fourth of July, so theoretically you can put on your bikini and *then* decide if you want to go skiing or swimming. Since the season goes on nearly forever, no one bothers to look at the calendar before they hop in their car. People flock there because, quite simply, surf's up.

Two High: Skiers cruise the vastness of Paranoid Flats while the Minarets look on. (Photo: Tom Johnson)

Once they get there, they scatter into the woods along the enormous broad shoulders of Mammoth Mountain. Mammoth Lakes is strictly a crossroads vacation town built around the fortunes of the mountain. There is no real center of action, so everyone holes up in their condo. When they do come out to ski, they show the same lemminglike instincts they do when they head for the beach. "Everyone comes up, skis two runs, has lunch, skis two more runs, and goes home," one local told us. "And they all do it at the same time every day." The lines at the gondola can be an hour long during the crush, but when your seatmates could make Charlie's Angels look drab, who's keeping time?

Mammoth reveals a lot about itself even before you get on the ski mountain. In the parking lot, for example, you'll notice that every car and van has chains on its tires. Even the snowplows have them. Mammoth gets an awesome amount of snow, over 400 inches per year. You could drop the entire accumulation from a New England winter under the cornice of the mountain and no one would notice it had arrived. When we got there, the drifts had covered the third-floor windows of the Main Lodge and were heading for the chimney. The snowplows pile the snow up so high on the edges of the parking lots that you would need an ice ax and pitons to climb them. Chains are absolutely essential for getting up the steep roads that wind through the trees to the staging areas of the mountain. Installing and removing chains is a principal source of income for the townspeople.

Those chains are wrapped around the tires of an awful lot of Porsches and customized vans. Ninety percent of them seemed to have vanity license plates like SKI BUM and ALFIE 2 and SCHOONR. Very laid back. All of the skiers getting out of the cars seemed very relaxed. We guess it is part of the etiquette of a seven-hour drive. But then, laid back is the essence of Southern California. Mammoth has extended this idea even to their trail cutting. The broad, rolling flanks of the moun-

tain are an endless series of cloned trails. As Tolstoy said, all intermediate runs are essentially the same. Mammoth has literally dozens of them, served by over two dozen chair lifts. These runs are the freeway mentality applied to skiing. Long, four-lane cruisers with lane markers. The mountain is perfectly groomed, so that people too stoned to apprehend obstacles as such can go with the flow. It's nirvana for the I'm O.K., you're O.K., would-you-get-the-fuck-off-my-skis low rider. Bumps are reduced to the merest dimples on the face of the mountain. Outbreaks of mogul acne are scrubbed away by the grooming crews. The mountain is known for its racing program, so you see a lot of long skis here. The freestyle short ski frenzy never caught on at Mammoth.

There are exceptions to the smooth cruising norm here, of course. We had the time of our lives on Upper and Lower Dry Creek, where skiers are funneled from a wide-open bowl to a cliff-lined gully. These rock cliffs are colorful, glowing, incandescent sun caves. Solar collectors. One sunny day we spotted two pairs of skis stuck into the snow by the base of these rocks. Someone was seeking refuge on the other side of the snowdrifts for God only knows what purpose. Lower Dry Creek is just what its name implies: a zigzag ravine that tosses and turns, forming a narrow trail through trees. Lower Dry Creek is marked on the trail map, but hardly anyone skis it. It should be skied. Lincoln Mountain is another underutilized chunk of real estate. Even though it is surrounded by chair lifts, the only way to get to the top for the powder chutes and wonderful tree skiing is to take off your boards and hike—a long traverse and climb. Powder hounds make the trek after every storm, to cut tracks in the steep chutes that rake the sides of the peak.

Even with these two attractions the bottom of Mammoth merely provides the footlights for the real action. The stage begins up above the treeline. Mammoth is a dormant volcano (they did have a fairly severe earthquake there two years ago) and the upper part of the cone forms the expert ski slopes. At the

Set your sights on the sun: The chairs at Mammoth are freeways to the sky.
(Photo: Tom Johnson)

very peak, accessible from the gondola and one chair lift, is a long cornice, a breaking wave of solid rock. Paranoid Flats drops 1,200 feet over the edge—fall and it's a non-stop slide to the bottom. But if you make your first turn with no problem, you can find a rhythm. This part of the mountain is perfect for wide, sweeping giant slalom turns. Blow one and you can always traverse a mile or two and coast to a stop. Just turn off the engine, pull out of the fall line, and taxi into the next county.

The steeper runs off the cornice are sometimes closed because of avalanche danger. But a few days after a storm, when the snow has settled, the cornice offers some of the steepest powder skiing in America. The snow may be "Sierra cement," but with the gravity assist of a near-50-degree slope you can bank your turns and float. There are drawbacks to terrain this smooth and steep. We saw one poor wretch fall in Hangman's Hollow and tumble about 800 yards. He looked like the corpse of an outlaw being dragged across the desert by the Vigilantes. Gravity just galloped away in a cloud of dust. We never did figure out how he got his skis back, since the safety brakes had parked them up under the lip of the cornice.

Another unusual aspect of skiing up here is the sense it imparts of wandering across a vast white desert. Paranoid Flats and the entire area under the cornice are so wide and deep that you can ski across the area for five minutes without making any apparent progress. Skiers become fly specks in a surreal, bleached moonscape, gradually fading from view feet first, like ships heading over the horizon.

A few days after our first crack at these steep slopes, we found ourselves back up there talking to a lady who was following the pro race circuit. We ended up exchanging business cards with her in an avalanche chute under the cornice at about 11,000 feet. A few molecules of metal on the edge of our skis was all that was keeping us from pitching down this 45-degree slope. Once again we felt the heart-stopping awareness of edges. Then this woman turned, tucked, and took the rest of the chute at about 65 miles per hour. It was life in the fast lane, Mammoth style.

BEST BETS

LODGING

Although the lodging at Mammoth sprawls, it can generally be divided into three areas. The Main Lodge is the farthest up the mountain, but the housing there is mostly undistinguished. The *Mammoth Mountain Inn* has just been renovated, however, and you could check into this place if you want to be right at the center of the action. The area with the best accommodations is over by Warming Hut no. 2, which is at the base of four different chair lifts. Condos like *Snowbird*, 1849,

and the *Ski and Racquet Club* all have very modern units with saunas, Jacuzzis, pools, and the usual range of amenities. The third area for lodging is down in the town itself, and we can recommend the very attractive *Wildflower* condominiums without hesitation. Although the Wildflower has no phones in the units and you do have to drive up to the lifts every day, it is easily the best value in the area. The reservation situation for any of these places is pretty chaotic. There are several competing reservation bureaus, and some of the condominiums prefer to book directly. Your best bet is to call the Mammoth Lakes Chamber of Commerce at 714-934-2712 and ask them to send you literature from all of them.

DINING

The Mammoth area has some really fine restaurants, and you can easily spend a week dining at a different jewel every night. Our favorites include *Roget's*, an exceptional French restaurant with a nice selection of California wines; *Whiskey Creek*, a popular spot that takes reservations and serves basics like barbecued ribs and steaks; and the *Mogul*, a steak place where you cook your own beef. Other local favorites include *Shogun* (new and Japanese), *Berger's* (softball-size sandwiches), and the *Captain's Table* (seafood). *Mountain Hideaway* serves fifty-five variations on the omelet theme, among other things. In addition, there are two special places near Mammoth that you might like to try. The *Carson Peak Inn*, in June Lake, serves complete dinners of steak, chicken, ribs, and seafood, and *Convict Lake*, about ten minutes from downtown, serves elegant Continental fare along with a splendid view of the Sierra Nevada range.

TRANSPORTATION

Cars. Period. Mammoth is about seven hours from L.A., three or four hours from

Surf's up: In late April skiers catch a big one off the cornice at Mammoth. (Photo: James R. Petersen)

Reno, and six or more from San Francisco. Even if you are staying near the lifts, you'll want a car to buy groceries and go to dinner. Be sure you have chains.

RANDOM NOTES

Après-ski life is surprisingly diffused at Mammoth. People gather at the Main Lodge as the afternoon wanes, but then it's off to the hot tubs and dinner. Some carousing takes place at *Andersen's Saloon* (adjacent to Pea Soup Andersen's Restaurant), and the bars of *Whiskey Creek*, the *Rafters*, and the *Cask and Cleaver*. The *Comstock Lodge* has a fireplace and a more intimate atmosphere.

If you can't get enough of the Sierras, Mammoth Heli-Skiing will take you up into the farther reaches of Inyo National Forest for downhill or cross-country skiing in the back country. Spring skiing at Mammoth, which doesn't really begin until the calendar says it's spring, around Easter time, is spectacular. In April there is a bikini parade and plenty of corn snow on the upper reaches of the mountain. You can also ski over the Dragon's Back of the mountain to a solid ice chute through a cave, Hole in the Wall. You can also ski down to the lakes on the back side. You'll need a car to pick you up, and don't try it alone.

Base elevation	7,953 ft.
Vertical drop	3,100 ft.
Number of lifts	27
Skiable acres	3,200
Average skiers per day	14,000 (weekends)
	6,000 (weekdays)
Average snowfall	400 in.
Number of trails	80
Trail breakdown	30% beginner
	40% intermediate
	30% expert

9
MOUNT WASHINGTON VALLEY, NEW HAMPSHIRE

BEST DAYS: Mount Washington Valley

"One day I was teaching a class of children at Mount Cranmore. I had a bunch of five-year-old girls. We went down everything on the mountain. Through the trees, running some gates, everything. It was all the giggling behind me that made it special."

PHIL HAYNES

Viewed from a small airplane buzzing a couple of thousand feet in the air, the Mount Washington Valley is quick to reveal many of its main attractions. The four ski areas strung out along the broad, 20-mile-long valley are clearly visible. So is the imposing bulk of Mount Washington itself; at 6,288 feet it is the tallest mountain in the Northeast and a bit hard to miss. If the winds aren't too furious, the pilot can dip down into the legendary Tuckerman's Ravine, where the rites of spring skiing are raised to a high art every April and May. Careful inspection also reveals enough cross-country ski trails in the valley to exhaust a Finnish border patrolman. At the south end of the valley is the main village, North Conway, with its outskirts of neon-lit, fast-food flotsam and a collection of interesting shops clustered around a picturesque village green.

But the real soul of the valley, the reason people keep returning year after year, is not so obvious. Scattered along the side roads off the main highway is a series of wonderful old country inns, genuine New England classics. They are the kinds of places that wrap guests up in the ambience of down comforters, four-poster beds, and roaring fireplaces. No other ski area we visited has kept the tradition of the country inn more alive or more accessible to skiers. It is a form of hospitality that draws guests from as far away as Norway and Venezuela, an attraction that would (and does) make the Mount Washington Valley a prime vacation destination even without the skiing.

The lure of accommodations at the Christmas Farm Inn, the New England Inn, the Dana Place Inn, the Wildcat Inn, the Eagle Mountain Inn, and several others in the area was powerfully illustrated during our stay there. None of the ski areas in the valley have really adequate artificial snowmaking (although Attitash is about to install it on 80 percent of their trails and Wildcat is covering 7 more miles), and a shortage of the natural stuff combined with a driving rainstorm one day to reduce skiable acres in the valley to zero. But no one was leaving. The lodges were full. "The attitude of our guests is a lot like that of trout fishermen," one owner told us. "They have made the decision to get away.

Sometimes you catch fish, sometimes you don't. The skiers who come here make the same kind of choice. They expect from a lodge owner what a fisherman expects from a guide: patience and camaraderie." So we contentedly settled back and tucked into the next installment of the 25,000-calorie-a-day diet these inns invariably dish up. Then we hoped the weather would clear enough so we could get outside and burn it off.

Skiers who can tear themselves away from their fireplace, or from a second helping of muffins at breakfast, can find some fine skiing in the valley. There are basically three gentler, novice and intermediate areas here: Attitash, Mount Cranmore, and Black Mountain, plus one stern challenge, Wildcat. Cranmore and Attitash both have respectable verticals of about 1,500 feet or so (Black has about a thousand) and are usually warmer and sunnier than Wildcat, which sits in the shadows of Mount Washington at the top of the valley. Cranmore, of course, is famous for its skimobile, a quaint conveyance built in 1938 that resembles an Art Deco bumper-car ride at your favorite amusement park. Plenty of people still come to Cranmore simply to ride the skimobile to the top and enjoy the view and the sunshine without any intention of skiing down.

Wildcat is situated across Pinkham Notch from Mount Washington, focal point of some of the fiercest weather conditions imaginable. Mount Washington is most famous (notorious is perhaps a better word) for being the scene of the highest wind speed ever recorded on the face of the earth, 231 miles per hour. During our visit we were treated to the spectacular sight of a narrow plume of pinkish clouds streaming directly off the summit of Mount Washington at sunset and dipping down into the Notch and then up the side of Wildcat Mountain. Gorgeous, but intimidating. The locals do have a sense of humor about the weather sometimes. We spotted a poster in the ski shop that showed a Western powder hound cutting up the fluff

and the caption penned on it read: "You guys really missed it yesterday."

Wildcat is a top-to-bottom mountain. Skiers use the whole vertical on every run, a feature that isn't always apparent until your thighs start to hum like the strings of a cello. The conditions at the top of the mountain encourage rapid descents, too. For one thing, winds can be so strong they have to string a rope out the gondola door for skiers to hang on to lest they get blown clear into Maine. Also, there aren't any rest rooms up there. Much of Wildcat consists of solid intermediate runs with a touch of expert near the top. These ratings are based on good weather and snow conditions, though, so all bets are off when the elements act up. (In fairness, conditions down valley at Attitash, Cranmore, and Black are usually much more benign.) Polecat was our favorite intermediate route, and we were told that in the spring, the picnic crowd gathers on one of its gentle curves, occasionally adjourning to a glade in the woods for more strenuous workouts. Wildcat and Lynx are sterner stuff. We didn't see too many kamikazes bombing down this mountain. Wildcat seemed to be full of fiercely competent skiers who respect their mountain, hardy stoics who take pride in their ability to handle conditions that send other people to Florida for the season.

The toughest trail in the valley, however, as well as the run with the biggest vertical in the East, is not found at Wildcat. Well, actually, it *starts* at the top of the Wildcat gondola and descends a total of 3,400 feet over 11 miles. The trail is part of the Jackson Ski Touring Foundation, which maintains about 125 miles of groomed and marked trails that wind all over the valley. The Foundation calls itself the Vail of cross-country skiing, and it's probably right.

One day we showed up at the Foundation headquarters, right off the main square in Jackson, and headed out for a tour with Foundation director Thom Perkins and an instructor, Annie Bardach. Nordic skiers gen-

There's no escaping the awesome view of Tuckerman's Ravine from Wildcat.
(Photo: Peter Wingle)

erally had impressed us only as full-tilt masochists on their funny little skis, but when we took one look at Perkins and Bardach flying along, we started to understand the wisdom of their ways. They had as much fun going uphill as down. They led us to ledges that gave us spectacular views of the whole valley. Never mind that we were passed by a pregnant lady and two grandmothers. We stopped for lunch at the enormous old Eagle Mountain Inn (open continuously for 102 years, they boast) and learned that in the spring the whole town retires to a 40-acre meadow on a warm day. Everybody gets pulled up the hill behind tractors, and they set up piles of food and drink. There are races and lots of general mischief, and then everybody skis down to Jackson at the end of the day.

So there are plenty of appealing reasons to come to this valley to ski. There is one primeval reason, too. Those wild winds atop Mount Washington continually dump snow over the edge of a cliff/headwall and into Tuckerman's Ravine, where it piles up as high as 75 feet. Sometime after Easter, the spring avalanches settle down and the snow turns into a solid wall of frozen energy. The rangers then give the O.K. Skiers who have stared across the valley into Tuckerman's from the slopes of Wildcat all season now sling their skis and boots over their shoulders and make the three-hour climb up a rocky path to have a go at the Headwall. They arrive at the mouth of the bowl, perhaps fortifying themselves with a nip of wine and the encouragement of the droves of sunbathers arrayed on the rocks, and then they ascend the 45-degree slope as high as their nerves allow. The slope is so steep you can reach out

Wildcat sometimes lives up to its name. Other times it's a winter wonderland.
(Photo: Jim McElholm)

The rites of spring: When the lifts close, you can always head for Tuckerman's.
(Photo: Dick Smith)

and touch it with your hand. At whatever point their death wish surrenders, they turn, carefully put on their skis, and face the music. If they fall, they endure the original alpine slide to the bottom, unless they hit some rocks on the way. The walk and the climb are what it's all about. You earn your pleasure with sweat, just as in the days before chair lifts. Showing up at Tuckerman's in the spring qualifies you as a true skier, just like checking in at one of the inns down the road qualifies you as a true hedonist. The games are different, but the pleasure is the same.

BEST BETS

LODGING

There are dozens of places to stay in the valley, ranging from elegant old inns to motels that specialize in water beds. Under no circumstances should you miss the former. Tops for atmospheric settings and ambience (not to mention delicious food) are the *Christmas Farm Inn*, the *New England Inn*, and the *Dana Place Inn*. All three have bedrooms in their main buildings, and Christmas Farm has a wonderful rebuilt maple sugaring house with a four-poster bed and fireplace and a two-room log cabin. The *New England Inn* also has some delightful two-room "cottages" that are perfect for couples who like fireplaces, and has its own network of cross-country trails. The *Wildcat Inn* is across the street from the Jackson Ski Touring Foundation and is a popular gathering place for cross-country skiers. The rambling old Eagle Mountain House, with its Grand-Hotel-goes-to-the-country atmosphere, is right above the town of Jackson and has about a hundred rooms open in the winter. If your tastes run to motels, try the *Red Jacket* in North Conway, and if a condo fills the bill, Attitash has many of them, including *River Run*, which is located right on the ski slopes. All of the

above can be booked by calling 603-356-3171, except for *River Run*, which is 603-374-2386.

DINING

All of the above inns operate on the Modified American Plan, which requires you to eat breakfast and dinner at the lodge. Considering the really superb meals their kitchens lay out, this is not exactly a hardship, but there are at least forty other dining spots in town. The well-known *Scottish Lion* (which also has a few simple rooms upstairs) has a varied menu, with Scottish oatcakes and irresistible breads on each table. Across the street is *Stonehurst*, an imposing old mansion of truly Hearstian proportions. Dining takes place in the magnificent downstairs rooms, and if you can take your eyes off the scenery, the food is very nice, too. There's a superb dining room at the *Bernerhof Inn*, where the emphasis is on carefully prepared appetizers and delicious fresh veal that the owner butchers himself. *Le Bistro at Chez Alain* is a French place highly regarded by the locals. A few casual spots worth noting are the *Red Parka Pub*, a popular steak and salad restaurant, and *Papa Mike's*, the only Mexican restaurant in the valley.

TRANSPORTATION

A car is really essential for getting around in the 20-mile-long valley, the main road of which is New Hampshire Route 16. The drive from Boston is about two and a half hours, and you can fly into Boston or Portland, Maine, which is about 60 miles away. Rental cars are available in North Conway if you arrive by Trailways or Vermont Transit Bus, both of which have regular connections three times a day to and from Boston.

RANDOM NOTES

Night life in the valley ranges from quiet conversations around the fireplace at your inn to rowdy goings-on at places like the *Al-*

pine at the base of Mount Cranmore. When the lifts shut down, many skiers head for two places, the *Up Country Saloon*, which has live music both afternoons and evenings, and the *Red Parka Pub*, with its lively bar. *Barnaby's* also has the three D's—dancing, drinking, and dining. The valley has a seemingly endless string of things to do besides skiing, and the local Chamber of Commerce (P.O. Box 385, Mt. Washington Valley, NH 03860) will be glad to fill you in. Lift tickets for any of the areas in the valley are interchangeable for the others, plus Loon, Water-ville, Cannon, Bretton Woods, and Balsams/Wilderness. Don't miss the local TV weather forecasts, which are live from the summit of Mount Washington. Also don't miss a chance to take a plane or helicopter ride up over the valley from the White Mountain Airport. Prices are reasonable for the spectacular flight, and tell Bunky we said hello. Be sure to check and see if the Inferno ski race from the very top of Mount Washington down over Tuckerman's Headwall is being brought back by popular demand. If so, make plans to be there.

	Wildcat Mountain	Attitash	Mt. Cranmore	Black Mountain
Average skiers per day	NA			
Base elevation	1,950 ft.	625 ft.	500 ft.	1,100 ft.
Vertical drop	2,050 ft.	1,675 ft.	1,500 ft.	1,200 ft.
Number of lifts	5	4	6	4
Skiable acres	204	215	300	NA
Average snowfall	100 in.	100 in.	100 in.	100 in.
Number of trails	24	29	17	16
Trail breakdown	9 beginner	5 beginner	5 beginner	5 beginner
	7 intermediate	19 intermediate	7 intermediate	6 intermediate
	8 expert	5 expert	5 expert	5 expert

10
PARK CITY, UTAH

BEST DAYS : Park City

"It wasn't just a best day, it was a best weekend. Late in March, when lots of people had called it quits after a lousy snow year, everything came together. On Saturday we skied in new powder at Deer Valley in the company of a woman so beautiful she could make grown men cry, and when you cry in Smith goggles, the damn things fog. Sunday at Park City was so warm that skiers were taking off their jackets and sweaters and piling them up in heaps at the bottom of the lifts. They skied in shirtsleeves, or less. You could smell suntan lotion everywhere on the mountain. Deep powder, endless love, and Miami Beach in one weekend. As the song says, who could ask for anything more?"

THE AUTHORS

Let us begin with a short story—a confession, actually. For years we would arrive at the Salt Lake City airport on our way to Alta for a quick powder fix. The airport was always a zoo, overrun with college kids throwing Frisbees and rejoicing over driving the flight crew crazy on the trip over from California or Boston or Chicago. Each time we would murmur a quiet prayer: Please, God, let them go to Park City. Sure enough, a bus with the sign "Park City Institute for the Criminally Uninhibited" would pick them up. We would sigh thankfully and head for Alta, wondering what kind of ski area would harbor such animals.

Now jump cut to two consecutive days at Park City last March. On Day One we are skiing in our sweaters under a warm, cloudless sky. We are overdressed. Beautiful women are skimming by us wearing only Danskin tops and gym shorts. We try to ignore them. We are searching instead for the blonde in the white top who walked into the breakfast café in the plaza at the base of the lifts this morning. We had experienced im-

mediate, undying love. Food fell out of our mouths. Now we can't find her, but her entire sorority seems to be skiing by us. We give up the search and start contemplating a statue honoring the inventor of Danskins.

On Day Two we are standing at the top of Jupiter Bowl. It is as far back into the Park City limits as you can get without setting off overland for Heber or Provo. We have been skiing the steep walls of this beautiful, wide semicircle and also keeping an eye on a rope strung between two pine trees near the top of the lift. The sign on the rope says, "Scott's Bowl is closed," but we know the ski patrol is working over there and the sign will come down soon. About twenty skiers have assembled to watch the patrolmen work their way along the overhanging lip of the bowl, tapping the edge with their poles to dislodge the loose stuff, checking the avalanche potential. The crowd is quiet. It feels like a family gathering. When the rope comes down, we tear off for Scott's along a narrow trail full of huge, rippled compression bumps. A few wipe out and a few smash into the trees. No

Look before you leap: Skiers assess McDonald's Ridge near Park City. (Photo: Pat McDowell)

one stops. It's the powder Nazi version of the Oklahoma land rush. We all sidestep up the steep ridge and there is one magical moment when everyone is poised but no one leaps. Virgin snow is about to be sacrificed. Finally, we launch ourselves into waist-deep powder. We hardly need to make turns. The snow is so deep that if you turn sideways, you'll stop dead. Instead we throw up rooster tails, jet streams of white dust. We start to understand how a lynch mob feels as powderlust rises in us. We peel off through the thick pine trees and come back for more. All afternoon the same cast of maybe two dozen skiers lays down lines in Scott's Bowl, like a musical score taking shape.

If you haven't already got the message, we are trying to say that Park City is one of the most surprising ski areas in the Rockies. It is also one of the most underrated. Park City has a reputation as a "family" area, with lots of wonderful intermediate skiing and incomprehensible drinking laws. No one prepared us for all the powder and all the beautiful women. Perhaps best of all is the fact that Park City is a great place to visit with a group of friends of different skiing abilities, because it really does have something nice for everyone. Sixty percent of the trails are rated intermediate, but the expert and beginner runs don't have to apologize for their existence. Even the restaurants seem to be undervalued, and the accommodations are more than just adequate. So why has Park City been overlooked? Well, the Church of Latter-day Saints may have something to do with it. Plus there being no national media attention focused on Utah very often.

But no matter. Once you get to Park City you mingle with all those Californians (60 percent of Park City skiers hail from the coast), mostly college kids who come here on charters or by bus. All those lovely California girls go head to head with the local crop and the confrontation even inspired Seals and Crofts to pen a song to those "Park City Ladies."

The town of Park City itself is about one mile from the lifts. Back in the late 1800s miners took $400 million in silver out of the holes that cover the ski mountain, and the town was a Victorian gem. Today it is no great beauty (no one will ever mistake it for Telluride), but the town and the mountain seem somehow perfectly integrated: You get the remains of the mining industry all over the mountain with the skiers on top. The mountain is so full of old mine shafts that they have to blow extra snow on some places to keep the warm, trapped air from melting the base cover. (Be sure to look out for the mole people when you go around a curve.) It's difficult to calculate the effect of skiing history, but Park City seems to teach you downhill touring. We were always stopping to inspect the worn timbers on the side of one of the old buildings that dot the ski area, or the rusted towers that were used to haul ore buckets up to the mine shafts. They make great backdrops for your snapshots.

If you point your camera up from the base of the lifts, you see two ridges, Payday and King Con (for Consolidated). Payday, the one on the left, is also the name of the famous intermediate trail that runs along the spine of the ridge (it's even lit up for 1¼ miles of night skiing), and it tempts you to go fast. You can peel off Payday down Nail Driver or Widow Maker, short, unexciting expert runs. This is where, one day, we came across a little girl about nine years old. She had missed her turnoff and found herself staring down a black-diamond run, groomed but still steep. We asked her how she skied and she said she had a bombproof snowplow. We started to talk her down and she proceeded to make nine or ten beautiful linked turns. By the bottom of the slope she was poling to pick up more speed. Born to cruise. Someday she'll be dangerous.

The right-hand ridge, King Con, has a couple of steep giant slalom runs that face the base lodge. They are often unpacked and usually uncrowded. We found ourselves cutting figure eights on them one day in about ten inches of new snow, like some precision drill team, the Blue Angels or Thunderbirds. You can drop off the back side of this ridge

Downhill touring: Old mining ruins are a prime distraction at Park City. (Photo: Tom Passavant)

onto eight or nine very fine intermediate cruisers like Climax, Shamus, or Liberty, or you can work your way in the other direction back into the mountain and catch the bump runs off the Motherlode and Thaynes chair lifts. There are a half-dozen good ones back here, and any one of them will give your legs a workout. Glory Hole and Ford Country have pitches as abrupt as any on the mountain, the kind where a forward fall will leave you airborne before you smash into the tops of the moguls on reentry. Double Jack and Hoist are more of the same. All of the runs splayed out along this ridge start out flat, letting you get loose, and then take a nose dive, like Highline or Blue Ox at Vail. One unique trail in this set is the Hoist, which has a sign at the top that restricts the run to people

with skis at least 190 centimeters or longer. The idea is to keep the bumps big and rounded, not short and chopped off as they are when short skiers have at them. We couldn't detect any difference in the moguls on the Hoist, but it's a nice gesture all the same.

From the top of Thaynes, which is also at the top of the endless (twenty-three minutes) gondola from the base, you can have lunch at the Summit House restaurant or maybe lose your lunch dropping off the edge of the earth into Blueslip Bowl, a short, steep plunge gouged out of one side of the peak. It used to be off limits because of avalanche danger, and any employee caught skiing it was given a blue dismissal slip. The face of Blueslip is definitely a rush, and the long runout through the woods is more downhill touring at its best.

From the summit you can meander along the Jupiter Bowl access road and down through the trees to the base of the Jupiter lift. At the top a chalkboard says, "Welcome to Jupiter," with a three-color sketch of the planet. From there you can traverse as far as you like around the rim of this gorgeous semicircle and then pick your line. It has trees and wide-open slopes and it is all an expert's delight. The ridge right under the chair is the most precipitous—Jupiter is 1,100 feet of vertical, and most of it is in the first 10 feet of horizontal. If you get bored with Jupiter, there is Scott's Bowl right beside it. All of this is at Park City, and we haven't even mentioned Deer Valley, the new area being developed on the peaks and ridges adjoining Park City. Deer Valley will be open beginning with the 1981–82 season. Its trails are well-designed, continuous fall line runs that eventually will be scattered across three separate mountains. Even though it will be a few more years until the entire area is open to skiers, what's there right now is delightful. There's even more skiing in the Park City complex when you consider Utah Powder Guides, who offer helicopter skiing in the lightest powder on earth in the Wasatch and Uinta mountains. If you remain unconvinced, we've included a portfolio of Park City photographer Pat McDowell's pictures to quiet any remaining doubters.

BEST BETS

LODGING

Park City is undergoing a construction boom of large proportions and the housing situation is changing (mostly for the better) practically every month. The resulting urban sprawl is not the last word in aesthetics, but most of the condos (hotels are scarce) are new and attractive, at least on the inside. Our favorite is *Snowflower*, a short walk from the lifts and village plaza. The units here are spacious, modern, and equipped with wonderful Jacuzzis. *Village Plaza* condos have the best location of all, right above the shops and restaurants of the mall. There is a two-story penthouse with two bedrooms that fills up fast every season; the others are a bit small but tastefully furnished. *Shadow Ridge* is a brand-new, red-brick box that squats at one end of the main parking lot. These condos are as graceful on the inside as they are ordinary on the outside. Also brand-new and highly recommended is the *Copperbottom Inn*, a small (thirty-one units) and elegant condo/hotel about a quarter mile from the lifts with its own shuttle van. Also, *Prospector Square* has over 300 units scattered about a mile from the lifts, and it features a gym and health club, plus its own restaurant. Central Reservations can book all the above at 801-649-8266.

DINING

We've enjoyed an unbroken string of fine meals in our visits to Park City, at places like *Adolph's* (delicious Swiss food, especially the veal dishes), *Janeaux's* (Continental), and *Car 19* (eclectic, very good). Downstairs from Car 19 is the slightly dressier *Shannon's*. Good steaks and casual atmosphere can be found in the *Claimjumper*, which is part of the hotel of the same name in town. The *Park City Yacht Club* serves fish dishes at its location right in the village, and *El Papagayo* has good Mexican fare. Breakfasts are a special treat at the *Corner Store* right on the main level of the mall: great omelets on hard rolls, fresh juices, and the like.

TRANSPORTATION

You aim for Salt Lake City. A snap. Once you are there, catch one of several regular shuttle buses for the fifty-minute trip to Park City. Easy. You can also share a cab or even a helicopter if you can't wait. Unlike Alta or Snowbird, Park City boasts that you'll never get snowed in or snowed out. A four-lane superhighway (Interstate 80) guarantees access. Once you get there, the local shuttle bus will get you around. It could run more often and the schedule could be more accessible, but it does work O.K.

RANDOM NOTES

Most of the après-ski action takes place in the various bars located in the plaza, and on nice days everybody seems to sit outside in the sun and check out the action. Alcohol can be had at the *Rusty Nail, Leibo's,* or the *Park City Yacht Club* right in the Plaza. Live dance music can be found at the *Rusty Nail,* upstairs from the base café, and on Main Street at the *Cowboy Bar* and the *Black Pearl* (a.k.a. Jody's). The local hot-tub emporium is called the *Health Spa.* Ski touring out at the White Pine Touring Center features some spectacular multiday treks into the mountains. There are shuttles over to Alta and Snowbird (under an hour away) daily from Park City, and your five- or six-day lift ticket can be exchanged before you go over. Want some local color at Park City? Try the *Alamo,* a serious bar on Main Street in town. P.S. Susan, we love you.

Base elevation	6,900 ft.
Vertical drop	3,100 ft.
Number of lifts	12
Skiable acres	2,200
Average skiers per day	NA
Average snowfall	300 in.
Number of trails	65
Trail breakdown	11 beginner
	30 intermediate
	24 expert

Don't they ever get tired of this? Photographer Pat McDowell calls this shot "Peaches and Cream."

It's another boring day in paradise as the Utah Powder Guides go to work. (Photo: Pat McDowell)

Enough is enough. Dave Cotter cuts perfect, lazy tracks near Park City. (Photo: Pat McDowell)

11
SNOWBIRD, UTAH

BEST DAYS : Snowbird

"One day I caught the last tram of the afternoon and I noticed that the ski patrol had finally opened up Little Cloud, a steep, high bowl off to the side of Regulator Johnson. It was an open invitation, like having a lover turn down the sheets to a bed. I just jumped in. All the lifts had closed and I could hear screaming laughter echoing off the rocks. The voice was yelling, 'This is fun!' *a good half mile away. It was."*

SUSIE KAY

There is a rumor that Texas oilman Dick Bass built Snowbird because he got a good deal on a warehouse full of black-diamond trail markers. Maybe they came from his brother Harry, who helped build Vail. No matter. Snowbird quickly provides new and greatly enlarged understanding of the terms *steep* and *deep*. A few ski areas like Jackson Hole have a fourth class of trails beyond the usual green circles, blue squares, and black diamonds—a yellow triangle with an orange exclamation point inside it that means "Expert, Use Extra Caution." At Snowbird these exclamation-point trails would barely merit an intermediate rating. If they even bother to mark a trail with a black diamond, it means "This is the easy way down." The unmarked parts (i.e., most of the mountain) are a monument to getting your act together and taking it on the tram. An obstacle course for the courageous and competent.

What Snowbird ought to figure out is a way to indicate the power of their trails, the gravity assist. Snowbird's terrain would be suicidal in New England, but when it is covered with 450 inches of snow a year, in-

cluding 85 and 79 inches in March and April respectively, the steeps become necessary if you are going to move at all. One day after a March blizzard we made first tracks down parts of Chip's Run and Silver Fox and found that the flat sections were almost impassable. We had to break trails and slog along like the peasants in *Dr. Zhivago.* We realized that gravity and snow depth are related. It was like setting the gears of a truck: STEEP INCLINE: USE FIRST GEAR. Other slopes get packed out and let you shift into fourth. Deep cancels out steep. Cold comfort at the top of the Snowbird tram, when you are surrounded by an endless choice between drop-offs and elevator shafts, but true just the same.

You don't have to be an expert skier to enjoy Snowbird, but it does help. Strong intermediates who are aggressive on challenging terrain can have a wonderful time, but Snowbird, like Stowe, attracts some of the hottest skiers on the planet. The morning after a big powder storm we saw enough skiers with classic, flawless techniques to make us think that a ski movie was being

Dave Bodgner unfurls his powder wings and heads for the office. (Photo: Pat McDowell)

On a clear day you can see forever, or at least all the way down to Salt Lake City. (Photo: Snowbird)

shot on every steep pitch and cornice on the mountain.

A single ride to the top of the tram is all it takes to sense the abruptly vertical nature of Snowbird. The Wasatch Mountains form a solid wall that stares back at skiers all the way from the parking lot of the Salt Lake City airport. Snowbird is a mere 31 miles from the runways, so the wall closes in very quickly. By the time you reach the mouth of Little Cottonwood Canyon and start to wind your way up this narrow sliver of valley, the scenery appears to be just across the room. At the end, a series of small canyons—mini-amphitheaters—marches along the south side at right angles to the main road. The last two in line are named Albion Basin and Germania Bowl, and they are the Alta terrain. The next two, Peruvian Gulch and Gad Valley, make up Snowbird. Viewed from the road, Snowbird looks like the screen of a drive-in movie, only dented.

The meteorological effect of this tight squeeze is that clouds get trapped up at the end of the box canyon and astonishing snowfalls get wrung out of them for days on end. Each flake has had all the moisture leached out of it by the long trip across the salt flats. The result is the stuff of legend: dry Utah powder. White smoke. It falls gently and piles up like feathers shaken out of a goose-down quilt. Skiers who have never been in deep powder, who have been pampered by years of skiing groomed trails, can get the surprise of their lives here. We heard about one fellow who rode up to the top of the tram without gloves or ski goggles and proceeded to ski off a cliff. This is not an amusement park or an air-conditioned ski arcade. Snowbird punishes the unprepared.

The people who ski here regularly become tuned in to mountaineering: the right equipment, the right weather sense, efficiency in adverse conditions. They ski with precision bearings. Quick as a hiccup. Sharp as a tack. Most of the time they stay on the 125-person tram that runs up the middle of the ridge which splits Snowbird into its two halves. The upper reaches of both amphitheaters—the cheap seats, as it were—are for experts only. These crags are full of chutes, couloirs, and steep, open powder faces like Peruvian Cirque and Little Cloud. Off the very top to the southwest of the tram you'll find Pipeline, the hairiest chute at Snowbird. This Pipeline has two things in common with Hawaii's Pipeline—rocks underneath you and rocks on both sides. The climb getting to it is a minor religious experience or, if you blow it, an afterlife all its own. Then there is Regulator Johnson, probably the biggest, most wide-open deep powder terrain south of the Hobacks at Jackson Hole. Regulator begins off the west side of the tram and is half a mile wide and 1,100 feet down. A Big Burn for adults. Above and to the left of Regulator is Little Cloud, another astonishing expanse of steep, open slope hard up against a rock wall. The new Little Cloud chair lift has made this area much more accessible (you used to have to traverse over from the tram), but Little Cloud is still often closed because of avalanche danger and poor visibility.

Another option is to ski right down the center ridge off the tram and not peel off down Chip's Run or Regulator. Skiers who elect to do this had better be prepared for some tough going. All along the knife-edge ridge are ropes with "Open" signs fluttering in the wind out over impossible-looking descents. Both sides are full of secret powder shots and a bewildering variety of landscapes. "See that old dead tree just up ahead?" our guide told us one day. "Go down beyond it about ten feet and turn left. You'll love it." One day we were thrashing through the moguls on Silver Fox and heard whoops coming from a section of Dalton's Draw up above us. Four skiers came hurtling out of the trees from an angle that revealed no possible route down except by parachute. We still haven't figured out how one gets to Dalton's Draw or its neighbor, Mach Schnell, in the first place, but we can't wait to go back and learn. This sort of thing happens all the time at Snowbird. You look up at cliffs that Sir Edmund Hillary would balk at climbing and they are always covered with tracks. Skiers keep popping out of the damndest places, and you ride back up the mountain determined to try it yourself.

Intermediates stick mostly to the bottoms of the valleys on both sides of the ridge, especially on a series of runs such as Bassackwards, Bananas, and Election that come off the top of the Gad II chair. Unfortunately (or fortunately, depending on your point of view), those parts of Snowbird that aren't dizzyingly steep are usually heavily moguled. The saving grace is that they are not rock-hard humps of ice like most moguls. These are usually freshly formed and soft. "One day in April the sun was shining and the moguls were so soft the mounds of snow would explode on contact," a woman told us. "It was human trail grooming."

The most sensible way to learn your way around is to take one of the free guided tours offered by the green-suited Snowbird hosts and hostesses. They gather on the plaza at the Snowbird Center above the tram base, as does the Mountain Experience, a gung-ho group that will, for a fee, guide you to what they euphemistically call "challenging terrain."

This kind of skiing obviously does not make for late nights and wild parties. It's a good thing, too, since Snowbird night life looks exciting only if you're staying up the road at Alta. We sat and listened to one newcomer rattle off a list of French and Austrian resorts while complaining about the lack of *joie de vivre* in Little Cottonwood Canyon. "You know what's wrong?" he said. "No night life. Dancing should start at four-thirty. There should be an ice bar at the foot of the mountain. Oh, for the glorious days of the Austrian ski instructors, who could party till dawn and then ski like angels in the morning." We left him babbling and pointed him in the direction of Colorado.

A third of all Snowbird skiers come from California, but they know better than to expect beach-blanket bingo here. They discovered Utah during the snow drought a few years ago and they seem to feel comfortable in the concrete high rises of Snowbird. Alta is

Attack of the powder hounds: LeRoi Williams obliterates himself in Wasatch powder. (Photo: Mike Epstein)

not so much to their liking. A third of all skiers here are single, and a third are female, which seems to show that black diamonds can be a girl's best friend. Snowbird has some astonishing lady skiers.

Some detractors call Snowbird concrete city, but we like the architecture a lot better than quaint Tyrolean nonsense. These tall buildings, three condos and one hotel plus the Snowbird Center, have a power and quiet that matches the raw rock of the mountains. Besides, the balconies make great launching pads when you get snowed in for three days and you take to diving into the heated pools of your lodge from the second or third floor. The go-for-it mentality with a side order of cabin fever.

Finally, Snowbird is where many of the lesson sequences you see in the ski magazines get shot, usually late in the season. These pictures have helped make a star of Corky Fowler, Snowbird's director of skiing. He is also the author of a fine book called *The Hidden Skier*. Corky told us, "I'm deceptive, an illusion maker. I ski to experience grace. I look at a slope and see energy lines, rivers flowing down. I just join the flow of one of those lines. When I play golf, I can see tunnels in the air, the path of the ball. It's the same thing." We skied with Corky one day and watched him drift down the slope like a leaf in the current. The secret of most sports, he said, is that there is no resistance. If you are doing it right, it should be effortless. Skiing does not have an opponent, he adds, only friends.

Say hello to Snowbird.

BEST BETS

LODGING

The *Lodge* at Snowbird, the *Turramurra*, and the *Iron Blosam* have a total of 409 condominium units. They include single bedrooms, studios with kitchen and foldout beds, one-bedroom suites, and some larger units that sleep six or more. The *Cliff Lodge* is a 162-room hotel. All four are clean and modern and have many amenities like saunas and outdoor heated pools. We personally feel that the studios in the condos, especially the ones in the Lodge at Snowbird, are the best deal for a couple, if you don't mind sleeping on the sofa bed. Reservations for all units at Snowbird can be had by calling 801-742-2000.

DINING

There are five places to have dinner at Snowbird, plus a few casual spots in the Snowbird Center for ice cream, snacks, and lunches. In addition, there is a small grocery store where you can stock up on supplies for the condo. The *Steak Pit*, located in the Center, is one of our favorite ski-country steakhouses. They have tasty salads, excellent beef, and our favorite dessert, mud pie, a concoction of coffee ice cream covered with chocolate sauce inside a chocolate-cookie pie crust. A model of its kind. The *Mexican Keyhole* has the usual tacos and enchiladas, and the *Golden Cliff* dining room and the *Lodge at Snowbird Club* are private dining rooms (that means you have to pay a membership fee to get in, but then they can serve you liquor) with Continental menus. The *Forklift* has informal dinners in the Center.

TRANSPORTATION

Same as for Alta (see Chapter 1). Cars are really unnecessary here unless you plan to drive into Salt Lake. Take the shuttle bus from the airport instead.

RANDOM NOTES

The Utah liquor laws are actually more confusing than restricting. In fact, since the miniature bottles they sell contain about twice as much booze as you would normally get in a drink ordered from a bar, they probably encourage you to get bombed faster. At any rate, the *Tram Bar* in the Snowbird Center is the hub of what passes for après ski here. The big attraction is the chance to watch the giant inner workings of the tram through a glass wall on one side of the bar. Otherwise, you're pretty much limited to the pool, the sauna, or a predinner drink in your condo. Don't forget the alternative of dinner up at Alta. The *Alta Lodge*, the *Rustler*, and the *Shallow Shaft* steakhouse have very good food, and if you call in advance they'll try to squeeze you in. Transportation up to Alta is good during the day but chancy at night, so check carefully lest you get stranded. If you still want more powder, Wasatch Powderbird Guides offers helicopter skiing from a pad right at the ski area.

Base elevation	7,900 ft.
Vertical drop	3,100 ft.
Number of lifts	8
Skiable acres	1,900
Average skiers per day	2,200
Average snowfall	450 in.
Number of trails	NA
Trail breakdown	20% beginner
	30% intermediate
	50% expert

12
SNOWMASS, COLORADO

BEST DAYS : Snowmass

"To be on the Big Burn on a sunny day is my idea of screaming happiness."

GRACE LICHTENSTEIN

Riding up the Elk Camp chair lift at the far eastern end of Snowmass one day, we spotted a skier moving toward us in a tight tuck at about fifty miles an hour. We knew that Snowmass was famous for its high-speed cruising terrain, but this guy in the skin-tight blue outfit was carrying things a bit too far. As he hurtled directly under our chair, he looked like a smoothly muscled cerulean panther about to spring. Then he took some air to prejump the lip of a knoll and was gone in a few swift seconds.

It turned out that the Aspen Ski Club was holding a race on Elk Camp that afternoon (Aspen and Snowmass are just 10 miles apart and share a common lift ticket), but you don't have to be a member of their downhill air force to fly Snowmass anytime you want. The secret of Snowmass's appeal is that no matter how good a skier you actually are, this place will make you feel like you're ready to challenge Franz Klammer for king of the hill. Snowmass combines an enormous, gently sloped mountain, bigger than all three other Aspen areas combined, with first-class trail grooming and ego snow of the softest,

most forgiving variety. It all adds up to ultimate skiing bliss, high-speed cruising division. At Snowmass you don't have to worry about skiing off a cliff or into mogul minefields. You just aim downhill and turn 'em loose.

"I keep coming back because it's fun," said a friend who is good enough to ski any mountain she chooses. "I love the wide-open spaces and the bright sunshine." She reminded us that not every skier who *can* ski Snowbird or Jackson Hole *wants* to all the time. Some would rather just relax and cruise at times, and Snowmass was made for those times.

On our most recent trip here we spent three days skiing the Big Burn under blue skies and 40-degree temperatures. The Burn is just one section of Snowmass but is easily the most famous intermediate run in the world. This huge open face is at least a half mile wide and has 1,800 feet of vertical drop. It's bigger than most entire ski areas, and at Snowmass it only gets you about halfway down the mountain. Legend has it that the Ute Indians set fire to the slope so that the

settlers who forced them off their sacred land couldn't make any productive use of it. They didn't count on the invention of the chair lift. On our trips down the Burn the soft powder airbrushed all our mistakes away and we took the entire 1,800 feet in one deep breath. Look out, Franz.

Later we hooked up with a lady who had skied Snowmass for seven or eight years and she told us why she kept coming back. "I know this is supposed to be a place for former swingers who've gotten married and had kids. Dentists and doctors buy up all of the condos. They get lots of people from Chicago and Detroit and Texas, and lots of ski clubs, too. For them, the attraction is a big mountain with a condo right on the slopes and a place to leave the kids during the day. Snowmass is three fourths the size of Vail, and there are enough lifts so the lines aren't too long. The new number-nine lift going up the Burn has made a big difference over there. I know I can come here when Ajax has taken its toll on my legs and Snowmass will make me look good and feel good. A day spent cruising Snowmass is hard to beat."

A lot of people think of Snowmass only as the Big Burn and put it down for being an unending series of cloned runs that get boring after a few days. Since there are eighty runs here, common sense suggests that there might be some variety after all. Even the Burn is not monolithic. It gets tougher as you move from west to east across the face, and by the time you reach the far-left side there are some nicely pitched black diamonds like Glissade and Garret Gulch. There are at least four separate sections of Snowmass, without counting the broad lower flanks of the mountain that seemed to be used mostly as access to the upper trails.

"On a typical day we like to go up to the top of Elk Camp first thing in the morning," another frequent visitor told us. "The view from the top back into the Maroon Bells is spectacular. Later in the morning my hus-band and I work our way over to High Alpine for the steeper stuff over there. We like to ski Chair Nine on the Burn, which is really nice and not as crowded as Four, especially around lunchtime. In deep, fresh snow it has the best powder terrain on the mountain, except maybe for High Alpine. Better skiers have an advantage at Snowmass because intermediates come here to ski the easier stuff. The tougher trails have smaller lines."

High Alpine deserves special mention. It has perhaps the three steepest runs on the mountain plus another, Green Cabin, that reminded us of Jackson Hole, with big cirques of solid brown rock towering overhead and gnarled trees sticking out of the rocks at odd angles. Who would expect this at boring old Snowmass? Who would expect Hanging Valley, a dense glade of trees that is barely recognizable as a run, much less a trail? It is poorly marked, just sort of disappearing into the evergreens at the far side of High Alpine. One person we talked to insisted on skiing it with a companion because she feared she might never make it out of the thick closet of spruces and pines by herself.

Snowmass is not exactly an underpopulated mountain, but the thousand feet of vertical below the Big Burn and High Alpine and Elk Camp seemed to be deserted every time we encountered it. What other area that puts eight or nine thousand people on the ski slopes every day has that much open space? The sight of all that nicely groomed, gently rolling terrain made us wonder if Snowmass shouldn't rent some of it to Telluride or Snowbird, both of which could use it. As matters now stand, most skiers seem to use these runs only when they are cruising back to their condos for lunch or dinner.

Skiing directly back to your condo is, of course, exactly what the developers of Snowmass had in mind when they designed the place. Although the Aspen Ski Corporation owns and operates the lifts and maintains the ski hill, the Snowmass Company manages everything else. Snowmass is a totally master-

Sergeant Preston lives: a cross-country skier near Ashcroft, site of the old TV series. (Photo: Russell/Kelly)

planned resort, from the sidewalks to the electrically heated main thoroughfare, Snowmelt Road. It claims to be the only ski area with every bed right on the slopes, and the promise of a condo or hotel room that lets you ski directly to and from the lifts is gen- erally well kept. At first, back in the 1960s, it was called Snowmass-at-Aspen, but as the area has matured it is seeking its own iden- tity away from Big Brother. Snowmass makes no bones about its family and intermediate- skier orientation. It is also no secret that

Where there's smoke: letting it rip on the Big Burn, scene of endless linked turns.
(Photo: Snowmass)

when the sun goes down a lot of Snowmass skiers make the twenty-minute drive to the big city for food and frolic. In a sense, Snowmass, with its large pool of high-quality housing, is a bedroom community for Aspen, the way Greenwich is an extension of New York. They are close enough so that you can soak up the culture and good food and night life of Aspen the way people in Greenwich sample New York. One advantage of being the younger brother of Aspen is that Snowmass has learned from Aspen's mistakes. This is an area that builds low-cost condos and sells them to employees at bargain rates, thereby keeping the staff happy and cutting down their commuting time.

"Snowmass is well run and the people are very nice," concluded one regular. "Even the lift attendants are great. They always play nice music at the bottom of their lifts. I really do think that if you enjoy skiing anywhere, you'll enjoy Snowmass."

BEST BETS

LODGING

Snowmass consists of five lodges and nineteen condominiums that are built right up the side of the ski hill, stairstep fashion. On one side of these accommodations are the ski trails and lifts and on the other side is Snowmelt Road and the parking lots. About halfway up the hill is a pedestrian mall lined with shops and restaurants, which is accessible via some steep sidewalks and stairs or by a shuttle bus that runs up and down the road. Our favorite condos are the very luxurious *Top of the Village* units, with fireplaces and private balconies (no. 303 even has a private Jacuzzi in the master bedroom), just completed *Woodrun V*, and the similarly brand-new *Enclave*, whose spacious units are at the bottom of the mountain. The top lodges are the *Stonebridge* and the centrally located *Silvertree/Eldorado*. The most unusual and romantic place to stay is *Aspen House*, an absolutely spectacular private chalet that consists of four master suites built around a central living area. Reservations are scarce and the price is high, but Aspen House is truly special. There are a number of

Easter Sunday: tracks laid down by skiers with skinny skis near Snowmass. (Photo: © 1980 Robert Chamberlain)

other private homes for rent, including one seven-bedroom palace with its own swimming pool that rents for $2,500 per week. Not a bad deal if you have a dozen friends to bring along. Reservations and information on all of the above lodgings can be had at 303-923-2000.

DINING

The combination of easy access to the restaurants of Aspen and a large number of condominiums with their own kitchen facilities seems to have kept Snowmass from developing really first-class dining. The *Pepper Mill* seems to be everybody's favorite and the continental menu is very nice. The *Refectory* has a surf-and-turf menu, and *La Piñata* is the standard-issue Mexican restau-

rant. The *Stew Pot* is a pleasant, informal place for homemade soups and breads, and we enjoyed the quick, tasty breakfasts at the *Village Deli*. All of the above are located in the Mall in the center of the village. Locals speak highly of *Mama Maria's* pizza down the road a bit, and the lunchtime food at *Sam's Knob* and especially the *High Alpine Restaurant* on the mountain is first rate, rivaling the on-slope meals served at Vail and Sun Valley.

TRANSPORTATION

The directions for reaching Snowmass are the same as for Aspen (see Chapter 2), except that when you leave the airport you turn left for Snowmass instead of right for Aspen. Taxis are inexpensive and convenient. During the day skiers are shuttled to any of the four ski areas for free, and we have found that the Pitkin County bus (exact change only) will get you to and from Aspen at night as long as you don't linger much past midnight.

RANDOM NOTES

Après-ski activity at Snowmass seems to consist mainly of taking a dip in one of the many pools scattered around the premises (we like the one at the *Timberline* with its Jacuzzi jets) or getting ready to head into Aspen. There are a few comfortable watering holes around the Village Mall, including the popular *Timbermill* and the casual *Casa Che*, where you can ski directly to the bar or into the pool if you get up too much speed on the homeward run. Also note that the mid-mountain *Ullrhof* short-order restaurant has a pay phone on its outdoor deck. It's the perfect spot for calling the office and making everyone back home jealous.

Base elevation	8,208 ft.
Vertical drop	3,600 ft.
Number of lifts	13
Skiable acres	1,420
Average skiers per day	8,000–9,000
Average snowfall	300 in.
Number of trails	76
Trail breakdown	15% beginner
	60% intermediate
	25% expert

13
SQUAW VALLEY, CALIFORNIA

BEST DAYS : Squaw Valley

"A storm had come in and the headwall was windpacked and firm. I would make a turn and kick up a 20-foot rooster tail that would hang in the air, ethereal. We get this firm windpack, with a touch of silk, and you ski something so steep that the snow from the previous turn will move down the hill faster than you. It explodes, billows, and floats up into your face, stinging your cheeks."

JUDY LEE

At the moment we are perched on the edge of a headwall, a cliff that mellows out far below into something called Siberia Bowl. The face below us is so steep that we could drop a snowball at arm's length and it would land thirty or forty feet down the hill. We peer tentatively over the edge and try to figure out the technique for skiing vertical snow. As we are thinking about it, a guy comes hurtling past us, completely nonchalant, and jumps the cornice like it was a sidewalk curb. No contemplation or hesitation at all, just aim and fire. This bravura display of the right stuff neatly illustrates two important points about Squaw Valley. The first is that this mountain defines the term *challenge*. Skiers who can't find something at Squaw to scare themselves silly must be on industrial-strength Valium. The second is that there are skiers who live here precisely because of those challenges, people who go higher, faster, and farther, who ski the edge.

If any mountain in the world is appropriate for taking it to the limit, it is Squaw Valley. The place is huge. The skiable terrain is so vast they don't bother to rate each trail,

they just rate the lifts. KT-22, for example, deposits you in exclusively black-diamond territory, while the Shirley Lake chair has more moderate, rolling acreage beneath it. One day we heard a message squawk out of a ski patrolman's walkie-talkie: "You are within a city block of the accident." A city block. The absurdity of the remark had the ski patrol in stitches. Some of these guys haven't seen a city in years.

If you lay the place out flat, the way it appears on the trail map, Squaw Valley is shaped like a fan. The main base area looks up a narrow canyon toward Squaw Peak, one of four separate mountains that form the top points of the fan. The lower part of the mountain is mainly a funnel down which everyone flows at the end of the day. The exception is off to the left of the main base area, where the notorious slopes of KT-22 and Red Dog beckon experts whose psyches and knees crave the supersteep or bungalow-sized moguls, or both. Of the other two peaks, Headwall and Emigrant (named for the settlers who came over the ridge on horseback), the latter isn't visible from the

From here to eternity: Skiers drop over the edge of Upper Sun Bowl at Squaw.
(Photo: James R. Petersen)

bottom. You've got to go up to the second staging area, elevation 8,200, before the entire panorama opens up. Up here the entire spine of the Sierra Nevada is strung out in front of you, and from the highest points you can see Lake Tahoe glistening in the sun. Above elevation 8,200 is the best intermediate and beginner skiing, an endless variety of plateaus and shoulders. There seems to be more of everything up here: tree skiing, bump runs, cornices, headwalls, cruises. The four peaks of the fan have a webbing of ridges that undulate down to give you bowls that could swallow most Americans in one gulp.

Squaw Valley has plenty of room to play, and a lot of the time they need every acre of

it. Squaw is a favored destination of weekend skiers from the San Francisco area, and on a busy Saturday or Sunday there can be as many as 14,000 people on the mountain. With so many skiers piling into this vast arena, it makes sense that the hard-skiing locals would find their way above and beyond the lifts. They climb up to the cornices, chutes, and headwalls at the very top of the four peaks, out to the edge of the white envelope, where they can hang it out and haul it back in again. We rode up the KT-22 chair one day. In front of us was a cliff face split by a narrow chute that had managed to hold snow despite its steepness. Gracing the middle of the chute was a set of linked turns, the kind of tracks that mean something to someone who had climbed and hiked over the rocks to claim that thin alley of snow. Squaw is a mountain of signature runs like that, and the people doing the signing are among the boldest, craziest skiers alive. Their detractors sometimes sarcastically refer to them as the Jerry Brown Ski Team for their alleged public-assistance lifestyles, but they are the skiers who define Squaw Valley.

For example, under the tram on a rocky buttress known variously as Little Granite Chief or the Rock Pile is an impossibly steep sliver called Sylvester's Slot, a line of descent executive by the man who skied off a 3,300-foot cliff while doubling for actor Roger Moore in the opening sequence of the James Bond thriller *The Spy Who Loved Me*. He was also the first (and thus far the only) person to ski off El Capitan in Yosemite Park. A parachute on his back made these leaps possible.

"It was just one of those things," Sylvester told us when he described his first of several trips down his namesake trail. "It had been a big snow year and the gully was filled in. It seemed so obvious that day, like it was almost beckoning me. It took a half hour of climbing to reach it. Stylistically, the skiing wasn't really a great job, but it was a place where ski tracks had never been set before. It was very intimidating. They tried to get me suspended from the ski patrol and have my pass lifted for doing it, but technically I hadn't skied a closed trail, because no one had ever considered the possibility of skiing it before. My boss refused to suspend me. Instead, we have a designation for ski classes that rates them from A through F, with F being the most demanding. He had a sign painted with a G on it and stuck it at the lip above the chute, and it stayed there all year.

"The average skier has a good time here because Squaw has some very good beginner and intermediate terrain, and it is on the upper part of the mountain, which often has snow when the bottom doesn't," Sylvester continued. "But Squaw definitely has more than its share of expert skiers who are not put off by the steep terrain. Adventure has sort of been institutionalized here. The only other places that struck me like that are Jackson Hole and Alta, where you want to make fresh tracks down every run. When I was on ski patrol and was assigned to KT-22, I could make first tracks down East Bowl, Seventy-five Chute (named for the size—75 millimeters—of the gun they used to fire to bring down avalanches), Women's GS, and West Face, at my leisure. Nowadays, to have a chance to do that on one slope you have to get in line an hour before they open the chair after a big dump. You have to ski in a blizzard, and even then the competition is getting fierce."

Steep and deep aren't the only challenges of Squaw in general and of KT-22 and Headwall, its two most expert peaks, in particular. Just about every square foot of KT-22 is crammed with serious moguls. Skiing these bumps is like facing 1,800 feet of hand-to-hand combat. There is not a lot of time for reflection or thoughtful analysis. You have the sense of being outnumbered in a gunfight, a barroom brawl. Moguls like these are a no-nonsense appraisal of your reflexes, resilience, and knees. Those who are slow on the draw need not apply.

As if all this spectacular terrain weren't enough, Squaw is blessed with some of the most prodigious snowfalls on earth. As much as 500 inches or more of mostly wet, heavy flakes (Sierra Cement and California Concrete are the nicknames) fall every year. "Sometimes we get these amazing snowfalls that just don't stop," says Sylvester. "You go out and lay down tracks, and the next morning you get up early and do it all over again. It's like being at a river when the fish are running. The mountain just keeps being replenished. Some days, just about the only thing you can ski is the west face of KT-22," he continues. "The snow is so deep you have to point your skis straight downhill and use both poles to get moving."

What do you mean, Sierra cement? Debbie Thomas cuts tracks off East Bowl. (Photo: Al Bourdet)

If only Squaw Valley delivered off the mountain like it delivers on the slopes. "What nature put here is fabulous, but what man added is just about the opposite," one person put it. The 1960 Winter Olympics were held at Squaw, and the games put the place on the map, but it is best to forget about all that now. The relics from the Olympics, a few tired buildings at the base, are in serious need of replacement. The lift system is much maligned, and after the disastrous tram accident of 1978 that killed four people and injured many more, the management has poured a lot of money into upgrading the system. There is the promise of new and better lodging, but few skiers choose to stay at the base of what cynics call "Squalor Valley." Most guests opt for the vacation condos tucked into the trees on the roads leading to the area, or for the lodges and hotels in nearby Truckee, Tahoe City, and other small lakeshore communities. The après ski in the valley is defined by the locals, just like the atmosphere on the mountain. One night we partied at a bar called the Lone Star Café, dancing swing to the hot licks of a country band called Bandit. The girls all looked like Margot Kidder and the guys like Jimmy Buffet. We danced next to a couple named Risk and Wink, and met somebody named Cool Breeze who, after three drinks, became Hurricane Force. Later we hooked up with some members of the ski patrol, who quickly absorbed three or four pitchers of margaritas. The dialogue went along the lines of "Oh, waitress, we're a little short. Could we wash dishes for five minutes and then use an employee discount?" Later they staged a telethon to pay the check.

The facilities at Squaw do seem to be getting better each season, however. "I think this area has a lot of good qualities, but it won't reach its full potential for a while," says Sylvester. "I think it could stand out among ski areas the way San Francisco stands out among cities." For the present, even if you don't leave your heart in Squaw Valley—probably because it's caught somewhere in your throat—you'll certainly remember the high and windy hills.

BEST BETS

LODGING

The accommodations at the base of Squaw Valley's lifts are adequate and nothing more. The *Squaw Valley Lodge* is the choice for someone who simply must stay right at the lifts. A new ninety-four-room luxury development is supposed to replace their hotel units and open in time for the 1981–82 season, but check closely about this one. Probably the nicest place to stay is the *River Ranch*, a comfortable lodge with private balconies on most rooms (book direct at 916-583-4264). *Tahoe Marina Condos* in Tahoe City, 5 miles away from Squaw, is a good choice too. Several condo developments are now under construction at Squaw; for a more detailed list, call Squaw Valley Central Reservations at 916-583-5855. It is nice to remember that the casinos and bright lights of Tahoe are only 18 miles from Squaw.

DINING

Restaurants are scattered all over the Tahoe basin, but there are a lot more good choices in dining than in housing. *Le Petit Pier* is a first-class French restaurant with a superb wine list (this is California, after all), located in nearby Tahoe Vista. Another Gallic standout, *La Vieille Maison*, heads the list in Truckee, a classic western railroad town that is showing new signs of life. Other possibilities in Truckee include *Grey's Toll Station*, *O.B.'s Board*, the *Passage*, and *La Copa del Oro* (known locally as Famine's). Along the shores of Lake Tahoe in various communities can be found the *Charthouse*, *Hacienda del Lago*, *Victoria Station*, the *Tahoe House*, *Pfeiffer House*, and the *Swiss Lakewood Lodge*. Also, don't forget that the casino hotels of Crystal Bay on the north shore and South Lake Tahoe/Stateline at the other end of the lake offer some enormous buffets at very reasonable prices as an incentive to potential gamblers (check to see if coat and tie are required).

TRANSPORTATION

Most Squaw skiers arrive by car from the San Francisco Bay area, a 200-mile drive on Interstate 80 and U.S. 50. Skiers who fly in from the East should head for Reno and then rent a car for the hour-long drive. Since so few people stay in the valley itself, you'll definitely want a car. There is a shuttle bus route, known as TART (for Tahoe Area Rapid Transit), but its schedule leaves a lot to be desired. Stick to a car.

RANDOM NOTES

There are a few bars and snack shops at the main base lodge of Squaw. They are usually very crowded at the end of the day, and you won't have any trouble finding them. Most skiers head for the bars located in the restaurants mentioned in the Dining section of this chapter, especially *River Ranch* and *Victoria Station* and the *Hearthstone* in Tahoe City. The *Lone Star Café* (formerly the infamous Bear Pen) is another possibility, as are several other bars in Truckee and the entire South Lake Tahoe strip. You should note that a lift ticket at Squaw Valley is not good at the other Tahoe ski areas, such as Heavenly Valley, Alpine Meadows, Kirkwood, and the rest. This is a shame, since there are, by some estimates, nearly as many chair lifts surrounding Lake Tahoe as in the entire state of Colorado. Wouldn't it be nice if skiers could sample all of them on a single ticket? Cross-country skiing is possible in Squaw's beautiful meadow and at a variety of other locations. Night skiing, begun in 1980, is available on a couple of Squaw trails Thursday through Sunday nights. Ice skating is scheduled to resume by the 1981–82 season in Blythe Arena, scene of the original U.S. upset of the Russians in ice hockey at the 1960 Winter Games.

Base elevation	6,200 ft.
Vertical drop	2,700 ft.
Number of lifts	26
Skiable acres	6,500 (approx.)
Average skiers per day	9,000 (weekends)
	2,500 (weekdays)
Average snowfall	500 in. (varies)
Number of trails	NA
Trail breakdown	30% beginner
	40% intermediate
	30% expert

14
STEAMBOAT SPRINGS, COLORADO

BEST DAYS : Steamboat Springs

"Last year, on Christmas Day, the mountain was socked in under low, hanging clouds. Riding up the chair, I suddenly broke through them into bright sunshine and diamond dust sparkling in the clear air. The girl in the chair in front of me began to sing "Silent Night." It was the closest thing to a religious experience I've ever had."

JEANNIE RAMSEIER

Probably the first thing we noticed about Steamboat was the attitude of the people who live and work there. Although you can't exactly call a ski resort that sleeps 8,000 people a local area, the spirit of Steamboat is defined by its residents, not by its guests. One afternoon, for example, we had lunch up at the midmountain cafeteria and saw on the wall huge blowups of local heroes like Buddy Werner (Silver Medalist in the 1964 Winter Olympics who was killed in an avalanche) and Billy Kidd (the current director of skiing who also won an Olympic skiing medal and who may or may not have invented the cowboy hat). Now, it's a little hard to imagine Vail painting a picture of Jerry Ford on its restaurant walls, or Aspen immortalizing Hunter Thompson in acrylics in Little Nell's, but at Steamboat the idea struck us as just right. After all, 20 percent of the skiers on Mount Werner are locals, and everyone takes great pride in their hometown Olympic champions. Buddy Werner's mom still owns a ski shop down in the town of Steamboat, 3 miles from the lifts, and his brother Loris runs the ski school.

Later that same day we wandered into the Tugboat, a typical locals hangout: that is, a knotty-pine cowboy saloon full of Marlboro Country men drinking Budweiser from long-necked bottles. There was the standard-issue Neil Young clone playing guitar up front, and back by the pool tables were a couple of Space Invader electronic games so complicated you had to be on drugs to play them well. The only thing out of place was the bar itself, for it is located smack dab in the middle of Ski Time Square, a cluster of modern shops and restaurants right by the lifts, and who ever heard of locals hanging out up at the mountain with the tourists?

Steamboat is a friendly and unpretentious place, a mountain of old ski clothes. One day we saw somebody wearing an ancient ski sweater with *Playboy*'s rabbit logo on it, and then spied another antique with the late Spider Sabitch's emblem in the fabric. At Sun Valley they might pull your lift ticket for wearing styles like those. They haven't been on the racks for at least seven years, but they still worked very nicely here, thank you. But don't get the impression that Steamboat is

Happy trails to you: Heavenly Daze at Steamboat catches the last few rays. (Photo: Ron Dahlquist)

frumpy and boring. This is the place where we first heard someone use the phrase "cashing in my fun tickets" to describe a night of carousing in a Jacuzzi. Steamboat used to bill itself as a family resort, but a market research survey revealed that 62.3 percent of its skiers were single. Steamboat's the skier's equivalent of Maxwell's Plum in New York. Steamboat is also supposed to be overrun with Texans ("Y'all come on down here, Betty Sue," the burly guy in tight ski pants commanded his terrified girlfriend, who stood a hundred yards above him at the top of the mogul run), but we suspect that a lot of those $250,000 condos springing up all over the base of Mount Werner represent Aspen dropouts, Canadian bacon, and Denver high rollers as much as oilionaires and Houston surgeons.

Most people come to Steamboat on the advice of friends or because of exposure to the ubiquitous marketing image of Stetsons and horses with ski racks on their hindquarters (the famous old barn where all the promotion shots are taken is just down the road from the lifts—ask any local to point it out). After all, Billy Kidd, from Stowe, Vermont, was years ahead of his time wearing and promoting cowboy hats with feathered headbands that look like somebody rear-ended a chickadee at high speed. Some of those Stetsons may rest on the heads of balding easterners out on vacation, but some of those hats also keep the sun off real ranchers and cowboys. That's why the sign in the Tugboat reads: FAST TIMES, HARD LAUGHS, GRUB, SUDS AND LIQUOR.

The ski mountain itself consists of four separate peaks, each with different attractions. The area feels like Disneyland—theme skiing, mostly for beginners and intermediates. At the very top Storm Peak can be spectacular after heavy weather, when the hoar-frost settles on the pines and aspens and turns them into ghost trees. Wide-open runs come off the top here, including the popular Buddy's Run. The spiritual skier heads over

to the other upper peak, Sunshine, and peels off down Shadows or Twilight, arguably the finest tree skiing in the land. The secret is not to ski the trees at all but to ski the spaces between the trees. We quickly learned that the thin aspens can crowd you, like Hitchcock's version of a slalom course, with gate poles four or five inches thick. Skiing the trees provides an instant elimination round for fools, cowards, amateurs, and bombers. Shadows is a steep slash through the trees that starts out innocently in the pines and then inclines to get serious in a hurry. The combination of large moguls and clusters of silver-gray aspens is an exhilarating challenge.

The lower parts of the mountain sprawl out in two or three directions at once. There are great intermediate runs everywhere, the kinds of trails that hypnotize skiers. Switch on the cruise control and fly. The runs are white frozen rivers long enough to give a sense of journey. Once in a while, though not too often at Steamboat, you'll run across some Class Five rapids, mogul runs like Ted's Ridge or Vertigo. A knowledgeable friend tried to remind us that the trees may be spiritual but bumps definitely are not. Moguls are merely the Rocky Mountain's answer to racquetball, she insisted, and the skier is the ball. At the very least, Astraltunes are required equipment. They ameliorate the pain of the moguls, like the Muzak in the dentist's office. The bumps under the Four Points chair are an exhibitionist's delight, the equal of many of the showcase runs at Vail or Sun Valley. When a skier gets it right, the whole world applauds. The trail-grooming crews shave Steamboat on a regular cycle, so that what was a knee-jerker one day is a smooth cruise the next. You have to chase the moguls around the mountain—a modern-day shell game.

If Steamboat has a problem, it is that the mountain faces south, and even with abundant snow, keeping its sunny side up means that conditions can easily become less than

Barb Johnson has a close encounter with the trees in the Twilight zone. (Photo: Ron Dahlquist)

ideal. Also, even though it is a jumbo mountain with excellent beginner and intermediate terrain, the chairs and trails interact so that a skier never takes the whole thing from top to bottom. Steamboat is a benign giant. An intermediate can ski the limits of the terrain, take all the mountain has to offer, and squash it flat, turning his skis every which way but loose. At Jackson Hole, the same skier might panic, frustrated by the large chunks of raw nature that are beyond his skills, forced to measure his disappointment by what he did not ski, rather than simply enjoy what he did ski.

Finally, there is ski touring at Steamboat. This is where we got the best advice we heard all year, on a late-night schnapps-powered cross-country tour: "The only way to survive cross-country is to get a good set of buns in front of you." We looked at the woman he was referring to and sure enough —kick and glide, kick and glide. The Steamboat Touring Center has 20 kilometers of four-lane superhighway trails. At first you think these high, wide, and handsome paths are too easy; then you realize that they are indeed very handsome and also very high. At 7,000 feet no trail is too easy. If you are more adventurous, there are guided tours up on Rabbit Ears Pass, about ten miles from Steamboat itself. You glide across meadows and gaze out into the Yampa Valley below. The broad vista hangs in front of your eyes like a tapestry, or a rear-screen projection of an idealized mountain scene. You move through the breathless quiet air, into the picture, and back down toward Steamboat.

BEST BETS

LODGING

Until just recently (say, last year) Steamboat's lodging was a lot like the mountain itself—mostly intermediate. Big money is coming into the area now, it seems, and the result is some very luxurious new housing,

mostly condos. Right at the base area, for example, is the *Lodge*, a set of very nice two- and three-bedroom condominiums with huge fireplaces and picture windows. About 150 yards up the main ski slope is the plush *Bearclaw* development, with its own health spa. Conventional lodges that are well situated include the *Sheraton* hotel, which adjoins the gondola shed, and the remodeled *Thunderhead Inn*. More secluded and more romantic is the *Ranch*, a group of townhouses just over a knoll about a quarter mile from the lifts. Nice views from these, too. For even more isolation, consider the *Rendezvous Lodge*, which consists of just four three-bedroom suites with kitchens and is set in the woods just behind the Burgess Creek chair lift about a quarter of the way up the mountain. Call Central Reservations at 303-879-0740.

DINING

No one will ever confuse Steamboat with Aspen or Vail, but that doesn't mean you can't eat well here. Perhaps the top spots are the *Gallery* and the *Thunderhead*, both of which have reasonably formal Continental dining, and *La Trattoria*, which is in the Ptarmigan Inn and has fine Italian fare. Other standbys in the village include the *Butcher Shop, Dos Amigos*, and the *Great American Cowboy*, which serve exactly what you'd expect with names like those. Heading toward town, there's the *Pine Grove Ranch* and the extravagantly Victorian *Brandywine*, which is everyone's favorite for a romantic drink. Farther out of town (ask for directions) is the *Riverbend*, with great ribs and pizza in a funky atmosphere. For late-night food, remember that the bar of the *Old West Steakhouse* serves a terrific prime-rib sandwich at 1 A.M.

TRANSPORTATION

Many people heading for Steamboat rent cars in Denver and, if the weather is good, enjoy the beautiful 157-mile drive up to the resort. Even though having a car is not abso-

Into the mystic: The Steamboat gondola plays tag with the clouds. (Photo: Ron Dahlquist)

lutely necessary here, we do recommend it, since many of the best places to stay and eat are not right in the village center. Budget, Dollar, and National have offices in town. Other alternatives include Trailways buses or flights from Denver on either Frontier or Rocky Mountain Airways to the Steamboat airport, 6 miles from the village. Frontier also flies to Hayden, 23 miles away. The local shuttle buses seem O.K., but somehow we always found it easier to get there in our car.

RANDOM NOTES

There are some nice funky bars up at the ski area, including the *Tugboat* and *Dos Amigos*, which are local favorites, plus the *Afterglo* pub. The downtown gathering place is the *Landing*. For genuine cowboy gear (need a new blanket for your horse?) ignore the F.M. Light ads and head for *Harwig's* or the *Cowboy's Mercantile* downtown. Want to really meet the locals who work at the ski area? Join Charlie's Breakfast Club, which meets at 8:15 every morning at the Mount Thunderhead midstation restaurant. Skiing with Billy Kidd takes place every day at 1 P.M. at the midstation and is great fun. Steamboat's Winter Carnival, held the second week in February every year, is the definitive version of these frolics. Sleigh rides up on the hill that feature nighttime steak barbecues are popular here. Check with the marketing office. You can rent private hot tubs at the Water Works in Ski Time Square. The springs for which the town is named don't go *chug, chug* like a steamboat anymore, but they still bubble through sinkholes in a park in downtown.

Base elevation	6,900 ft.
Vertical drop	3,600 ft.
Number of lifts	16
Skiable acres	614
Average skiers per day	5,000–6,000
Average snowfall	300 in.
Number of trails	61
Trail breakdown	23% beginner
	49% intermediate
	28% expert

15
STOWE, VERMONT

BEST DAYS : Stowe

"It was the kind of day where for no apparent reason I got five percent better with each run. Lessons I'd had six months ago clicked in, suddenly made sense. I got smoother, more efficient, the longer I skied. At a place like Stowe, being in total command of what you're doing makes runs like National and Hayride pure pleasure instead of torture. On that day I was the master of the mountain."

PETER SHAW

There is only one lead for a chapter on Stowe. It is four words long. Starr, National, Goat, and Liftline: the notorious Front Four trails. They're the most famous runs in the East—the first thing everyone wants to hear about when you come back from Stowe. Even without the embellishments that most legends undergo, they are impressive. National and Liftline are a mile long and a hundred moguls wide. Goat is a mile long and about two moguls wide, and it's littered with boulders the size of Volkswagens. Starr is just as narrow and even steeper than Goat—the average gradient is 36 percent and the first hundred yards are so precipitous no one has ever bothered to pull out a plumb bob. Goat and Starr may be legends, but very few people have ever actually seen them. If you stand at the top of Starr, for example, there's a heavy fence and a sign that says something like Terminal Experts Only. A couple of hundred yards out beyond the cliff edge there's a tiny notch in the treetops, but that's all you get to see of Starr unless you ski it.

On the days we skied Stowe, both Starr and Goat had been closed all season for lack of snow. One morning after a substantial storm, however, we lucked out and got to cut under the ropes with some accomplices from the ski patrol. The first thing we noticed was a suspicious number of moguls on a trail that had not been open all year. When we paused about a third of the way down, five outlaws came sailing over the crest of the steep drop right above us. Then another four came into the trail through a narrow cut in the trees. The patrolmen reluctantly started to pull lift tickets. Three more skiers came over the falls above. It was starting to look like the stateroom scene from *A Night at the Opera*, where everybody who's least expected shows up with the Marx Brothers. Who, me? There were guys in the crowd who had deliberately bought half-day tickets so if they got caught they wouldn't be out so much cash. One season pass holder even bought a day ticket, apparently as an offering to the ski gods. Not only did we learn about how moguls build up on closed trails, we learned a lot about the skiing at Stowe. How many trails can you name that are worth a lift ticket?

One of the nice things about Stowe is that

while the famous attractions live up to their reputation, the place has lots of other virtues no one ever tells you about. If everyone talks about the Front Four, no one mentions all the great intermediate cruising terrain scattered over Mount Mansfield and on Spruce Peak, the mountain across the road that is an integral part of the Stowe operation. The gondola up the side of Mansfield deposits skiers at the top of thousand-turn trails like Perry Merrill and Switchback or the tough, challenging Chin Clip. These runs unwind like a Slinky going down a staircase—long-winded intermediate challenges. If you don't know how to turn at the top, you'll learn by the bottom. One afternoon we ran Chin Clip until we dropped from exhaustion and the sheer pleasure of all those dips and bucks and turns.

Spruce Peak has the misfortune to face south into the sun, and it can be hard-boiled on the wide-open lower flanks. "I've looked across at Spruce and seen the sun reflected in the deep blue mirror of glare ice over there, but something inside me still wants to go over and ski the sucker," one person told us. The upper parts of Spruce are narrow, gentler cruises like Smuggler and Sterling that roll and slide through canyons of trees and sometimes rock. What they need here are starting gates at the top to send skiers off at four-minute intervals so the chain collisions in those tight walls won't do heavy damage.

Another joyful surprise about Stowe is the tree skiing. Mount Mansfield is set at just the right angle to wring snow out of the storms that roll across Lake Champlain, and the

New England charm: If they take one more picture of that steeple, it may collapse. (Photo: Stowe)

snow hides in the trees for a long time without blowing off the slopes. One day we cut into the glades just to the right of Nosedive and nearly had a heart attack when we found a full foot of light, dry powder tucked among the maples and ash and birch. The last thing we ever expected to be doing at Stowe was skiing Alta powder in Steamboat trees, and that made every turn so much sweeter. There is more tree skiing on the other side of Mount Mansfield down below the top of Toll Road, the 4-mile beginner run that is a splendid Hobbit trail with a canopy of trees arching overhead.

The bad news is that Toll Road (which is one of the original trails at Stowe and used to be a real toll road that ran up to a big hotel perched on top of Mount Mansfield) and the small area at its bottom, called Toll House, is about all there is to occupy beginners at Stowe. This creates a situation in which Stowe has three of everything—rental offices, ticket windows, ski schools, all linked by shuttle buses that run between Toll House, Mansfield, and Spruce—and skiers can be forced to split up during the day if they have different skiing abilities. It's a drawback that management is well aware of, but they still haven't figured out just how to overcome it, although there are plans afoot for the summer of '82 to close Toll House and move the beginner area up to Spruce Peak. Luckily for Stowe, however, only 3 percent of their skiers rated themselves as beginners in a survey that the area conducted. Forty-three percent rated themselves intermediates, and an astonishing 54 percent said they were advanced. The amazing part is that hardly anyone seems to have lied. The median level of experience at Stowe is ten years, and six skiers out of ten are return visitors. The practical effect of this is that we saw more archetypal skiers on this mountain than anywhere east of Snowbird. Stowe skiers are conscious, alert, and intelligent—so focused on the task at hand that watching them ski is like watching a bowling ball roll down the mountain. They project an atmosphere of intense concentration that is almost tangible.

But lest you think that Stowe is all hotshots and know-it-alls, we heard from one of the Stowe Hosts, who act as moving information booths to help skiers get around, that he'd seen at least two people take off their skis by stepping out of their boots and walking into the lodge barefoot. Another woman asked if she could go to the bathroom with her skis on. The host thought about it and said, "Well, if you can get down the stairs in them, go ahead."

One more thing that no one mentioned was that Stowe is the kind of place where skiers take off their skis and climb up above the lifts just for the fun of it. In fact, Stowe is the only mountain we know of that has a cut trail up above the highest lift. Upper Nosedive is the top of the legendary old racing trail that was hacked out of the trees in 1933. Since then a nose job has been performed on some of its more exotic changes of direction, and now the trail rises a quarter mile or so above the top of the Mansfield chairs. Upper Nosedive just hangs there, like a plume of white smoke in the mountain air. One day we spotted a trio lugging their skis up the left edge of the untracked trail. They paused at the top while a crowd gathered to watch below, and then they floated down that stretch of blank white canvas, signing their names in smooth brushstrokes in the new snow. We introduced ourselves and signed on for a bit of even more serious climbing above the gondola on the opposite flank of the mountain. After a trek too painful to recount, we skied down something called Profanity and then into what the locals have named the Miniboos, for Miniature Cariboos. After 2,000 feet of tricky snow and tight clusters of trees, we emerged in a sweaty, exhausted heap somewhere near the bottom of Chin Clip. More Vermont powder and trees. Just be sure to take a guide who's been there before, and don't forget that this is out of bounds.

Past experience means a lot at Stowe, and it's one of the few mountains we've visited where you have to understand its history and development to fully appreciate what goes

*Would you believe a trail above the lifts? Skiers cut fresh tracks on Upper Nose-
dive. (Photo: James R. Petersen)*

on there today. The very first trails, like Nosedive and Perry Merrill, were cut by hand as Civilian Conservation Corps projects during the Depression, and skiers had to hike up the mountain to ski them. In 1940 a wealthy insurance magnate, C. V. Starr (yes, they named the trail after him), and ski school director Sepp Ruschp began expanding and consolidating the area in a big way. Everybody involved with Stowe in those days ran first-class lodges and restaurants, but nobody really much cared about public relations. Stowe had its reputation as the ski capital of the East, but it also had the image as a refuge for a lot of crusty, elitist, hard-nosed skiers who viewed any "improvements" like the ones in Nosedive as merely ways to let more sissies ski their mountain. Stowe, for example, was the last major ski area in America to institute any kind of package vacation or even have a multiday lift ticket.

In the last five years or so things have loosened up quite a bit at Stowe as the old guard has discarded some of the out-of-date practices but still retained the ones that today's skiers appreciate. The old-fashioned style takes the form of a silver-haired gent and his wife calmly slicing up a delicious-looking whole roast duck that they had packed into a hamper and brought up to the Octagon restaurant. New England's version of brown-bagging it. Another much-cherished habit from days gone by that's still around at Stowe (and nowhere else as far as we know) is the blankets you get at the bottom of the two Mansfield chairs. Skiers borrow these black ponchos with plaid linings and throw them over their heads so that they look like the Clint Eastwood character in all those Sergio Leone spaghetti westerns. Too bad they won't let you ski down the hill in them like a gang of desperadoes.

We ran across some behavior of a more modern sort when some locals told us about the gondoliers, people who have had sex on the seven-and-a-half-minute ride in the enclosed cars. The quarters are cramped and your time is limited, they told us. You have to plan your positions in advance and start taking off your clothes in the lift line. The crew at the top of the gondola used to applaud the cars that arrived with steamed-up windows, until somebody got the bright idea of rubbing no-fog cloths on the plexiglass for a better view. We asked a couple of gondoliers if seven and a half minutes left much time for foreplay and they said, "What's foreplay?" At Stowe, of course, foreplay is a romp on the Front Four, the kind of turn-on every skier understands.

BEST BETS

LODGING

Most of the sixty-odd places to stay around Stowe are strung out along the 8-mile stretch of Route 108 that runs from the village of Stowe to the base of the lifts at Mount Mansfield. There are no lodges right at the mountain, but those closest to it are among the choicest. The *Inn at the Mountain* is a very nice, modern hotel run by the ski corporation, as are the *Mount Mansfield Condominiums*, which are luxurious units located right at the Toll House slopes. A bit down the road is the famous *Topnotch* resort, a deluxe lodge that lives up to its name with ease and is our first choice in the area. Slightly farther away up a side road is the *Stowehof*, a clubby, intimate inn with soaring ceilings and rooms that are decorated in various styles. Farther back toward the village are innumerable smaller hotels and lodges, mostly family-run and warm and comfortable. Some favorites include the *Scandinavian Inn*, the *Yodler*, *Edson Hill Manor*, and, right at the intersection of Route 100 and the access road, the *Green Mountain Inn*. The famous old *Trapp Family Lodge* has promised to rebuild after its disastrous fire of 1980. Check for reopening dates with Central Reservation at Stowe, at 800-451-5100 (December to March only) or 802-253-7321.

Can I call a taxi from here? Skiers atop Mount Mansfield contemplate the drop. (Photo: Clyde Smith)

DINING

If ever there was a well-kept secret in ski country, it is the abundance of wonderful restaurants in the Stowe area. Every restaurant in the area is family-run, and there are no chain operations whatsoever (someone told us that the Colonel came to town once, but nobody dropped in so they packed their buckets and left). *Topnotch* has an excellent (and expensive) dining room, as does the *Inn at the Mountain*. Favorites of ours include the *Hobknob*, where you must try the lemon chiffon pie for dessert, the *Swisspot*, in downtown Stowe (chocolate cream pie here), the *Shed*, a local favorite, and the *Spruce Pond Inn*. Then there's the *Partridge Inn, Charda*, the *Golden Horn East* (a cousin of its Aspen namesake), *Steen's, La Bicoque*, and others too numerous to mention.

TRANSPORTATION

Stowe is a long but easy drive north on I-89, 40 miles from Burlington and 10 miles off the Interstate. Fly into Burlington and rent a car, which is indispensable at Stowe, or face the seven-hour drive from New York (it's about four hours from Boston) up Interstate 91 to I-89. There is a continuous free shuttle between the three base areas during the day, as well as buses that ply the access road up from the village, but at night you're on your own.

RANDOM NOTES

Stowe has the biggest, liveliest night-life scene in New England, and it's better than a lot of Western ski areas as well. Everyone gathers in the *Den*, at the base of the Mansfield chairs, to eat free popcorn and listen to John Cassell play the piano in the afternoons. Others head down the road to the *Matterhorn*, a loud, lively spot in the afternoons and evenings. Later at night there is a choice of quiet or not-so-quiet live music at the *Playhouse*. Loudest of all is the *Baggy Knees*. *Sister Kate's* is also popular, and the elegant *Buttertub* bar at Topnotch resembles a subdued hangout on the Upper East Side of Manhattan. The *Whip* and *B. K. Clark's* are two other popular gathering places. The *Pub* is the authentic British article, complete with a dart board and English owners. The *Stowe Cinema* has a bar inside where you can imbibe and watch the movie at the same time. Great idea. Cross-country skiing is very popular at Stowe, and there are innumerable trails and at least four major touring centers. One special feature is a Mountain Top Tour that guides experienced ski tourers across the summit ridge of Mount Mansfield. For information about the myriad activities going on in Stowe, check with the Stowe Area Association, right in downtown. Finally, those trails on the other side of Spruce Peak belong to *Smuggler's Notch*, a completely independent ski resort (there are some package deals that permit you to ski both mountains, and you can actually go over the top from the back of the Spruce chairs) with a delightful modern cluster of lodges and condominiums on the other side of the notch itself. The mountain is interesting when the snow conditions are good, especially for beginners and intermediates. For more information call toll free to Smuggler's Notch at 800-451-3222.

Base elevation	2,243 ft.
Vertical drop	2,150 ft.
Number of lifts	9
Skiable acres	330
Average skiers per day	5,000 (weekends)
	2,500 (weekdays)
Average snowfall	250 in.
Number of trails	35
Trail breakdown	7 beginner
	19 intermediate
	9 expert

16
STRATTON, VERMONT

BEST DAYS: Stratton

"One weekend at Stratton I had the most amazing two days of skiing in my life. On Saturday the clouds settled onto the valley floor in an air inversion, and when we broke through the top layer on the chair it was like looking down on a big, fluffy, white pond under a blue sky. I'd never seen that before. On Sunday it snowed over a foot and I skied fresh powder for the first time ever on the East Coast. I turned a lot of somersaults in all the fluff, tumbling and rolling over in the snow. It was definitely my all-time best weekend."

SANDY SHORTER

We had heard that Stratton was more like a country club than a ski resort, a collection of scrupulously groomed white fairways surrounded by the second homes of wealthy New Yorkers. Our first impressions did little to dispel this notion. Standing in the lift line one weekend we saw a gray-haired executive type getting on the chair with a copy of the Sunday *New York Times* under his arm. We figured maybe he wanted to tackle the crossword puzzle on the way up. A little later someone explained that he probably lived in one of the houses near the mountain and was just doing his shopping on skis. "This place wouldn't exist without the *Times* and the *Wall Street Journal*," he said.

Stratton's connection to the upscale New York market was even more obvious once we got a look at the fashion show around the base lodge. Men and women paraded around in an array of gaudy and expensive plumage unequaled outside of Manhattan. The men put on a virtuoso display of the latest Fila and CB Sports jackets, and a pair of quilted gray Roffe leg gaiters was *de rigueur* for every young male. As for the women, Strat-

ton is the only place we've ever seen where eyeshadow is color-coordinated with the latest Bogner and Anba zip-together suits. A friend of ours reported that the ladies' room resembled the makeup counter at Bloomingdale's. Only at Stratton can you stand in the lift line and smell L'Air du Temps and Chanel drifting above the crowd.

If we were feeling a bit defensive about Stratton when we arrived, it was because it was the one exception to our rule that all of the resorts in this book had to have vertical drops of over 2,000 feet. True, the back side of the mountain, the south-facing Sun Bowl area, just does squeak in at 2,003 feet, but the main part of the mountain on the north side is a relatively gentle 1,750-foot drop. We had selected Stratton over some of the bigger mountains in the Pacific Northwest because Stratton's impact on the skiing world far exceeds the scale implied by this one statistic. First of all, the area is a major destination resort not only for New Yorkers but for all of southern New England. It sponsored a World Cup race in 1978 and had the good fortune to have both Mahre brothers, Phil and Steve,

Intermediate Mecca: Stratton is cruiser heaven—high, wide, and handsome.
(Photo: Hubert Schriebel)

win races. Stratton currently hosts four of Morton Lund's Superlearning Ski Weeks and three Women's Way Seminar weeks every year. It's the permanent site of the Stratton Mountain School, a prep school for young racers that has produced many members of the U.S. National and Olympic teams, including Heidi Preuss, who was fourth in the Lake Placid downhill. What this means for the average skier who spends a week at Stratton is that there always seems to be something going on like a race or a festival. The social calendar is so crowded that we thought the place must have a cruise director, like on "Love Boat"—a full-time employee who dreams up all this stuff. One day, for example, we were waiting for a lift when we saw a figure falling out of an airplane above the mountain. As we rode up, the parachute popped open, and he hit a target set up near the top of the Standard Chair. A bunch of people helped him into a pair of skis so he could run a course of gates on the trail. It seemed like a great way to beat the lift lines, but it actually was part of the annual Winter Carnival. Finally, Stratton is a great place to go to with a group of friends. You rent one of the big, elegant new houses up on the hill off the access road, eat together, talk together in front of the fireplace. It's right out of a Michelob commercial, but it's real and it feels very nice.

After we'd been here for a few days we began to notice the exceptions and the ironies to our clichéd notion of Stratton as the winter extension of the Hamptons or the New York Yacht Club. A local ski store was selling bullshit repellent in spray cans. And everyone we saw was having the time of their lives. One of the operative rules of skiing is that you generally get what you pay for, whether it's a pair of boots or a week's vacation. Stratton is one of the more expensive places in our top-25 list, but what it delivers in return is a high-quality experience. There is plentiful skiing at Stratton itself, plus Bromley and Magic Mountain, each of which is within a half hour's drive of the others. On Stratton there is immaculate

grooming and snowmaking. Scattered in the triangle of roads that connects all three ski areas is an abundance of high-quality lodging that ranges from luxurious condos and private homes to romantic old inns tucked away on some of the most peaceful, typically New England country roads you would ever hope to find.

Of course, none of this would matter if the ski mountain didn't make people happy. Stratton specializes in the kind of intermediate, middle-of-the-road skiing that never has to apologize for its existence. Even if there is nothing terrifying on the mountain, even if none of the expert slopes would really rate an expert designation out West, it somehow doesn't matter. You're still in front of a jury of your peers. Hubert Schreibel, the Austrian skier and photographer, who works at Stratton, explained the differences between the trails for us one day. "I like the fall line trails in the middle of the mountain, like Slalom Glade, Liftline, Spruce, World Cup, and Rimeline," he said. "Skiing the fall line is like working out in a gymnasium. All of the equipment, the apparatus, is right there in front of you. You simply perform the exercise, the right moves. This mountain also has cruising trails, like Black Bear and Grizzy Bear, that wander more. On them you tour, you take in the scenery. You can do it on autopilot. It's the difference between concentration and fascination." Since Stratton has some fifty-three trails to choose from, you've got plenty of chances to decide what kind of skiing you prefer. For all its attention to fashion we noticed that the kids, the families, the moms and pops, all skied the mountain until the lifts closed and they had to be shooed away by the ski patrol. Yo-yo skiing, where you go up and down as many times as possible without any of this two-runs-and-a-cup-of-hot-chocolate nonsense, is the rule rather than the exception here. Stratton lets the experts show off and the intermediates and beginners keep up with the group. Everyone can sample the mountain at his or her own pace without having slower skiers banished off to some distant Fanny Hill of their own.

Linked turns: A cross-country skier explores Stratton's golf course. (Photo: Neil Stebbins)

We did notice that beginners, however, can be subjected to something called a Dopplemayer Carousel, a set of long spokes that revolve around a hub. Novices who need to get the feel of being on skis without having to point them downhill hang on to one of the spokes and get pulled around in a circle. While this is a terrific idea for people who've never felt a ski glide over snow, the effect is something out of those grade-B Bible movies where the slaves turn the gristmill while a Roman sentry in sandals cracks a whip on their backs. The first time we saw it we could not figure out what crime they had committed. Now that we know better, we think that a variation of this machine with shackles on it would be a dandy place to chain up those idiots who bomb the beginner hill or ski across your tips without bothering to apologize.

All of Stratton's unending cruiser runs can turn into bruisers when the weather doesn't cooperate. Stratton does a first-class job of snowmaking, but things can get icy on the most popular trails. On days when this happens you should ignore the follow-the-leader mentality that keeps most skiers right in the middle of the mountain under the chair lifts and head off to the sides of the mountain and search for snow on the edges of the trails.

We had the good fortune to hit Stratton after a storm had dumped a foot of snow on the mountain one Sunday night and all the other skiers were heading for home. On Monday we unpacked our knees and followed the Hubert Schreibel formula of skiing right down the fall line, cutting sixteenth notes where previously we had only managed quarter notes. The moguls were covered with soft snow, the kind you can smash right into head on and then decide in midair what course corrections you want to make. Off to the sides on Wanderer and Drifter we found untracked powder until after lunchtime, since the few people who were there at all were, again, right under lift line with the other sheep. We swooped and banked, feeling the natural contours of the mountain under our feet instead of the packed-out sur-

faces pushed around by a thousand skis. We tried to take everything the mountain would give us, and if it wasn't Jackson Hole, it didn't make any difference. Any trail, taken confidently in a foot of fresh snow, is still perfection. Quality, as opposed to quantity, always carries the day.

BEST BETS

LODGING

The Stratton area sprawls all over the roads that connect the three local ski mountains: Stratton, Bromley, and Magic. Starting right at the base of the Stratton lifts, there are three very fine lodges: the *Birkenhaus*, with its highly regarded restaurant, the modern *Stratton Mountain Inn*, and the more casual but still highly rated *Liftline Lodge*. As you wind your way down the long access road (which has no development on it at all) you'll see lots of luxurious private homes that can be rented through Stratton Real Estate (802-297-2323). At the bottom of the road is a turnoff to the *Red Fox Inn*, popular with younger folks. You can turn either right or left on Route 30 at the bottom of the access road. Left takes you toward Bromley and the modern *Kandahar Lodge*. A few miles to the right is the junction of Route 100 and the popular *Fundador Lodge*, with its big, warm living room and grand piano and excellent restaurant. A left turn up 100 brings you to the atmospheric *Londonderry Inn*, and at the end of a forty-minute journey down Route 30 lies the famous *Newfane Inn*, one of the best-known country retreats in Vermont. *Styles Brook Cluster Homes* or *Shattarack* around on the other side of the mountain are the best bets in the condo department. Call 802-297-6915 for all of the above, except the private homes.

DINING

Once again, you can wander all over the area in search of food and not be disappointed very often at all. The *Birkenhaus*, the *Stratton Mountain Inn*, the *Peppermill* restaurant in the Fundador Lodge, the *Londonderry Inn*, and the *Newfane Inn* all have excellent cooking. In addition, there is the *Sirloin Saloon* and the *Mill* for steaks and the *Three Mountain Inn*, which received high praise from several people in the area for its small but first-rate menu.

TRANSPORTATION

The entrance to Stratton is off Route 30 in Bondville, Vermont, not in the town of Stratton, which lies to the south of the ski area. There's really no practical alternative to a car here. The nearest places to fly into if you're renting a car are Albany, Boston, and Hartford. New York is 235 miles away, a solid five-hour drive. There is a free shuttle bus between Stratton and Bromley.

RANDOM NOTES

Après-ski activity begins at the base lodge of Stratton, where the *Bear's Den* and *Theodore's* are jam-packed every afternoon. On Thursdays and Saturdays be sure to catch a performance of the Stratton Mountain Boys, who come complete with lederhosen and Tyrolean music. The Stratton Mountain Inn has a popular bar on the premises, but most skiers head down to *Haig's* or the *Deli* at the bottom of the access road. The *Mill* and the *Red Fox* are also popular. The *Liftline Lodge* has a spa with saunas, hot tub, and massage facilities. If you just can't take another day on the slopes, there is interesting shopping at the Jelly Mill in Manchester Village on Route 7.

Base elevation	2,125 ft. (north face)
	1,872 ft. (south face)
Vertical drop	1,750 ft. (north face)
	2,003 ft. (south face)
Number of lifts	8
Skiable acres	350
Average skiers per day	6,000 (weekends)
	2,000 (weekdays)
Average snowfall	230 in.
Number of trails	53
Trail breakdown	45% beginner
	30% intermediate
	25% expert

17
SUGARBUSH, VERMONT

BEST DAYS : Sugarbush

"It was the day in late March when I skied in the morning and then went horseback riding through the woods in the afternoon. People were out sugaring in the maple trees as we rode by. It was glorious."

JEAN SHERMAN

There are days in the life of every skier when you can do no wrong in the morning. You ski smoothly and sweetly. Then you break for lunch, and when you head back up the mountain you discover that whatever sweet spot you were hitting earlier is gone. Lunch legs has struck. We're not sure exactly what causes lunch legs, but it always hits us right after a large, terrific midday meal, especially those served in peaceful, sunny restaurants and accompanied by good white wine. If the Center for Disease Control ever investigates this phenomenon, the first place they'll visit in New England will be Sugarbush.

Sugarbush has the two things a ski area needs to become a source for the dread lunch legs. First, there are restaurants like Chez Henri that are on or very near the slopes. The people who run these places believe that homemade onion soup, fresh pâté, and quiche were meant to be eaten in pleasant surroundings and with real napkins, even if the patrons are all wearing down-filled clothing. Second, there are lots of long, steep runs like Rumble or Stein's Run that seem like ideal trails to tackle right after a leisurely

lunch and some good wine. If the ingredients are taken in proper sequence, the victim of lunch legs usually finds himself a few thousand feet directly above Chez Henri accompanied by a set of knees that have gone to sleep.

We bring up the subject of lunch legs here because the combination of tough skiing and good food, not to mention excellent lodgings, is what Sugarbush is all about. The resort is blessed with a broad-rimmed natural bowl as a main ski mountain, and it is laced with trails that rank just behind Stowe (partisans say they are equal and Sugarloaf supporters demand recognition here, too) in the toughest-skiing-in-New England sweepstakes. Sugarbush makes excellent use of the full 2,400-foot rim of this bowl, and its runs drop continuously without a lot of cat tracks or unreasonably long runouts. In the bottom of the bowl is the closest thing to a self-contained ski village in Vermont, a small cluster of excellent restaurants, attractive lodges, and condos, plus a few shops and an indoor sports complex. On the 4-mile access road from the village to the main highway is a scattering of

Who says it's not nice to fool Mother Nature? Snowmaking guns at Sugarbush. (Photo: Chan Weller)

condos, a wonderful old inn or two, plus some more restaurants. Out on Vermont Route 100 are the towns of Warren and Waitsfield, which have more of everything but not so much that you feel overwhelmed and frantic.

From the time Sugarbush was built in 1957, the resort carried the reputation of a glamour spot for jet-set skiers, an image that usually comes back to haunt a resort if the reality doesn't keep pace. Sugarbush used to be called Mascara Mountain or Vogue Valley. It was the ski area in the East where magazine editors came to do fashion layouts and blondes in Bogner stretch pants sipped drinks in outdoor cafés. The aura of Peter Estin and Stein Erikson, the early directors of skiing at Sugarbush, and of fashion nabob

Oleg Cassini lingered over the valley like woodsmoke on a still morning. In those days management cut a trail especially for Ericson (called, logically, Stein's Run) so that television cameras could come to Sugarbush to have an unobstructed top-to-bottom view of a ski race or record Stein's revolutionary flips and aerials.

Today, the glamour ghosts seem to have faded even while the qualities that attracted the glamour remain and have been smoothly updated. One sunny day we enjoyed an old-fashioned indolent lunch with some people who had just flown in from San Francisco for a few days of skiing. If we closed our eyes we could have been transported to Sun Valley in an instant. The kids who were bashing the bumps on Stein's Run seemed to be showing off for the ghosts of those old cameras. Even though the lift line goes up a different trail, Mall, it is still an audience run, 1,200 feet of steep and bumpy ego alley. The Bogner outfits were still around, too, but they stayed in the lift lines even when the temperature hunkered down into single figures, a sure sign that there are serious skiers inside those suits.

If you think of Sugarbush as being shaped like the cupped palm of your right hand, everything on your three middle fingers is rated intermediate or expert, so serious is a good thing to be here. The lift that is the ring finger, Valley House, opens up Stein's Run and Mall, plus Twist and Moonshine. The middle finger is the gondola, and from the top there is a long, joyful cruise called Jester. Jester twists and turns and offers at least half a dozen chances to make scenic turnoffs and enjoy the view. Jester also runs into Glades, a cluster of thick hardwoods and birches scattered in the trail to produce a wide-angle slalom course with bark-covered gates. The sterner challenges off the gondola include Paradise, Spillsville, and the lift line underneath it, called Organgrinder. This series of stairsteps is known locally as grinder-air-grinder. You come flying straight down a series of ledges (grinder) and every hundred yards or so you blast off like a rocket (air).

The first finger is the Castlerock chair, the only lift that doesn't start at the base. This is solid black-diamond territory, a handful of very narrow, tricky runs that face south into the sun, so that exposed rock is an added incentive to perform carved turns as precise as the school figures in ice skating. Runs like Middle Earth and Castlerock, with their undulations, dives, and ticklish corners, are trail skiing at its absolute best. Toughest of all is Rumble, a trail so narrow that it's invisible from the chair lift right next to it. Rumble used to be a goat path and it has been grudgingly widened to accommodate maybe two goats shoulder to shoulder. Skiing Rumble is like riding one of those toy slot cars that are

trapped on a track. Hesitate just a little and you quickly learn what it means to have a trail ski you instead of the other way around. If you are really adventurous and have some pull with the ski patrol, you can cut off into an area called the Powder Chutes, a kind of unlisted directory of tree skiing for hearty bushwhackers. Be sure to take a guide if you go.

Sugarbush offers a couple of alternatives for people who want to avoid the conundrums of Rumble or the threat of lunch legs. You can head over to Sugarbush North, which used to be called Glen Ellen, and enjoy the wide-open beginner and intermediate terrain or a few steep sections on the upper part of the mountain. Sugarbush bought Glen Ellen a few years ago and has tried to lure skiers over there with a free shuttle bus for the ten-minute ride, an interchangeable lift ticket, and (especially) new snowmaking machinery to the summit. They have succeeded so well that anytime the snow is less than perfect at Sugarbush, everyone immediately heads over to North for the rest of the day. The purchase of Glen Ellen and the decision to install lots of snowmaking there has been a boon for Sugarbush. A string of snowless winters had been producing jittery feelings in all the locals. For example, we woke up one morning to a booming noise, and later in the day we jokingly told a Responsible Person at the area that we thought it might have been an avalanche control gun. "Oh, no," he explained, "it was just one of the lodge owners committing suicide." Grim humor. Eventually Sugarbush and Sugarbush North will be connected by lifts and trails, but the Forest Service, which the locals regard as a cross between the army, the telephone company, and a country club, requires an act of God to touch anything above 2,500 feet on the mountain, so no one is holding their breath.

If you want to be absolutely certain of avoiding lunch legs, you can make the twenty-minute drive over to the third and

Harvest time in the powder fields: Chan Weller and Mike Manson plow it up. (Photo: Clyde Smith)

oldest of the local ski areas, Mad River Glen. Mad River is the skiing equivalent of a brown-bag lunch, not very fancy but definitely nourishing to your skiing. Mad River has had the reputation as a place for serious skiers since it was founded by a guy who thought that Stowe had become too commercial. This was in 1947, mind you. The pride and joy of the area is the terrain that spills off of the main chair lift, a quaint conveyance called Single Chair for a couple of good reasons. There is space for only one person per chair, and for years it was the only way up the mountain. With hairy trails like Liftline and Chute and plenty of steep shots through the trees that only Mad River veterans can find, this area lives up to its reputation as a place for hardy, single-minded skiers. It's the antithesis of Sugarbush as far as ambience goes, and that makes it a perfect complement to its more glamorous neighbor.

BEST BETS

LODGING

The Sugarbush area has at least forty lodges and a dozen condo developments to choose from, and they include the largest selection of high-quality accommodations in the East. Tops in location are the *Hotel Sugarbush* and the brand-new *Village Gate*, two condo-hotels situated right in the village at the base of the lifts. Along with *Mountainside Condos*, they represent ideal lodging for couples since they offer studios and one-bedroom units with kitchens almost exclusively. (Many have fireplaces.) If you need more space, try the luxurious *Castlerock* units just off to the side of Village Gate. Down the access road is the elegant *Bridges* development, which comes complete with its own indoor pool and tennis complex, plus a shuttle bus to the lifts. The white clapboard *Sugarbush Inn* is a first-class country inn, a bit bigger than most, but well cared for and

featuring a host of extras. The *Club Sugarbush* condos, sprawling across the street from the Sugarbush Inn, are very spacious and modern, definitely deluxe. Finally, up on the road toward Mad River Glen there's the classic old *Tucker Hill Inn*, with a fine restaurant and some cross-country trails right outside the door. For reservations at all of the above call toll free 800-451-5030.

DINING

Plenty of good choices here, too. We would go first to the *Phoenix*, which is right in the village, for the delicious Continental cuisine and especially for the dessert selections, which you can't miss under any circumstances. *Chez Henri* has good bistro-style French food, and a short distance down the road is *Sam Rupert's*, which specializes in fresh fish. *The Common Man* is probably the best-known restaurant in the area. This beautifully restored 100-year-old barn has some delicious European food prepared by a Swiss chef, plus a nice wine list. Nearby is an interesting Mexican place, *Las Cuevas*, at Fox Hill. It's on the main floor of an old hotel, and the rooms have been converted into a series of arched white stucco dining alcoves. Finally, don't miss Ben & Jerry's ice cream, which is made in Burlington and served at a few of the local dining spots; Heathbar and Oreo Mint are among the flavors. If you still aren't full, *Waffles* has more ice cream in the village center, and *Ron's Deli* can come up with bagels and locally renowned Freihofer's pastries when the munchies strike.

TRANSPORTATION

Sugarbush is one place where you can get by without a car, but still, we think it's a good idea to have one if you want to ski Mad River or eat at some of the outlying restaurants like the Common Man. Otherwise, the shuttle over to Sugarbush North runs smoothly and freely.

RANDOM NOTES

Sugarbush is a lively place with an attractive, well-to-do clientele. When the lifts close, people stop into *Chez Henri*, up by the lifts, and especially the *Blue Tooth* and *Gallagher's*, both of which require a car to reach. These last two places are very popular and crowded. Later at night there is music in the casual, downstairs room of *Fox Hill*, and disco dancing at *Downstreet* and the *Back Room* (of Chez Henri again). The Sugarbush Sports Center, a tennis/swimming/handball/exercise center just below the Village, is a complete and very popular facility.

Memberships are available in a variety of passes and package plans. *Waterworks* on Route 100 is the local hot-tub emporium; redwood tubs can be rented by the hour. There are at least three large cross-country facilities in the area, at Tucker Hill, at the Sugarbush Inn, and at the village itself. If you ride the gondola on a sunny day, be sure to climb to the observation deck in the rocks up above the top station. When the weather is clear you can see all the way to Whiteface Mountain in Lake Placid, New York, up to Stowe to the north, and into the White Mountains of New Hampshire to the east.

	Sugarbush	Sugarbush North	Mad River Glen
Base elevation	1,575 ft.	1,483 ft.	1,600 ft.
Vertical drop	2,400 ft.	2,600 ft.	2,000 ft.
Number of lifts	8	6	4
Skiable acres	330 (for both Sugarbushes)		NA
Average skiers per day	NA	NA	NA
Average snowfall	275 inches	275	NA
Number of trails	34	39	25
Trail breakdown	4 beginner	13 beginner	7 beginner
	14 intermediate	19 intermediate	9 intermediate
	16 expert	7 expert	9 expert

18
SUGARLOAF, MAINE

BEST DAYS : Sugarloaf

"I had been out at Sun Valley for a month. After thirty days of bashing soft moguls, it was terrific to come home to something challenging. I didn't want the snow to forgive me, especially if I'd done something wrong."

TOM HILDRETH

When we arrived at Sugarloaf the powers that be were lamenting a magazine article that stressed how zany the place was. "Zany?" they said. "We're not zany. We're polished and cosmopolitan." As we stood there listening to this, a television set was tuned in to Sugarloaf's own closed-circuit TV station, WSKI, which was replaying highlights of the annual White, White World Week. The screen showed the National Bodysliding Championships. The winner was dressed in a polyurethane bag that he'd doused with silicone spray. As his competitors flailed away far behind him on pieces of cardboard covered with red wax, he slid down the slope backward, waving a bottle of champagne in one hand. Cut to the World Heavyweight Skiing Championships, with 400-pound adults running slalom gates for fame and fortune. Cut to Canoeski, the downhill race where contestants paddle a canoe down the slopes. As they said, polished and cosmopolitan. It was only later that one of them admitted that his best day on the mountain was when he skied down Widowmaker buck naked except for his gloves and ski boots.

Why is it that some of the most inaccessible resorts, places like Telluride and Jackson Hole and Sugarloaf, attract the best and most fun-loving skiers? Sugarloaf, for example, is as far north as you can get in these parts without having to take French lessons. (To avoid confusion with Sugarloaf, Michigan, this one is officially called Sugarloaf/USA.) It is located in the most isolated part of a state that is bigger than the rest of New England put together, but has about the same number of residents as Columbus, Ohio.

No matter how or why it happens, the isolation is what makes Sugarloaf unique. "We are trying to be a positive alternative to New Hampshire and Vermont," one of the Responsible People here told us. "Our main asset is the mountain, plus the special events and the spontaneous happenings that break out all the time." He could have added that the folks who live here know how to entertain themselves in the kind of extravagant style you'd expect in a frontier setting like this.

What Sugarloaf has to offer besides friendly and fun-loving locals is an absolutely first-class ski mountain with a small,

The snowman cometh: What if there really is someone in there? (Photo: Chip Carey)

Sugarloaf's wide-open snowfields offer a taste of alpine skiing in the East. (Photo: Chip Carey)

highly centralized ski village right at the base of the lifts. There is a tight cluster of restaurants, condos, shops, and bars literally astride the slopes, and some more accommodations a hundred yards or so off to the sides and below. It's all so compact that you can easily stop after a run, drop into your condo or one of the bars to reload, and then walk right over to the gondola in a matter of seconds.

As for its "main asset," the ski mountain, we think that with the exception of Stowe and possibly Sugarbush, Sugarloaf has more to offer the New England skier than any other area. The ski terrain consists of a single broad, cone-shaped peak that is gentle at the bottom, steeper in the middle, and very steep up top. There is a good balance of trails for all levels of skiers, too. The 2,600-foot vertical of the mountain is skiable from top to bottom without interruption, except possibly for cardiac arrest at the top of runs like Boom Auger, Wedge, and Bubble Cuffer. Sugarloaf arguably has the greatest working vertical in the East—only Killington and Whiteface Mountain at Lake Placid claim more, and both of those places give up that vertical only occasionally and with a good deal of effort. Sugarloaf also is the only mountain in New England with a taste of true alpine-style skiing: the crest of the mountain above the timberline that they call the Snowfields. When the conditions are right, usually in the spring when the snow accumulates enough to cover the rocks and the scrub trees, you can throw yourself out into the stratosphere, the vast tilted desert that funnels you into a series of steep bump runs the equal of anything in the country. We skied Boom Auger, Wedge, and Bubble Cuffer when the moguls were manageable, but we still didn't have the nerve to take them from the very steep top chutes that start in the snowfields. All three trails are very uneven— they kept pitching us from side to side, so it was like skiing on the deck of a sinking ship during a storm. All that tossing around combined with the moguls made these the only trails we've ever seen that require two Dramamine tablets before you ski them.

A funny thing happened to us on the way down Narrow Gauge. This top-to-bottom trail is the most popular intermediate run on the mountain (and it's the first one to get the attention of the snowmaking crews). A local magazine points out that Narrow Gauge isn't really very steep; it's just that there is this thing right in the middle of it called the Headwall, one short but very precipitous pitch that looks like one of the big ones off Waikiki. When the ice is up, it's sometimes blue. Anyway, the intermediates who love this trail tend to line up at the top of Headwall like a picket fence and review their life insurance policies before taking the plunge. One day we came to a set of empty skies pointed off into the woods at one edge of the Headwall. We peered over to see if their former occupant was alive. Someone called down to see if he was all right, and he yelled out from the underbrush, "Sure. I saw what was going to happen. I made my move." Say what? As near as we could tell, his move was to flap his arms wildly and hope he could fly over the trees.

Narrow Gauge is also the scene of some serious, high-speed cruising at Sugarloaf. One morning we were passed by a skier on this trail who was moving at about Mach 2. It turned out he was just practicing for the local Nastar race. Sugarloaf is the only mountain in America we are aware of where the weekly Nastar competition is a downhill instead of a slalom or giant slalom. Every morning we saw squads of kids walking toward the lifts wearing helmets and carrying those bent racing poles like Klammer has. The locals love these competitions and they take them very seriously. The races usually draw over a hundred contestants, including one group that holds training breakfasts (steak, eggs, and tequila) at a restaurant in the mall. The weapon of choice for these affairs is a pair of hand-me-down 223-centimeter racing skis, usually acquired at a severe discount from Karl Anderson, the popular local hero who is the most successful downhill racer on the U.S. Ski Team.

Some of the participants in these local competitions turn out in the skin-tight racing suits you see in the World Cup. The usual Sugarloaf ski wardrobe is put aside for the day. For men, this generally amounts to a dirty CB Sports parka, a set of baggy pants from Johnson Woolen Mills, a pair of old Rossignol Strato's, cracked Uvex goggles, two mismatched poles, and a pouch slung around the neck to carry green leafy substances. Women tend to dress exactly the same, except that off the slopes they all wear big airforce winter survival boots that make them look like Olive Oyl.

Unfortunately, we arrived at Sugarloaf after a heavy rain had eroded much of the snow cover. Everyone was busy pitching in to help get the mountain back into shape for the weekend, running the snowmaking and grooming machinery nonstop day and night. (Sugarloaf covers 110 acres of trails, including two 2,600 vertical-foot runs, with manmade snow.) By the third day after the storm most of the mountain was open and skiable, but the locals race was canceled since everyone was still on duty. They didn't cancel the regular postrace party at Maxwell's bar, though. The free Busch beer and hors d'oeuvres flowed on as usual, with everyone from the owner of the ski area to the snowmaking crews drinking shoulder to shoulder, laughing and talking. Basic New England camaraderie prevails here. Everyone we turned to had a story to tell, and very few of them were designed to highlight the polished and urbane side of Sugarloaf. Before we arrived here we'd heard that the local motto was "Everything to excess," so we weren't too surprised to hear about the toga party where Saran Wrap was substituted for bedsheets, or wet T-shirt contests that were remarkably short of T-shirts. We met the ski patrolman who came to town in a van and held a party in it every night for three weeks as a way to break the ice. It also figures that since Sugar-

Just imagine it's an L.L. Bean catalogue. Two locals tackle the Maine woods.
(Photo: Chip Carey)

loaf has a gondola—or "eighteen minutes of privacy," as one person put it—they would have a Club Car Club—a group of veterans with altered states of consciousness who ride the gondola, get high, ski fast, ride the gondola, get high . . . say, where was that gondola again?

When we left Sugarloaf they were still a bit worried about that "zany" business and trying to figure out how to market skiing up here in Maine when everybody yearns for a Caribbean island instead. As far as we're concerned they're doing a great job right now. Don't change a thing; we like Sugarloaf just the way it is.

BEST BETS

LODGING

Sugarloaf has about 220 condominiums and a couple of lodges right at the base of the ski mountain. Our top choices are the *Sugarloaf Inn*, an elegant place about 200 yards below the village center (it has a lighted walkway and its own chair lift going up the slope), and the units of *Mountainside Condos* that are located directly above the shops in the mall. Other mountainside units are a short walk away at the bottom of Buckboard Trail, and *Birchwood Condos* are right next to the Sugarloaf Inn and are run by the same owners. There are some nice accommodations 2 miles from the lifts at the *Capricorn Lodge*, at the *Left Bank Condominiums and Chalets* 6 miles down the road toward Kingfield, and at a wonderful old mansion, *Winter's Inn*, in Kingfield proper, 16 miles south of the ski area. More condos are planned up by the lifts, so check carefully when you call 207-237-2861 for information and reservations at all of the above listings.

DINING

Here again, there are three main centers of activity. Up at the ski area is the *Truffle Hound*, an elegant but unstuffy establishment with good veal and a delicious spinach salad. The Sugarloaf Inn runs on the Modified American Plan for its guests but also takes reservations from outsiders for its excellent restaurant. There are a number of informal places in the village center for lunch and dinner, including *Gepetto's* (also favored for breakfasts), *Jake Cassidy's*, and the *Bag*. Perhaps the best food in the area is served at the *Country Mile*, an unassuming place in nearby Stratton with a large wine list. Two-for-one nights are popular in these parts. On Mondays locals head for *Macho's* and dig into Mexican food. Tuesdays they trek up to Eustis (don't miss the turnoff or you'll end up in Canada) for two-for-one prime rib and lots of local color. Wednesdays it's the *Red Stallion*, back in Valley Crossing. *Tufulio's* has reliable Italian fare, and down in Kingfield there's elegnat Continental dining in *Le Papillon*, the restaurant in *Winter's Inn*, and at *One Stanley Avenue*.

TRANSPORTATION

There is no town named Sugarloaf up here, so if you're looking for it on the map, run your finger 16 miles north of Kingfield, Maine, on Route 27. Although you can spend a week up at the ski slopes without getting in your car, especially if you're staying at the Sugarloaf Inn, there's really no other way to get here in the first place. Lots of skiers come here from Canada and from as far off as Washington. Boston is about five hours away by car, and you can fly into either Portland (two and a half hours) or Bangor (two hours) and rent a car from there.

RANDOM NOTES

Sugarloaf is a lively, friendly place where you'll feel at home immediately. Après-ski activity, also known locally as "avalanche control," starts at the base of the lifts, at the barnlike *Maxwell's*, where there is usually a band, and at the *Bag*, *Gepetto's*, and *Jake Cassidy's*. Later on in the evening you can have a quiet drink at the upstairs bar of the *Truffle Hound*, too. There are other shops besides bars and restaurants in the mall. The *Schusspa* offers a relaxing combination of sauna and whirlpool for about five dollars, the *Orient Express* has takeout Chinese food, and *Gail's Garb* has some very interesting knitted ski caps for adults only. Sugarloaf has about 80 miles of cross-country trails, including one beautiful trek that follows the bed of the old narrow-gauge railroad along the Carabesset River all the way down to Valley Crossing. Great for those really frigid days. The *Irregular* and *Sugarloaf* magazine are maybe the best of the breed at any ski area. Very informative. Nice Touch Department: When you get your lift ticket at Sugarloaf, you can attach it to your jacket with a pipe cleaner instead of the usual wire wicket. It lets you change ski jackets without hassling with another ticket. Other ski areas should immediately follow suit.

Base elevation	1,600 ft.
Vertical drop	2,637 ft.
Number of lifts	11
Skiable acres	250
Average skiers per day	5,000 (weekends)
	1,200 (weekdays)
Average snowfall	160 in.
Number of trails	43
Trail breakdown	14 beginner
	15 intermediate
	14 expert

19
SUMMIT COUNTY, COLORADO

BEST DAYS : Summit County

"Have you ever watched champion surfers do cutouts? They race down the wave, then hesitate. The wave lifts them and they re-wind their ride, climbing back up the crest and over the top. At Arapahoe the skiers treat cornices like ten-foot waves off Malibu. Surf's up. They drop down the face of the ridge into the gully at the top of Pallavicini, then make a hard carved turn back up the face and over the crest of the ridge. I watched a couple of skiers doing it and tried it myself. It's like teasing the mountain, taunting it like a bullfighter. Forget fall line skiing. This was like skiing on a trampoline."

DEE DEE ASH

Summit County, Colorado, represents a high-water mark of the American dream. During the gold rush of the 1880s thousands of prospectors and loggers swarmed into the front range of the Rockies just west of Denver and established a rich, raucous mix of boom towns, lumber mills, and gold and silver mines. Today the hills are alive with the hum of clusters of chair lifts that have sprouted off Interstate 70, but you can still explore the old ghost towns and mining sites or party in the carefully preserved Victoriana of Brecken-ridge. The Continental Divide arches its ragged spine right through the district, but the snow-covered ripples and creases that once caused so much hardship for the settlers are now the groomed trails of Keystone and Copper Mountain and Breckenridge and Arapahoe Basin. In just a hundred years the territory has gone from being the pan of gold at the end of the prospector's rainbow to the skier's equivalent of the Virgin Islands: It has something for everyone. There are four ski mountains within a half hour's drive of one another, 180 miles of trails, and a total

vertical drop of 8,673 feet, all on one inter-changeable "Ski the Summit" lift ticket. In addition to the Victorian gold-mining ambience of Breckenridge, the county has one of the best hotels in ski country, hundreds of lovely condominiums, some excellent restaurants if you know where to look for them, and even a Club Med at Copper Mountain.

There used to be a formula that said skiers should stay at Keystone, party in Brecken-ridge, and ski at Copper (and Arapahoe if they were feeling lion-hearted). We played this tune. We liked it. The variations aren't bad, either.

The Keystone Lodge may be the most tasteful hotel in the Rockies. The lodge and all the condos and shops that cluster around it are understated marvels of thick timber, lush, hanging plants, and expansive views out across the mountains. Our window looked out over a wide ice-skating lake that was encircled by twinkling white pinpoint lights. Skaters glided around a Christmas tree strung with colored lights that was an-chored in the middle of the ice. The last faintly blue shades of twilight deepened into the purple night and backlit the towering forested mountains to the south and west of the condo. Keystone has the reputation of a refuge for the upper middle class—doctors and lawyers and corporate nabobs who shun the limelight and come here because Keystone is deliberately low key, a sort of miniature Sun Valley without the publicity. But luxury is a lure and an aphrodisiac no matter how rich or poor you are. By that measure Keystone is a turn-on even if you don't go near the ski slopes.

Party at Breckenridge: This town may not be as quaint as Crested Butte or Telluride, but it is no slouch in the Victorian charm department, and once the sun goes down it can hold its own with any town. Start with a terrific Mexican dinner at Mi Casa and then hit the bars. The Briar Rose, named after an old mine on Peak Ten, is a restaurant and bar with a honky-tonk piano. A nice warmup. A block up off the main drag is the so-called Devil's Triangle. It consists of two funky bars and one poolroom/roadhouse, the latter with a crowd that was so tough there were quick-release bindings on the picture window and shock absorbers on each pool cue. (Just when chaos seemed inevitable, a local legend named Murph gave a lady companion a rose. It was Valentine's Day and he was saying thanks for the memories, even though they'd never met. Very suave, that Murph.) Cool down in Andrea's Pleasure Palace, a fireplace-and-candlelight lair with deep couches and flocked wallpaper. While away the rest of the evening playing the Breckenridge Bar Crawler's board game (it really does exist), which has cards like "You left your jeans in the car—lose one space" or "Stop at hot tub party—lose two squares." A serious party town.

Skiing at Copper: Copper is a broad mountain with some long, intense bump runs and an endless string of expertly cut and groomed trails for the less experienced. It sits right on a curve of Interstate 70, and between the road and the mountain is a new village (Copper opened in 1971) with lots of

shiny condos and the even newer Club Med. Copper is so new, in fact, that it still doesn't really have the variety of shopping and dining attractions of its cousins, but it is coming on fast. Of course, you can escape from the world into Club Med and hide there all week gorging on the lavish buffets. The bumps on runs like Brennan's Grin and Two Much, and the steep glades of Drainpipe, come close to the challenges of Blue Ox and Highline at Vail, which is just over the pass on the Interstate. Copper is a well-planned mountain, segregated according to skiing abilities. The gentler trails are on the west side of the area and things get more difficult as you move east, sort of like they do in real life. Copper is known for mile after mile of graceful, swooping trails like Soliloquy, Windsong, and Copperfield, runs as pleasant as their names imply.

But forget the formula and improvise. Take the skiing at Breckenridge. Of all the Summit County areas, Breckenridge may have the most to offer all by itself as a destination, from lodging and dining to skiing. The mountain, which is a mile or so up from the town, has two separate but interconnected peaks which are mostly long, gentle intermediate and beginner slopes. In between the two peaks is a more precipitous valley with some underrated expert terrain. We got a close look at it when we were invited to join a regular group of veterans who, we were told, "ski the mountain just for fun every Thursday." We met them in the Bergenhof cafeteria of Peak Eight (the other area is on Peak Nine in the Ten Mile Range). We got a little nervous when one member of this group was introduced to us as a former colleague of Stein Ericson on the 1956 Austrian Olympic Team. "Say," we asked, trying to sound nonchalant, "just how fast do you guys take this mountain?" We got a chorus of disclaimers that would have bluffed Amarillo Slim. We heard about bum knees, pacemakers, blurred vision, exotic infections, the works. Our first run was off a high Poma lift that lets you traverse to the top of a very steep, smooth bowl called

Ski the Summit: A cross-country skier explores the ghost towns outside Keystone. (Photo: Neil Stebbins)

Horseshoe. Someone tried to bet us that Trygve, the former Olympian, could ski all the way back down to the cafeteria with a dollar bill held between his knees and not drop it. No takers.

Since no one embarrassed himself too badly on Horseshoe, we moved over to the other peak and tackled Tom's Baby. Our group leader went over the crest of this trail with the abruptness of a scuba diver jumping out of a boat. He just vanished feet first. Devil's Crotch and Mine Shaft were more of the same, trails that swallow you up in their narrow confines and spit you out into the valley far below, exhausted and sweaty. On the other flank of this valley is a new chair that opens up some absolutely beautiful open-bowl skiing. We frolicked over there until the lift attendants strung a rope across the chair-lift entrance, and even then we asked if

we could sneak under for another ride back up. Save the last dance for us, darling.

Keystone is a surprise of a different order. It is a cruiser's paradise, where familiarity breeds confidence. It's the only mountain we've seen that has subtitles, signs on the lift towers that direct skiers: "Smooth cruising—Frenchman or Flying Dutchman." They also get history lessons, Burma Shave style. "What's a go-devil?" one sign asks. "A go-devil is a sled used to haul lumber," its successor replies. "What is a jackwhacker?" "A jackwhacker is a mule driver." The area tries to connect with its past, and with nature. Another sign reads, "Look for gnawed trees. Porcupine." Keystone has an enviable design that lets beginners go to the top of the mountain almost immediately. The view of the Gore Mountains and the Divide and the Ten Mile Range is magnificent, and the trails are as smooth as inlaid mother-of-pearl. Schoolmarm, one of the longest novice trails in America, may be the best: 2,340 vertical feet, top to bottom, strung out over 3 gentle miles. Keystone is a great place to bring a lover who wants a learner's permit.

The biggest variation from all this low-key luxury is Arapahoe Basin. Arapahoe is just 5 miles up the road from Keystone, but it takes you back to the basics in a hurry. The area is mostly a huge, wide-open bowl hard against the side of the Continental Divide. The raw energy of colliding land masses seems to blast its way into your skiing here, making you more aggressive, more aware of gravity. The primitiveness of the area makes you an instant ski veteran. There are no lodges, no fancy restaurants, just a parking lot, a cafeteria and bar, a couple of chairs, strong, swirling winds, and lots of snow. Always there are towering rocks on your left side as you ride up. Not for nothing is this called Summit County. All four areas have base elevations above 9,200 feet, and Arapahoe has the highest lift-serviced skiing in America, up to a breathtaking 12,450 feet. Most of Arapahoe is wide open, and you get used to finding your own way down. This is appropriate since there is a history of curious, adventurous skiers up here. The big attraction for them used to be Pallavicini, a steep slash of gully that looks like somebody drew a giant fingernail down the face of the mountain. Pallavicini used to be something to write home about, bragging how you traversed halfway around the mountain for 1,000 feet of insane pitch down an avalanche chute. Now there's a chair alongside and it's an insanely steep mogul field. On our first trip down it was more a question of survival than a triumph of technique. At one point the chute seemed to funnel to a slot exactly one mogul wide. Bush pilots know better than to fly into a canyon that doesn't leave any escape hatches. Skiers aren't always so smart. One thing that hasn't changed is the prodigious snowfalls at Arapahoe; 450 inches a year means you can ski until June here, and when the condos just down the road are book-

ing golf tours, skiers from Denver are wailing down Arapahoe in their cutoffs.

The biggest variation of all is the one you invent yourself on cross-country skis. Summit County is one big touring complex, and you can trek virtually anywhere if you are good enough. Keystone even provides a topographical map to the ghost towns in the area. We recommend the trail to Sts. John, a cluster of ancient cabins that is apparently just beyond the range of vandals and is in good shape considering its age. You drive to Montezuma and climb for half an hour until suddenly you are a hundred years back in time and a million miles from nowhere, sitting on a rusted ore cart eating a picnic lunch, talking about the gold rush and the dreams of your ancestors. Spread out in front of you is a staggering panorama, the Rocky Mountains' greatest hits sparkling in the crisp blue sky. Paradise is being in the middle of nowhere with a Jacuzzi just down the road. You talk about luck, about striking it rich in Summit County. Past tense and present perfect.

BEST BETS

LODGING

Keystone not only has the best lodging in Summit County, but it probably has, on average, the nicest, most tasteful accommodations of any ski resort in America. That's not to say there aren't a few standouts at Copper or Breckenridge, but the overall quality of the *Keystone Lodge* and the sixteen condominium complexes that surround it are hard to top. We especially like *Lakeside* condos because they adjoin the lodge itself, but *Edgewater, Argentine, Mall,* and *Plaza* are all beautifully appointed (they even restock the firewood every day) and within easy strolling distance of the shops and restaurants in the center of the complex. Over at Breckenridge, the choicest spot is the huge (326 units) new *Beaver Run* condo-hotel. Beaver Run is a first-class operation, with every conceivable amenity from its own shopping plaza to a private shuttle bus into town from its location up on the slopes. Beaver Run has some especially pretty loft units with high ceilings and skylights, and the studio units are tempting romantic hideaways for couples. Over at Copper, where new condos appear like mushrooms after a spring rain, the pick of the crop as of this writing are *Foxpine* and *Bridge End*, plus the new *Mountain Plaza* and *Lodge at Copper*. For those so inclined, the Club Med/Copper Mountain has all-inclusive packages with lift tickets. In all cases call Central Reservations at Keystone (303-468-1234), Copper (303-688-6477), or Breckenridge (303-453-2918).

DINING

This is where a car really makes sense in Summit County. The *Blue Spruce Inn*, for example, may be the best restaurant in the area, but it is located in Frisco, at least 10 miles from any of the three areas. Without a car you would miss out on their wonderful homemade breads, desserts, and ice creams, not to mention the fresh chicken Kiev and other treats. No reservations, so go early. You'll also need wheels to reach the *Gore Range Inn* and its popular relative the *Snake River Saloon*, both on the main road to (and in the latter case, just beyond) Keystone. The *Keystone Ranch*, a restored ranch house that serves a three-entrée menu every night in rustic but extremely elegant surroundings, is also a drive away. If you're grounded at Keystone there are several nice places in the Keystone Lodge, including the formal *Garden Room* and the casual *Bighorn Steakhouse*. Over at Breckenridge, the standout is *Mi Casa*, which we think is the best Mexican restaurant in ski country. The *Miner's Camp* is the local steakhouse. The restaurants at Copper can't really compete with some of the

Wilderness it ain't: Keystone's condos are recommended without reservation.
(Photo: Clyde Smith)

best choices at other areas, but *Farley's, Compañero's* and *Tuso's* do a good job with steaks, Mexican fare, and Italian dishes respectively, and the Plaza serves more elegant continental fare on a pleasant outdoor patio. Your best bet is to stay at Club Med and enjoy the bountiful feasts they're famous for.

TRANSPORTATION

At the risk of sounding like a broken record, we want to restate the fact that having a private car is essential for getting the most out of a vacation in Summit County. All three areas are under a hundred miles from Denver, but public transportation is surprisingly limited. Keystone has a direct shuttle van that meets skiers at the Denver airport, but Trailways buses are the source of frequent complaints. The Ski the Summit Shuttle was improved somewhat last year with more express buses during the day, but it remains useless at night. Check with your airline for fly/drive packages out of Denver.

RANDOM NOTES

As we've noted above, the best après-ski and nighttime action is in the infamous Devil's Triangle at Breckenridge, where *Fatty's, Shamus O'Toole's,* and the *Angel's Rest* (known locally as the A.R.) are located. *The Briar Rose* and *Andrea's Pleasure Palace* are fun, and the *Ore Bucket* and the *Miner's Camp* are funky and loose. The *Gold Pan* was described to us as a "great place to catch a fight" if you really want to get funky, so be advised. All of the above are within walking distance of each other in Breckenridge. At Copper, most guests head back to their condos and Jacuzzis when the lifts close or to *Mountain Standard Time* for live music. And at Keystone they gather around the magnificent stone fireplace in the Keystone Lodge or head for the big swimming pool/Jacuzzi and bar just outside. One other local favorite is the Old Dillon Inn in Silverthorne, which features Mexican food and country music. Old Dillon itself lies at the bottom of Lake Dillon these days, having been flooded some years ago. The new town rises on the shores of the lake. An interesting alternative for cross-country buffs is the rambling old *Ski Tip Ranch*, a guest ranch that used to be a stagecoach stop in the days when a toll road ran over Argentine Pass from Georgetown to Montezuma. It's just outside of Keystone and perfect for touring enthusiasts who want some old-fashioned ambience and style. Out-of-bounds skiing is very big at Arapahoe, where the Divide Guide program will take you over the back side of the area into parts unknown but thrillingly beautiful. Our one quibble with Keystone is that the owners, Ralston-Purina, are so uptight that *Playboy* magazine is sold only under the counter. Give us a break, guys. Our favorite sign in Summit County? The one at Breckenridge that says "Do Not Ski in Parking Lot." And speaking of signs and owners, the only visible evidence of Twentieth-Century-Fox's recent purchase of Breckenridge is a few trails that have been renamed for the parent's hit movies, like *The Goodbye Girl* and *High Anxiety.* No word yet about *The Empire Strikes Back.*

	Keystone	Copper	Breckenridge	Arapahoe Basin
Base elevation	9,300 ft.	9,600 ft.	9,630 ft.	10,780
Vertical drop	2,340 ft.	2,450 ft.	2,213 ft.	1,670
Number of lifts	10	14	14	5
Skiable acres	460	725	800	350
Average skiers per day	3,500	3,500	3,500	1,000
Average snowfall	200 in.	250 in.	200 in.	450 in.
Number of trails	32	51	67	22
Trail breakdown	15% beginner	25% beginner	30% beginner	40% beginner
	65% intermediate	50% intermediate	45% intermediate	50% intermediate
	20% expert	25% expert	25% expert	10% expert

20
SUN VALLEY, IDAHO

BEST DAYS : Sun Valley

"In February of 1974 a classic storm dumped 30 inches on Baldy. The next day is still affectionately referred to as Big Wednesday. We bootlegged our way on the chair with the patrol. There was not a track to be seen anywhere. We did two runs on Exhibition for starters. I remember watching Bob Griswold rip Central Park to shreds. Charlie McWilliams smoked Christmas Bowl like never before, and Nick Jones made a run on Limelight that left everyone on the chair in awe. People went crazy that day, hooting and hollering down the mountain and then standing in the lift lines grinning like idiots."

GARY BRETTNACHER

We approached Sun Valley by car from Salt Lake City, through the prairie country and rolling hills well below the snow line. Gradually we rose through a gentle pass and came upon the Sawtooth Mountains, smooth, regular, barren peaks covered with snow. The only real vegetation was on their north slopes, which are in the shadows and hold the moisture. As we passed the airport in Hailey, 11 miles from Sun Valley, a private jet with a custom brown paint job flashed in across the runway. Along with Aspen, Sun Valley is one of the places where Lear jets come to mate. It provided our first sense of the layers of wealth and glamour, old money and new, that have come here to play since 1936.

Finally we approached Ketchum and Sun Valley itself. Bald Mountain loomed up on our left, a picture-book ski mountain. Baldy unfolds in a series of ridges, canyons, and bowls, as though someone started to unpack a ski mountain and stopped halfway; an origami ski mountain. At night Baldy glows in the moonshine—it's the center of attention in a way no other ski resort can match. In

fact, it looks like one of those little glass hemispheres you turn upside down to create a snowfall. There is a rumor that Sun Valley's trail crews merely turn the mountain upside down at night.

We drove one mile past Ketchum, a nice though hardly picturesque farm town, to Sun Valley Village, checking out the sprawl of new lodges and condominiums everywhere. In addition to Sun Valley and Ketchum there is now Elkhorn, a self-contained village 5 miles away, and Warm Springs, a cluster of accommodations right at the base of Baldy. Everything is a few miles from everything else, and Sun Valley itself is about five miles from the lifts, but the shuttle buses are very efficient. The Village is where most of the action is, and we headed for the legendary old Sun Valley Lodge, the place Averell Harriman put up in 1936 so that celebrities could ride out on his Union Pacific Railroad and play in the snow. And ride they did. Everyone from the Shah of Iran to Abbott and Costello came to Sun Valley. Sonja Henie swirled around the ice rink at the lodge and skated her way into America's heart in *Sun Valley Serenade*. It was Hollywood-by-the-ski-slopes from the very start. In the 1950s Sun Valley had two more attractions: gambling and Ernest Hemingway. The latter moved to Ketchum and sank familial roots into the town. The former took hold firmly, too. Slot machines lined the hallways just inside the entrance of the lodge, and high-stakes table games took place in Ketchum at the old Christiana Inn. Rumor has it that when the Idaho legislature outlawed gambling in 1953, the owners of the lodge squirreled away the slots in the storage tunnels under the outdoor swimming pool, figuring the law would soon be reversed. Everyone denies it these days and swears the machines were sold for scrap years ago, but it is fun to imagine them still down there whenever you are swimming through the steam up above.

This is the sort of reverie Sun Valley inspires so easily. It is not a mountain of bold-face challenges. You don't spend your days conquering the steep, the narrow, or the unrelenting. This is where skiers come to have permanent grins engraved on their faces. The girlfriend of a local photographer summed it up for us: "This is a cruise mountain. The trails are so long that if you don't know how to turn at the top you'll learn by the time you reach the bottom. I learned to ski over on Dollar"—the original ski hill located between the Village and Elkhorn, today serving beginners only on its 600-foot vertical—"but I measure myself by the big mountain. People come here and learn control. How to make turns. They keep coming back until one day, without breathing hard, they do the whole thing without stopping. My finest day on this mountain was when that happened to me. I made two runs, top to bottom. It was sunny and I was in control."

But Sun Valley also encourages audacity. With 3,400 vertical feet served by sixteen chairs (they brag about the lack of lift lines and they are right—one ski book even claims Sun Valley has *too many* chairs), the mountain is immense. Where other mountains fall in steps, Baldy has consistent, uninterrupted

pitch, and it sprawls over three sides of the mountain, so you can always stay in the sun if you wish. The trail map even has four separate views just to get it all in. On the far south side is Seattle Ridge, a series of well-groomed intermediate runs that look out across the bowls: Farout, Lefty, Mayday, Lookout, Easter, and Christmas. Christmas, for example, plunges 2,580 vertical feet in about 4,400 of length. Deep mountain. The bowls are like wide gullies with sustained steepness all the way. In good snow they are heaven, real leg burners. But the snow can also be heavy here—death crud that eats you up.

The shots you see from Sun Valley of lone skiers in a minefield of moguls are taken on Exhibition, Limelight, or Holiday. They are all ideal places to ricochet through waist-high bumps with the whole world watching. Every trail is steep, narrow, not really that long but staked out right near or directly under a chair lift. Sun Valley has tapped the sense of audience—perhaps because they are used to showing off glamorous folks—and they do it better than any other resort. Skiers can ride the Exhibition or Warm Springs II chairs to the top of these mogul runs and have their own public stage. Maybe that's why intermediates love Sun Valley. This is where they can make a debut.

Skiers tend to work their way around the mountain with ease on the clever cat tracks. Begin on River Run or College, terrific intermediate slopes which start from the very top of the mountain. It is no accident that the latter is named College. The ski school uses it all the time, and it is a remarkable place to learn, or just to cruise and share a slope with a friend. Over at Warm Springs there are more such trails, like Flying Squirrel and Grey Hawk. The only thing missing at Sun Valley is abundant snowfall. Sun Valley is one of the best mountains in America. We wish it were 2,000 feet higher or 100 miles away in any direction. The season is short here and the snow, just 200 inches a year, tends to come in big dumps that produce legendary powder days and all the publicity shots. The rest of the time it is up to the trail crews to make the most with the least, but they always seem to come through. Sun Valley has the best grooming of any resort, bar none.

The bottom of Warm Springs is a victory lap. There is a restaurant and bar right at the lift and crowds gather here in the afternoon. Sometimes a band plays, and the outdoor tables are filled with gorgeous people wearing fashions they don't get away with anywhere else. A girl in a beret and a green army jumpsuit. More beautiful women and handsome men. Did we really meet a woman here named Parked Car LaRue? Probably. It's all been going on like this at Sun Valley for so long that everybody knows how to maximize the pleasure. The guests, the waiters in the restaurants, the bellboys at the lodge. Even the resort owners who keep up the tradition of having a box of tissues and a set of simple hand tools at the base of every lift. It costs them a fortune in tissues, but they do it anyway.

One afternoon after we left Warm Springs and headed back to the lodge, we passed up the après-ski dancing (as opposed to disco) in the Duchin Room in favor of drifting through the steam in the circular pool. The waiters brought rounds of drinks out to us and we signed for the bill. We wondered if Sun Valley was deliberately designed to be so pleasurable or if it just worked out that way. We drifted some more and thought about it.

BEST BETS

LODGING

The overall quality of the housing at Sun Valley is higher than at most other Western ski areas. The centerpiece of the resort is the legendary *Sun Valley Lodge*. The lodge was built out of cement that is painted (very convincingly) to look like logs, and was refurbished in 1972. The rooms are really not

Fly like an eagle: That's Seattle Ridge in the background, poetry up front. (Photo: Gary Brettnacher)

the last word in luxury, but the atmosphere is delightful and the deluxe units and suites are particularly attractive. Ask for a room that faces the ice skating rink. Amenities range from the wonderful pool to a bowling alley and massage room, and the service is first rate. The *Sun Valley Inn*, built just after the lodge, is a bit more modest but also very nice. If you prefer a condo, our top choice is the *Lodge II Apartments*, right next to the lodge. These units are owned by folks with plenty of money and good taste, and if you can secure one of the eleven rental apartments, you're in luck. If Lodge II is booked, bypass the older Lodge I units in favor of *Wildflower*, a new condo development that's just a short walk from the village center. If you insist on staying right at the lifts, Warm Springs is your best bet. Sun Resorts (800-635-4441) has nice units with fireplaces and saunas. For all other listings, call 800-635-8261.

DINING

Sun Valley is blessed with many excellent and reasonably priced dining spots and cursed with long lines waiting to get into them. Always reserve early for such popular spots as *Le Club*, the *Fish Market*, *Ore House*, the *Warm Springs Restaurant*, and *La Provence*, the last of which was singled out by gossip columnist Suzy as the hot spot in town last year. The most romantic dining experience in town is *Trail Creek Cabin*, which you reach via a horse-drawn sleigh that glides across snowfields (actually it's the golf course, but who cares?) to a large, cheerful log cabin with a roaring fireplace and delicious food. Reserve early. For some reason Sun Valley restaurants have excellent wine lists with reasonable prices. Take special note of Idaho's own St. Michelle Vineyards, and try their Pinot Chardonnay. The best and biggest beefsteaks in town are

served at the *Pioneer Saloon*, and memorable breakfasts can be had downtown in Ketchum at the *Kitchen* and the *Kneadery*, or in the village at the *Konditorei*. Other local favorites include *Su Casa* and the *River Street Retreat* (for fresh fish). Finally, don't miss the new croissant-and-coffee cart at the bottom of the Warm Springs chair in the morning. A great idea.

TRANSPORTATION

Sun Valley isn't the most accessible resort, but at least there aren't any severe mountain passes to get over on the way there. The best idea is to fly to Salt Lake or Boise and then catch Gem State or Mountain West commuter lines directly into Hailey, 10 miles away. There are buses from either city and from Twin Falls, but you need to reserve in advance. Cars are really not necessary in Sun Valley since the free shuttle buses connect the village, Elkhorn, Ketchum, and the ski lifts very efficiently and run into Ketchum at night. Driving from Salt Lake is a relatively painless five hours over the flat terrain, and plenty of parking is available, except in Warm Springs. Again, call Central Reservations, 800-635-8261 for details.

RANDOM NOTES

Après-ski action abounds at the bars along Main Street in Ketchum, especially in *Whiskey Jacques*, the *Cedar Creek Yacht Club*, and the *Silver Creek Saloon*, plus the reliable *Pioneer Saloon*. Back over at Warm Springs everyone heads for the *Creekside Bar and Grill*, and in the village itself the *Ram* is lively and crowded. The local hot-tub rental (by the hour) emporium is the *Hot Spot Tubs* in Ketchum. Don't forget ice skating on the

The treeless peaks of the Sawtooth Mountains reflect moonlight over Sun Valley. (Photo: Gary Brettnacher)

Wasting away in Margaritaville: Waiters will bring drinks poolside at the Sun Valley Lodge. (Photo: Sun Valley)

indoor or outdoor rinks at the Sun Valley Lodge. Sun Valley's Nordic Ski School and Touring Center has excellent instruction and cross-country terrain to try out what you've learned. Finally, don't miss the photo of Shelley Winters in stretch pants that is framed on the cafeteria wall of the Sun Valley Inn.

Base elevation	5,750 ft.
Vertical drop	3,400 ft.
Number of lifts	16
Skiable acres	1,275
Average skiers per day	3,500
Average snowfall	200 in.
Number of trails	64
Trail breakdown	16 beginner
	32 intermediate
	16 expert

21
TAOS, NEW MEXICO

BEST DAYS : Taos

"Walkyries is a steep, moguled tree run, one of the most beautiful and unspoiled in the United States. When it's heavily packed out and/or icy, it can be scary, but one day, when I was the first skier on top of the mountain, I hit it under a deep blue sky, warm sun, and fresh, knee-deep powder. I just floated down through the forest as shafts of sunlight streamed through the trees. I couldn't imagine any greater joy than just being alive in this place, on this day."

DOUG BENSON

Taos is a world of its own, created in the image of its founder, Ernie Blake. Blake is the legendary Swiss gentleman who brought his vision of a small, European-style ski resort to an isolated valley in northern New Mexico twenty-five years ago. He nurtured Taos to its present lofty standing among the world's premier ski resorts and is still its guiding light. Every day he pops up all over his mountain, sometimes wearing his cap that says "Janitor." In an era when ski areas are owned by huge corporations that also market cattle feed or feature films, Taos bears the indelible stamp of this one man. He and his ski area are gracious, Continental, and perhaps a bit eccentric. If Taos had a motto, it could easily be "I'm Ernie, Ski Me," and then in parentheses it might add, "But First Sign Up for Ski School."

For most of its first quarter century everyone who came to Taos came for the same reason and was on the same schedule. "Everyone who was lucky enough to score a reservation also had to buy an entire ski week package that included lessons every day," one Taos veteran told us. "During the day you were

shown the area by experts, at a pace commensurate with your ability. The mountain was so unrelentingly tough that they didn't want you running around loose on it, so they gave you military skiing, with platoons and formations. Everyone was in control.

"Taos resisted GLM and Inner Skiing," he continued. "When the rest of the country was letting it happen, these guys were into technique. Taos produced scholars: articulate, accomplished skiers. Along with solid, basic technique they also taught respect for the mountain. They still do that today, but back in the old days Ernie would close the lifts at lunchtime so everyone could go back to their lodge and eat. At night, the dinner conversation would revolve around technique. It was like graduate school in skiing, the big difference being that dinner often included duckling à l'orange and baked Alaska. The food is still wonderful today, and the night life hasn't changed a bit, either. It's still almost invisible."

Dwelling on Taos's past is not only fun but also relevant to the Taos of today. The changes of the past few years have been

Skiing the steeps at Taos. If the bottom falls out, this must be El Funko Bowl.
(Photo: © 1976 Peter Miller)

additions that surround the unique core of your ski experience here, but they haven't devoured it. The skiing on the main mountain is still joyous and joyously steep, even though there is now enough new terrain to keep intermediates happy for weeks. The ski school is still among the best in the world, even if some pepole who come to Taos nowadays don't have the good sense to enroll in class. The food at the St. Bernard and the Edelweiss and the Thunderbird lodges is still the equal of any in ski country, but today you have the option of staying in some of the new condos that have sprouted in the tiny valley. The night life is still practically nil, and that's one thing that probably won't change. Taos and Alta are America's mountain monasteries. Changes or no, where else can you stay at a European-flavored ski resort, spend your morning winding down tree-lined trails reminiscent of the best of New England skiing, bash your way through powder bowls, chutes, and glades the equal of anything in the Rockies, and then spend the afternoon eating authentic Mexican food or visiting an 800-year-old pueblo inhabited by the Taos Indian tribe? Nowhere we know of.

The contrasts began for us long before we got to the ski slopes. We drove three hours from Albuquerque through the brown desert, past adobe huts, and through the dusty town square of Taos with its dozens of art galleries and craft shops. Nothing in this landscape prepared us for the sudden appearance of snow or for the sense of alpine seclusion as we wound our way up 8 miles of narrow, twisting canyon road. At the dead end of the valley, at about 9,000 feet above sea level, we came upon a small cluster of buildings huddled at the base of a very large ski mountain. A pair of chair lifts ran up alongside a trail so steep that it seemed to be climbing directly to heaven at the same angle taken by *Apollo 11*. This, we gathered, was the notorious Al's Run. Its companions, Inferno, Snakedance, and Edelweiss, cascade down the same front face like bumpy waterfalls. At the base of the lift is the famous sign explaining to the panic-

stricken that Al's is just a small fraction of the ski area and that you should *not panic*. The chair goes up over Al's Run and levels off for a while. From this point several superb intermediate runs also meander down the face, including one called Porcupine, which is our favorite. Porcupine reminds us of Flying Squirrel at Sun Valley or Naked Lady at Snowmass. This is where you practice the wide, swinging carved turns the Taos instructors pound into your brain and legs. Porcupine is the perfect warmup run and the perfect way to end the day, hooked up with your friends for one final cruise while the sun's last rays warm you.

A second set of chairs takes you to the very top of the mountain. Taos has one of the great summit vistas in America, out across the Sangre de Cristo Mountains, covered with brown brushstrokes of aspen trees against a jagged, snow-white canvas. Surrounding everything is the incredible New Mexico light that attracts artists and craftspeople to Taos and Santa Fe. When this gentle light rolls across the desert and up into the mountains, it seems to be on fire, agitated and astringent. Relax for a few minutes and enjoy the view before the skiing gets serious and you have to decide which way to descend. To the right is the West Basin and its series of chutes that go from steep to steeper: Castor, Pollux, Reforma, Blitz, Oster, Fabian, and finally Stauffenberg. Blitz and Reforma are the equals of Limelight and Exhibition at Sun Valley or Highline at Vail for serious bumps. Stauffenberg is perhaps the toughest of all of them. Jean Mayer, the famous Taos instructor whose influence on the area is second only to Ernie's, wrote recently that you simply can't be afraid when you ski these chutes. Instead, you look forward to the image of your first turn, and then you assert that image, impose your concentration on the mountain. You do it not for the rush, he says, but for the calm in the storm of adrenaline these runs induce.

If you turn east from the summit, toward the newer terrain in Kachina Bowl, you drop down into Walkyries, the best tree skiing this side of Steamboat. Walkyries is a cathedral of tall, thick evergreens. One day we drifted down among them and had the filtered beams of sunlight to use as slalom gates. Walkyries and Rubezal are trail and glade skiing at its best. Country roads winding through the trees. You are alone in the wilderness on this side of the mountain, out of sight and sound of civilization in a way only a few other ski areas can offer.

Once you reach the bottom of Kachina you can choose from beginner, intermediate, and expert runs. Taos is not a large area, but it is full of surprises. After coming here for five years we suddenly discovered Hunziker's bowl off the Kachina chair one day. We stood at the top of the open slope feeling like test pilots, as in "Let's take this sucker out and see what she'll do." Then we dove down through the powder, sinking into the snow as the acceleration took hold. A magic moment of discovery.

Along with the new terrain opened up by the Kachina chairs have come new skiers. Some are locals from Santa Fe and Albuquerque who have discovered that Taos is worth the drive. For people who live farther away and come by jet, Taos is trendy. One result, aside from the inevitable lift lines (one story has it that the first time Ernie saw a lift line, he sent somebody over to it with coffee and doughnuts), is that they now get skiers who don't understand or appreciate what Ernie Blake has tried to put together in this valley. Regulars still return every year to ski with their instructors, to be the sorcerer's apprentice, but Taos also gets people who are in over their heads now: the young gunslingers who go for it on guts alone, minus technique. You can spot them on Al's Run, trying to outduel the mountain by brute force alone. Taos is the kind of place where the go-for-it mentality can get you in real trouble.

It is also the mountain that inspires the best skiing of your life at any moment. We recall, for example, skiing down Walkyries in a blizzard, with the stately pine trees standing as silent sentinels to our pleasure. Taos was in a world of its own, and so were we.

BEST BETS

LODGING

There are five lodges and three condo units right at the ski area, and they are all within a hundred yards of the lifts. The *Hotel St. Bernard* and the *Hotel Edelweiss* are both charming, comfortable places with excellent meals (the Edelweiss is famous for its breakfasts, and guests take lunch and dinner at the St. Bernard). The *Thunderbird Lodge* also has excellent food and a pleasant setting. The *Hondo Lodge* is newer and thus may have a bit less personality than the first three. The *Innsbruck* is the most informal and least expensive of the group. The *Siera del Sol, Rio Honda,* and *Kandahar* condos are modern and convenient; their primary drawback is that it's difficult to get a dinner reservation at the lodges if you aren't a guest over at one of them. For reservations and information call 505-776-2295, and be sure to book far in advance.

DINING

In addition to the really superb food served at the St. Bernard, Edelweiss, and Thunderbird lodges, there is a pleasant restaurant, *Michael's*, right at the mountain. Another treat is the Mexican food at *La Cocina* down in the town of Taos, and *Casa Cordova* in Arroyo Seco.

TRANSPORTATION

The primary gateway is Albuquerque, 148 miles south of the ski valley. From there you can take an express bus on Saturdays or rent a car. Santa Fe is only 70 miles away, and the

There are other ways down Taos, but Al's Run is the most famous and direct. (Photo: © 1980 Peter Miller)

town of Taos is 18 miles from the ski lifts. A car is not necessary at the ski area at all unless you are planning frequent trips for sightseeing or dining in the area. There is a daily shuttle from the ski area to the town of Taos several times a day.

RANDOM NOTES

For many years the Taos Ski Valley had no TV, no radio, no newspapers, and almost no night life. Nowadays there are a few TV sets, and for the last three or four years there has been live entertainment every night until mid-night at the *Thunderbird, St. Bernard,* and *Hondo,* with the St. Bernard being traditionally the most lively. The best idea for a Taos ski week is to buy a "Taos Learn to Ski Better Week" package that includes a room, three meals a day, lift tickets, and a lesson every morning. The big attractions outside the valley are the Taos Indian Pueblo, which is open to visitors, and shopping for arts and crafts in the town of Taos. If skiing isn't enough activity for you, you might try staying at the *Tennis Ranch* at Taos (505-776-2211), which features indoor tennis courts in a location down the valley.

Base elevation	9,207 ft.
Vertical drop	2,612 ft.
Number of lifts	8
Skiable acres	1,090
Average skiers per day	2,000
Average snowfall	327 in.
Number of trails	62
Trail breakdown	24% beginner
	25% intermediate
	51% expert

The ride of the Walkyries: A lone skier drops through the trees at Taos. (Photo: Ken Gallard)

22
TELLURIDE, COLORADO

BEST DAYS : Telluride

"Once I arrived in Telluride in time to catch two friends on the last day of their vacation. As near as I could tell, they had signed a suicide pact, throwing themselves down the trails off Chair 6 until they dropped dead or beat the mountain. I don't particularly care for moguls. When I go to New York, I don't hang out in Central Park. I don't consider being mugged an integral part of my travel experience. But on this day, everything worked. I skied till I was falling asleep in the chair. My friends shipped themselves back to the city. I stayed another week."

PHIL McGUIGAN

Telluride has always been a very practical town in a very impractical location. Back around the turn of the century, when a waterfall of gold was pouring out of the Tomboy and Idorado mines up in the nearby hills, the town fathers didn't tax the citizens but instead ran the place with funds collected from the numerous brothels. During Prohibition, when very fine whiskey was being distilled here, they levied a tax on the local "soft drink" establishments and ran the city with that money. These days, they don't take gold out of the ground in Telluride, but they mine the American Express cards of the skiers who are resourceful enough to figure out how to get here. As we said, a very practical place.

Considering Telluride's impractical location, how else would you describe a town that is enclosed on three sides by very steep, 3,200-foot cliffs and is situated at the dead end of an 18-mile-long box canyon 127 miles from Grand Junction, Colorado, except as remote? Well, you could also call it impossibly beautiful or wildly poetic. Our advice is to call it all three, because what Telluride really looks like is a movie set. If the town didn't exist, a Hollywood film crew looking for a place to shoot a feature about a couple of gunslingers who love to ski steep slopes, deep powder, and huge moguls would have eventually wandered up the canyon and built Telluride out of cardboard and plywood.

Fortunately, the town's early boom days resulted in Telluride's being built out of solid brick instead of cheaper lumber, and the original article doesn't need any Hollywood tinkering. The New Sheridan Hotel, for example, has been almost totally restored to its original Victorian magnificence. The Senate bar still has on its wall the wooden roulette wheel that once ran nonstop for thirty-four years (all bets in gold or silver only). Since the whole town was declared a National Historic District in 1964, very little, especially the exteriors, will be changing. Telluride is therefore not only a fairly amazing place to ski if you crave the steep and deep, but also an intensely romantic destination, the perfect spot to bring a lover who skis like a dream and dreams like Elizabeth or Robert Browning.

If Telluride hadn't already existed, Hollywood probably would have invented it. (Photo: Alan Becker)

But the same mountains that feel so cozy can also make you claustrophobic and a little bit crazy. The ghosts of old miners seem to flash in the air, and the town attracts its share of eccentrics (that is, professional dreamers). We went into a local bar (*all* the bars here are locals bars) and saw a picture of the Flying Epoxy Sisters on the wall—three guys who ski on a single pair of skis at the same time while dressed as women. According to legend, when the trio first came to town, one of the locals took offense. He cornered an Epoxy Sister in a bar and began to question the virility of a guy who liked to wear dresses. The Epoxy Sister looked him in the eye and said, "Well, you can throw a punch at me if you like. Or you can buy me a drink. We can have fun any way you want."

They always seem to be fighting over something in Telluride. Politics is a sport here, like racquetball. At the same time, the town attracts Aspen dropouts and Hollywood celebrities, people who feel out of synch with the real world and come here to play in America's attic, this town full of old clothes and old buildings and new kitchenware boutiques. When we asked a Responsible Person about Telluride's marketing strategy, he thought about it for a while and said, "We want to attract as many rich single women as possible." One evening a few days later we stumbled into the Jacuzzi at our lodge sometime after midnight and ran into a naked woman cavorting there with three equally naked men. They casually adjourned to her room while we soaked our muscles. The marketing plan seems to be working, at least for some. But if you are a single male in Telluride, better be prepared for a cold visit just the same.

Outsiders view Telluride as the thoroughbred of ski resorts, high strung and elite. All this may be true, and the place is definitely hard to get to, but it attracts high-quality suitors, like the queen bee who flies so high that only the strongest males can reach her. Telluride promises a lot for expert skiers, and it delivers: 450 inches of powder a year, superb tree skiing, more moguls per acre than any area on earth, plus the Plunge and the Spiral Stairs, our votes for the toughest cut trails in America. But if you are looking for miles of long-winded intermediate cruises like at Steamboat or Vail, forget it for now (some potentially excellent intermediate terrain off to the south won't be ready for another few years). The problem here is that the ski mountain is shaped like a doorstop—a wedge. One side, the north-facing slope, is a cliff. The other side is gently rolling meadows, with maybe the best beginner terrain in Colorado. In between there's not much, especially since you have to ride three long chairs to get to intermediate slopes (to reach expert nirvana it takes four chairs and about a forty-minute commute).

But back to the steeps for a moment. There is a whole series of first-class expert runs off the top of Chair 6, but the Plunge and its neighbor, the Spiral Stairs (known locally as the Spiral Scares), are the Superbowl and World Series of bump runs. Each trail plummets 3,200 vertical feet (emphasis on *vertical*) and is cut about three skiers wide through the trees. As for the moguls, you can't figure out how they managed to park all those Buicks on such a steep incline, and then got the snow to build up over them. About a third of the way down, your knees surrender. Your lower body is abused, and if you cross your tips, even for an instant, the engine of fear kicks into overdrive and you think you might tumble directly into the pool of the Telluride Lodge a half mile below. What'll it be today? Backscratcher or full-gainer? Two thirds of the way down you hit a flat section and you think, thank God, it's over. You relax your concentration, so the surprise is a bit overwhelming when the whole front of the mountain drops away again and there, now a mere 1,000 feet below, staring you in the face through the gunsight of your ski tips, is the town. Only enough air for half a gainer from here. Your breath starts sounding like a Darth Vader soundtrack. Your body becomes a heat pump that is rapidly pushing you toward meltdown. You decide to make a pact with your

Into the valley of death rode the 200's: A skier takes the Plunge at Telluride. (Photo: Neil Stebbins)

knees—just get me out of this alive and I promise not to make love in the missionary position for six months. Honest.

Then you reach the bottom and you realize what you've done. You've passed one of the ultimate tests of American skiing. You walk away with no muscles, but the memory is like mental muscle tone. The memories will get you down every other bump you'll ever encounter, and you'll never be less than the person who skied the Plunge or the Stairs.

BEST BETS

LODGING

Telluride still has fewer than a thousand beds for skiers, and until recently there was no one ideal place to stay. But a lot of building is going on here, and some fine new lodging is in place. At the top is probably *Cornet Creek*, a small, deluxe condo unit with stained-glass windows, steambaths, and Jacuzzis, plus an excellent location. Right behind Cornet Creek (literally) is the new *Boomerang* condominium, and a few yards closer to the Coonskin lift is another very attractive development called *Greysill*. The new condo units of the *Manitou Lodge* have beautiful views over the town, and the Manitou has a wonderful all-night Jacuzzi. The one drawback is the stiff walk to and from the lifts if you miss the shuttle. For a truly special trip into the past, book the William Jennings Bryant suite at the *New Sheridan Hotel*, which may be the most extravagant Victorian restoration in Colorado. The hotel also has thirty-one other rooms and six other suites. You can book any of the above through Telluride Central Reservations at 303-728-4431.

DINING

As befits a town that attracts a sophisticated, well-to-do clientele, Telluride has some excellent restaurants. The *Senate* has very good food to go with its Victorian atmosphere, and *Julian's* serves high-quality northern Italian fare in the renovated dining room of the New Sheridan Hotel. Other worthwhile places include the *Powderhouse* for steaks and seafood, *La Paloma* for Mexican fare, and the *Iron Ladle* for wonderful breakfasts. Two new and worthwhile entries in the Telluride dining sweepstakes include *Dang's*, which serves Thai food, and *Sophio's*, a Mexican restaurant. *Baked in Telluride* can satisfy carbohydrate cravings with delicious pastries.

TRANSPORTATION

As we have noted, Telluride is a tough place to get to, and a visit requires careful planning. The best idea is to call Central Reservations and discuss the options with them. Currently, Montrose and Grand Junction are the best places to fly into, and connecting buses into Telluride can and should be arranged in advance. Rental cars are available in both cities, and lots of skiers drive here from Arizona and New Mexico, but Telluride does not encourage private autos (there is only one paved road in town) and snowfalls can be daunting. A local shuttle van should be augmenting or replacing the horse-drawn sleigh of last year, but don't count on it. Walking to the lifts can be painful in ski boots, but otherwise the town is very compact and easily manageable on foot.

RANDOM NOTES

Telluride isn't big on discos or fern bars, but saloons it's got. The bars at the *New Sheridan Hotel*, the *Senate*, the *Roma*, and the *Floradora* have plenty of atmosphere. They're the sort of places where you expect a grizzled miner to belly up to the bar any moment and pay for a beer with gold nuggets. If you fly to Telluride in a private plane (doesn't everybody?), the nearby town of Cortez has an excellent all-weather airfield.

Johnny Stevens samples the snow out of bounds at Telluride.
(Photo: © 1980 Robert Chamberlain)

Riding down the Coonskin chair is nothing to be embarrassed about. Everybody does it, and the view is great. KOTO, at 91.7 FM, is Telluride's entry in our Mellowest Station in the Rockies contest. During a recent snowstorm the disk jockey informed us that it was "snowin' like a sumbitch outside" and then played all of side one of Cream's *Disraeli Gears*. What may be the most beautiful grocery store in America is on the lower level of the Telluride Lodge. The Boiler Room and Sauna Bath is a communal spa on the lower level of the Opera House, with a Jacuzzi the size of Lake Erie. Finally, we'd like to know what the record is for most runs down the Plunge or Spiral Stairs (or both) in one day. So far we've heard the number four mentioned.

Base elevation	8,735 ft.
Vertical drop	3,105 ft.
Number of lifts	6
Skiable acres	462
Average skiers per day	828
Average snowfall	400 in.
Number of trails	37
Trail breakdown	15% beginner
	50% intermediate
	35% expert

23
VAIL, COLORADO

BEST DAYS : Vail

"I love the perpetual sense of discovery. One morning I made fresh tracks on a trail. There was an ermine on the side of the trail, watching. He was almost invisible against the snow. He followed me down the mountain, playing, sliding through the snow. I was not an intruder. We were part of the same world."

JEANNE TILKEMEIER

Look at any American town with the population of, say, 13,000 people and you're bound to find a few oddballs who should be kept in an attic. It makes sense, then (at least to us), that when you have 13,000 skiers on Vail Mountain on a busy day, you'll probably have at least a couple who don't, ah . . . fit in. One day we were skiing here with two of the attractive, green-suited Vail hostesses who help lost and needy skiers, and the conversation turned to some of the strange things they had witnessed on their mountain.

"Well, there was the lady who managed to step into her skis backward," said one hostess. "Then she asked her instructor what was wrong. She apparently thought the tips were supposed to turn up in back, like the spoiler of her husband's Porsche.

"Then," she continued, "there was the guy who told me his boots didn't fit. I told him to take them off. He was wearing his tennis shoes inside them."

"A man once came up to me in a total rage," added hostess number two. "He was hysterical and very rude. He screamed, 'I can't find my way. Where am I on this map?'

I looked at it and said, 'Well, for one thing, this is a map of Copper Mountain.' He threw it down on the ground and started stabbing it with his ski pole."

Vail has home-grown characters as well. Take the Ravinoes. Vail has outlawed aerials, like jumps and flips, so one day each year the Ravinoes get together and try to bring some airborne anarchy to the mountain. They get as many as 500 spectators together (many bring their lunches), and crank up a stereo as two or three dozen jumpers start doing illegal maneuvers. It's called the annual Get Upside Down Day. We heard a rumor that Gerald Ford was going to compete. We figure that any mountain that has room for the Ravinoes, a former president, his Secret Service guards, plus people who wear tennis shoes inside their ski boots isn't really the plastic town that it's supposed to be.

But these stories are the exception at Vail. Vail's wider reputation is that of a jet-set resort where the jets arrive from Cleveland or Houston (and, lately, from Mexico City and Caracas). It has the image of a *nouveau riche* town populated by fur-bearing airline

Bumps? What bumps? David Biska-Wingle conquers Prima in high style.
(Photo: Peter Wingle)

pilots and Republicans who have mastered the carved turn. Vail actually struck us as being closer to a theme park, like Disneyland on skis or Lion Country Safari. With trails named Simba and Bwana and a whole section of the mountain called Lionshead, they've got only themselves to blame for this impression. Another thing to remember is that just because a place is artificial doesn't mean you can't have a great time there, as Disneyland proves. Vail is one of the few ski areas that will keep any skier, beginner through expert, occupied for a full week. No small accomplishment, that.

Vail is arguably the largest single ski mountain in America in terms of groomed acres of trails (Heavenly Valley in California has been known to disagree). It has 57 *miles* of trails strung across its vast north face, plus superb powder bowls on its back side. One unconfirmed report has it that Vail employs more people in its trail-grooming operations than the state of Colorado has working on its highway crew. Vail isn't simply larger than most New England resorts, it's almost as large as New England, period. What other resort has a free shuttle service that is the third largest bus system in the entire state? We tried to ski every run at Vail in six days and didn't even come close. One friend of ours who worked and skied here for two full years claims he still hasn't skied the whole mountain.

Off the mountain, there are at least forty restaurants and innumerable shops and lodges tucked away among the quasi-Tyrolean architecture for which Vail is constantly being disparaged. It's hard to think of any amenity or activity that Vail doesn't offer for a price. We saw one place that featured sensory-deprivation tanks, as in the movie *Altered States*. It was located just under the local Baskin-Robbins. Sensory deprivation isn't our idea of what to do on vacation, but hey, who are we to argue? There is even a total tanning center so you can wear your ski goggles in and come out looking like you've conquered the back bowls. Something for everyone. Or someone for everything.

The drawback to all of this is that, like Disneyworld, everyone wants to come here to play. Vail can be so crowded that they have to stop selling lift tickets when they approach 15,000 for the day (they've only sold out four times). People have actually scalped lift tickets here and sold them for $35 or $40. The lift lines are generally manageable, but on a couple of occasions they were so long we thought they should have express lanes, like at the supermarket, for skiers who made ten turns or less. The restaurants, even the midmountain ones with sit-down service, sometimes require reservations made before you leave home. Maybe they ought to plug in to Ticketron. Wise skiers hit Vail in early December, January, or April, when the crowds are absent but the snow isn't.

But the crowding and waiting are redeemed by the quality of the skiing. Skiers of every stripe can find suitable terrain all over the mountain, and at the same time everybody gets to go to the top and enjoy the magnificent view across the Gore Range. There are more 14,000-foot peaks in this area than anywhere in the United States outside of Alaska. Beginners can stay on the eastern edge of the area, at the bottom of Golden Peak, if they feel uneasy. When they get their ski legs, they can move up the east side of the mountain, past the expert bump runs in Northeast Bowl, and ski their own mini-bowl over at Far East on runs like Flapjack, Tin Pants, and Sourdough. On the opposite side of the mountain they can meander the entire 1½-mile length of Lost Boy back in Game Creek Bowl and come down the front face of the mountain on Lion's Way or Simba into Born Free. Intermediates have similar clusters of runs all over the mountain. Game Creek Bowl is usually nicely groomed and easily negotiable. It tends to attract crowds who spend the day on Lost Boy. Vail is arranged so that intermediates can dig into as much as they want of lots of different kinds of skiing. You want trees? Just duck into the pines between Expresso and Cappuccino, or head for Riva Glade from the top of Chair 11 or 4. Bumps? Ski the edges of Look Ma or Riva Ridge. Challenging cruises with steep faces? Hit Northstar and Northwoods on the east side of Chair 11, or come down Pickeroon and Avanti over on the Lionshead side of the mountain. If you bite off more than you can chew, Vail's trails usually give you a way to bail out on alternate routes like Cold Feet, Compromise, Choker Cut-off, or Surrender.

We really started to get our bump technique together at Vail, even though we found some of the famous bump runs, like Look Ma and Prima, a bit disappointing. Look Ma is sweet but short. You have plenty of witnesses on the deck of the Mid-Vail restaurant, but not enough time to testify. Same with Pronto. The folks waiting for Chair 11 may love watching, but we preferred the more solitary challenges over in the relatively undiscovered Northeast Bowl. Blue Ox, Rogers Run, and Highline test the strongest legs. Blue Ox deceived us. It starts out as a mellow cruise and we thought we had our rhythm. Then the bottom dropped out and we made it a third of the way down on memory alone before a mogul the size of a white elephant threw us. Highline was more of the same: the kind of run that makes dental floss superfluous for a week or two. These runs can't be groomed because of their steepness, but

Forget the fox: A pack of powder hounds sniff out the back bowls at Vail. (Photo: Vail Associates/Peter Runyon)

that's what they said about the legendary Prima too. We had the misfortune to arrive right after this famous mogul monster had been reduced to a golf-course fairway tilted on its side. Prima to Pronto to Log Chute used to be a great triple play taken back to back, and mowing the bumps on any one of them is a serious error.

The biggest Vail tales of all are generated on the back side of the mountain. The entire south face of Vail is a wide-open, expert cruise through every imaginable kind of snow. On generous days there is endless powder. At other times you catch heavy death crud or corn snow. Before Vail was even built, the founders were smart enough to head into the back bowls to shoot a promotional film that induced rich investors to come aboard. Ever since then the back bowls have been the setting for pictures that make skiers all over the world drool. Once they arrive, it doesn't matter if they can't tell for sure if they are skiing in Sun Up Bowl or Sun Down Bowl, Yonder or Over Yonder, or on Cow's Face or Milt's Face, on Wow or Lower Wow, Seldom or Never. All of them are impressive. The lift line at the bottom of the bowls can be impressive, too. But, as on the front of the mountain, hardly anyone complains. The best attractions always sell the most tickets, and Vail delivers quite a ride.

BEST BETS

LODGING

Despite its image as a plastic, "Shake and Bake Bavarian" town, Vail offers some solid, high-quality lodging. The town is basically spread across the base of the ski mountain from east to west, with most of the lodging and restaurants located in Vail Village on the east side, and a smaller cluster to the west at Lionshead area by the gondola building of the same name. At the top of our list are the extremely luxurious *Northwoods* condominiums, one of the nicest layouts in the Rockies.

Only twenty of the seventy-eight units here are rentable, and many of the owners are wealthy and prominent foreigners, but the rates are reasonable, considering the quality of the construction. For more traditional housing, the famous old *Lodge at Vail* is loaded with atmosphere and has a perfect location. The two new wings of the lodge are condos, and you can rent the studio end of a multibedroom unit (ask for no. 535 if it's available) and have an intimate hideaway. Other good choices are the *Vail Athletic Club*, a slightly snobbish place with lots of amenities, the spacious *Mountain Haus* condominiums, and the smaller, newly redecorated *Hotel Sonnenalp*. Over at Lionshead, your best bet is probably *Mariott's Mark Resort*, although we've heard good things about a newer lodge called the *Spa*. Central Reservations books all these at 303-476-5677.

DINING

Vail restaurants have a sense of big-city exclusivity about them. This is the land of the never-empty water glass and the disappearing plate. Reservations are a must, and knowing which place is "in" far enough in advance to secure a reservation is a mark of your own status. Nevertheless, there are some very fine places to eat, including *Alain's Creekside Café*, a small, romantic room with delicious French fare and a lively bar in front. Other favorites are the highly touted *Left Bank*, *Ambrosia*, and the *Alpenrose Tearoom*. The *Vail Athletic Club* dining room is also a treat. For brunch the place to go is *Cyrano's* (and *Cyrano's Too* in the Spa at Lionshead), a chic hangout with delicious egg dishes. The best cheap burgers in town are at *Donovan's*, which is also the most popular bar when the lifts close. Over at Lionshead, *Alfie Packer's*, named after an old homesteader who barbecued his companions back in the 1880s, packs 'em in at lunch, and *Purcell's* is a popular steak and seafood house for dinner. Vail also is blessed with perhaps the finest on-mountain restaurants of any ski resort we visited. Both the *Stube* at Eagle's Nest and

Rise and shine: A flock of early birds greet Sun Up Bowl on Vail's back side. (Photo: Jill Vig/Vail Associates)

the *Cook Shack* at Mid-Vail offer very good sit-down dining (be sure you have a reservation) and cookouts on their decks in nice weather.

TRANSPORTATION

Vail is 100 miles from Denver and is literally astride Interstate 70, leading some wise guys to maintain that Vail is just another roadside attraction in Colorado. Whatever the case, you can catch a scheduled bus from Trailways (beware—they've been known to bump skiers, even those with reservations) or get four or five people to split a cab from the Denver airport. Rocky Mountain flies into nearby Avon, and special add-on fares can make this connection a great deal, so ask your airline about it. Rental cars can be had in Denver, but we would urge you to drop them off once you arrive (Hertz and Avis offer this service) since a private auto is unnecessary in the compact village.

RANDOM NOTES

Aspen may have a wider reputation for swinging night life, but they don't roll up the sidewalks at 7 P.M. here either. *Donovan's* is the most popular watering hole, and *Garton's Wild West Saloon* is rowdy, funky, and lots of fun. Other nice places to bend an elbow are the *Red Lion*, *Cyrano's*, the *Gore Creek Yacht Club*, and *City Limits*, whose latest transformation has been from disco to punk. At Lionshead, try *Alfie Packer's*. Got to go disco? Try *Shadows at the Mark* or *Holmes Underground*. If the back bowls seem a bit cramped to you, ask about tours of China Bowl and Teacup Bowl from the ski patrol. You'll find their headquarters up at the top of Chairs 11 and 4, in a shack that is officially addressed 11250 Skyline Drive. The Vail Ski School is experimenting with two-way radios —so the instructor can talk to a pupil as he or she skis along. So far, no word on how many students have picked up Stapleton Approach Control, received orders to descend to 6,000 feet, and hold. Vail has many beautiful picnic decks and tables all over the mountain that make great brown-bag lunch stops. Ask the green-clad hosts and hostesses on the mountain for directions. Try to find out which week in February all of the dentists in America convene at Vail (they do this every year). Make plans to go elsewhere unless you

want a cavity filled. Also avoid Easter week, when hordes of college kids and wealthy South Americans descend en masse. The best-kept secret at Vail is that the *Vail Golf Course* restaurant serves food in a very peaceful setting, far from the crowds. Vail is the only mountain in the West that deserves its own dictionary of trails. Before you ski Vail, we suggest you get a copy of *Up and Down Vail Mountain* by Sherry Oaks and Raymond Gruenfeld (Boulder: Westview Press). It is the kind of enterprise that could only result from a great mountain and a large potential market. See you in Hairbag Alley. Note that the tepee over near the top of the mountain by Peanut Park is a favorite trysting place for Vail employees. If the skis out front are crossed, be discreet in entering.

Base elevation	8,100 ft.
Vertical drop	3,150 ft.
Number of lifts	18
Skiable acres	1,750
Average skiers per day	8,000
Average snowfall	382 in.
Number of trails	100 (approx.)
Trail breakdown	30% beginner
	40% intermediate
	30% expert

24
WATERVILLE VALLEY, NEW HAMPSHIRE

BEST DAYS : Waterville Valley

*"One Monday morning in mid-January last year a storm dumped
16 inches of fresh snow on the mountain. We rode up to the top at
8 A.M. and the new snow was hanging in the evergreens, turning
them all pure white. It was super quiet. It made you feel so good
just being there. Five hours later we had skied it all up, whooping
and hollering with that special exhilaration you get when you
ski untracked snow."*

NICOLE GREGORY

The easiest way to understand the difference between ski resorts in Vermont and those in New Hampshire is to look at a road map. Interstate 91 brings a steady stream of people up into the Green Mountains from New York, while Interstate 93 shoots directly out of Boston and into the heart of the White Mountains of New Hampshire. The variations in style and temperament between New York and Boston are very clear, and so are the differences between their favorite ski resorts. Not better or worse, just different. Equal but separate pleasures, like a week in the Hamptons versus a week on Cape Cod.

Waterville Valley reflects its New England roots as surely as Stratton mirrors New York or Mammoth Mountain echoes Los Angeles. How else could we explain our contented feelings when we returned to our lodge every night after wrestling with weather and snow conditions that would make Admiral Byrd feel at home? Bedrock New England hospitality is the trump card that's played on top of gracious, subdued, and discreetly elegant surroundings. There are plenty of other Jacuzzis in other ski resorts to soak in under the

stars, but somehow ours at Waterville seemed to envelop us in a sense of well-being. Everyone and everything here, from the owner of the ski area to the ski week package customers, derives something from the location.

Waterville Valley sits at the dead end of an isolated valley 12 miles off the Interstate. The small enclave of condos and lodges is about two miles from the ski slopes on Mount Tecumseh, and the entire resort is surrounded on all sides by imposing wooded mountains. You reach the valley by driving through the vast White Mountain National Forest on a two-lane highway that cuts through a series of curving blue ridges. After you pass a small commercial cluster near the I-93 highway interchange, there is nothing to mar your approach through soothing mountains. Waterville is not just a retreat, however. It is also a convenient staging area for daytime jaunts a bit farther north to Loon Mountain, with its gentle swells of ego-building intermediate trails, and to Cannon, both of which are under an hour away.

Cannon is by far the most challenging area

Waterville Valley at night. The village is a snug cluster of lights. (Photo: Clyde Smith)

of the three, and the challenges come as much from the weather as from the lay of the land. This old ski area (it was founded in 1938 when the state installed the nation's first aerial tramway up the mountainside) is perched right in the bottleneck of towering granite cliffs that is Franconia Notch. The famous Old Man of the Mountains rock formation is right around the corner. Actually, he isn't all that old, he's just been out in the wind here too long. It was at Cannon that we learned one of the secrets of New England skiing. We shared the new, eighty-passenger tram up to the top of this 2,022-foot mountain with no more than a dozen people all day. On every run we faced a beggar's banquet of ski conditions: rock-solid ice, chopped ice, shredded ice, steep mogul runs with grass

sticking out of them, and other surfaces too painful to recall. The wind was blowing and the temperatures were in the teens. Not only were people still trying to get in one more run at four o'clock when the lifts closed, but they were having a great time. Even the army troops training on this state-owned mountain with their baggy fatigues and ancient ski equipment seemed content as they glided across the tundra in ragged formation. Most of the terrain here is challenging intermediate slopes, and the lower third of the mountain contains three steep bump runs: Zoomer, Polly's Folly, and Avalanche. Polly's is the bottom part of the Cannon downhill course, which Jean-Claude Killy sped down to win his first World Cup race in North America back in the 1960s. We'd heard that skiers try to follow Killy's route down the mountain fast enough to catch the same tram car they rode on the way up. "Well, some guys do like to try," conceded the granite-faced old-timer who punched our tickets. Top to bottom in eight minutes. Ayup.

What we figured out from all of this is that the reward you get from skiing here comes not from surmounting some vast topographical challenge but from the experience of each single turn performed perfectly in sometimes highly imperfect conditions. It's the mastery of technique over surface. All those people on the mountain were taking pride out of having fun on stuff that would cripple most western skiers. Adversity as the mother of adventure. Pilgrim's progress. It is a particularly New England pleasure to triumph over the elements when Mother Nature raises the odds and makes the game interesting. When we finally had left Cannon that night and were soaking in the Jacuzzi, we understood why people keep driving up I-93 out of Boston in the dead of winter.

Later that night we attended a party that was being held to celebrate the end of a week for ski school classes. Waterville Valley takes special pride and pleasure in teaching the skills you need to overcome whatever nature throws at you on the mountain. The packages provide unlimited lessons for five days, social gatherings every night, and a ski instructor who accompanies your group all week and acts as much as a personal guide as a slopeside pedagogue. "The most important technique an instructor can learn is the elbow rub"—that's how one Responsible Person put it. Tonight there was fondue, a buffet dinner for 150 people, and dancing to a German brass band. The ski school handed out a few serious and many playful awards. The slowest instructor got the coveted lead medal. The feeling was that of a revival meeting called to praise Saint Bernard, the patron saint of skiing. The notion of gathering places is strong here—the whole village is deliberately designed to draw guests out of their lodges for dinner, dancing, drinks,

whatever. The idea is to throw people together with others who are sharing the same week-long experience, but it's not the enforced gaiety of Club Med. Not in New England.

Waterville Valley has also tackled the problem of the postintermediate skier blues. How do you get over the hump into expert heaven? Waterville hosts a series of recreational racing camps for adults run by Steve Lathrop. They probe the secrets of running gates, the carved turn, and angulation. They teach the mechanics of tuning skis. At the end of our week there they held a Calcutta and sold teams on the auction block. The money goes into a pot and the winning team in the next day's race gets 60 percent of the loot. The night of the skiers' banquet we walked back to our lodge at about 11:30 and discovered a lone race camp member filing his skis in the lobby. We started to talk, but he said, "Don't break my concentration." Forget the Inner Skier, we thought; there's nothing like a little competition to bring out your serious side.

The idea of moving from courage to competence hasn't swept up every skier we saw at Waterville. Weekends draw droves from nearby Boston, and not all among them are as serious as the edge doctor we saw in the lodge. One Saturday we spotted a 250-pound teenager barreling down the middle of Sel's Choice at about 45 miles an hour. He was bent over at the waist, and with his bulk and dark clothes he resembled a piano on skis. We watched his descent, figuring that if he made it all the way to the base lodge, he'd blast a hole in the wall the size and shape of a runaway Steinway. Somehow, at about Mach 3, he managed to jump in the air, turn sideways to hill, and skid a bit before he blew out of his bindings and scattered himself and his wardrobe all over the slope. "These guys show up all the time," a ski patrolman lamented later. "They usually wear khaki camouflage jump suits and orange Budweiser caps with the bills turned up. There isn't anything on the mountain that's really dangerous, so they go for it, no guts, no glory. They like to scare themselves silly. I wish they would learn to control themselves."

The fact that there is not much that is really dangerous at Waterville doesn't mean you'll die of boredom here, though. The mountain is designed to be a series of long, rolling, uninterrupted fall-line trails laid side to side on the eastern face of Mount Tecumseh. There are no long traverses or cat tracks to stop the flow, and the wide, western-style trails resemble a set of white ribbons tied at the top where the Sunnyside and White Peak Chairs converge. The farther you wander off to the sides, the gentler the terrain becomes. Right down the middle you'll find Bobby's Run (named after the late Senator Kennedy, who was an early patron and supporter of the resort), Gema, and Ciao, all marked with black diamonds, but in truth there is nothing at Waterville that a solid intermediate can't handle. White Cap and Sel's Choice have been the site of three World Cup races in the past eleven years, though, and True Grit was the scene of the first two National Professional Freestyle championships.

Waterville Valley, under the leadership of its founder and owner, Tom Corcoran (a member of the 1956 and 1960 Olympic ski teams), is in the middle of an elaborate master plan of expansion that will produce a self-contained, European-style ski village between the slopes of Mount Tecumseh and the smaller Snow's Mountain on the other side of the valley. There will be plenty of new, mostly intermediate terrain on both sides, plus more lodges and condos and shops as plans move ahead. Even now, though, Corcoran's mark of New England gentility is everywhere. The condos and lodges are mostly very new and very tasteful, as are the limited number of restaurants in the village. There is a distinct absence of trash (literally as well as figuratively) and flash. People in these parts ski not to be a part of the "in" crowd or to watch celebrities, but for the

feeling of escape, the sense that winter has not gotten the best of them. "Come up for air," we kept hearing them say. If it is a high-voltage vacation you want, this isn't the place. But if you're after a deep breath of New England skiing, Waterville will do just fine.

BEST BETS

LODGING

As we've mentioned, Waterville Valley should be the focal point for a week of skiing along I-93. The area offers some very high-quality accommodations, including one of our favorite lodges anywhere, the *Snowy Owl Inn*. The Snowy Owl is a beautifully updated version of the old New England inn, with towering ceilings, lush hanging plants, and stone fireplaces. Another favorite is the *Valley Inn*, with the most complete array of amenities in the valley, including a fine dining room, an indoor/outdoor pool, and evening entertainment. The *Silver Squirrel* is a less expensive version of the Snowy Owl. The choicest condos are those managed by Waterville Realty, including *Noon Peak*, which features Jacuzzis in some units. Central Reservations at Waterville (603-236-8371) can book any of the above.

DINING

The *Fourways Restaurant* is the central dining place (and favorite après-ski watering hole) in the village because most of the guests who are on the Modified American Plan take their dinners here even while they stay in other lodges or condos. The food is high quality and reasonably priced Continental fare. On Saturday nights the Fourways sprouts an additional dining room, *Andre's Specialty Restaurant*, and chef Andre Meyer whips up spectacular treats for just thirty-five people who've had the good sense to reserve far in advance. In addition, the in-

This is New England? A skier on Cannon, with Mount Lincoln in the background.
(Photo: Dick Hamilton)

formal *Finish Line* serves casual dinners over at the base of Snow's Mountain. Away from the village, the *William Tell* is a lively Swiss restaurant that serves delicious veal dishes, rösti potatoes, and desserts. There is a crackling fire and lots of good cheer here, and the William Tell is deservedly the most popular place in the area. Up in Franconia, close by Cannon, is another special place, *Lovett's*, an old inn built in 1784 that is well known throughout New England for its fine food (it also takes overnight guests).

TRANSPORTATION

A free shuttle bus runs back and forth between the village at Waterville Valley and the ski slopes on Mount Tecumseh (a five-minute trip), making a car unnecessary during the days you spend on that mountain. Most skiers arrive by car anyway, and use them for excursions to Loon, Cannon, or wherever the snow is reportedly best each day. At night you're on your own unless you're dining in the Fourways, the Valley Inn, or the Finish Line.

RANDOM NOTES

New Hampshire liquor laws decree that there shall be no bars without adjoining restaurants in the state, a move that hinders, but does not eliminate, night life in Waterville. The base lodge at Mount Tecumseh is lively once the lifts shut down, and there are "tea dancing" and Swiss pastries served from a cart at the *Rustic Nail* lounge in the Fourways every Tuesday, Wednesday, and Thursday. Actually, the music varies from rock to jazz to country, but it's always good, and they do serve tea if you ask for it. Other gathering spots include the bar of the *Finish Line* and at the *William Tell* down the road. Note that five-day tickets for Waterville Valley, Cannon, or Loon are good for one day of skiing at either of the other two areas. Cannon, however, imposes a two-dollar surcharge for use of the tram. Since there is a T-bar that goes nearly all the way to the top, you may want to avoid that fee, especially if you just want to ski the bumps on Polly's Folly and its neighbors all day. The Waterville Touring Center has some excellent cross-country trails that start right at the village center and wind around for 55 groomed, double-tracked, patrolled kilometers through the trees of the valley. Good idea on cold days.

	Waterville	Cannon	Loon Mountain
Base elevation	1,815 ft.	2,000 ft.	900 ft.
Vertical drop	2,020 ft.	2,146 ft.	1,850 ft.
Number of lifts	9	7	6
Skiable acres	186	199	140
Average skiers per day	3,000 (weekends)	2,300 (weekends)	2,750 (weekends)
	1,300 (weekdays)	1,500 (weekdays)	800 (weekdays)
Average snowfall	156 in.	156 in.	125 in.
Number of trails	35	36	25
Trail breakdown	7 beginner	8 beginner	7 beginner
	16 intermediate	20 intermediate	14 intermediate
	12 expert	8 expert	4 expert

25
WHISTLER, BRITISH COLUMBIA, CANADA

BEST DAYS : Whistler

"My recipe for a great day here is simple: Sunshine, powder, and a group of skiers who enjoy discovering what Whistler has to offer. I get off on people's energy, the excitement of exploring this playground. It is perfectly acceptable to be astonished by this mountain."

LEANNE, A WHISTLER GUIDE

We first heard about Whistler from two Canadian kids who had saved up enough money to come to Portillo, Chile, for some summer skiing one year. They were out of place among the jet-setters and international racing elite who gather in Portillo every year (so were we, as matter of fact). They wore overalls and wool shirts. But they skied impeccably all day, taking the steep slopes of the Andes with total aplomb. The only other resort they had skied was Whistler. "You've got to do it at least once," they told us. "Whistler's a unique experience. It has the greatest vertical drop in North America, and you use it all. It's no-frills skiing. No night life. No town. Just the biggest motherfucker mountain you've ever seen."

The next time we heard about Whistler was when a 1979 World Cup downhill race scheduled at the Canadian giant was canceled because of poor racing conditions. The Pacific storms that move ashore into the Coast Mountains north of Vancouver had softened the snow too much, and the judges were calling the race course unsafe. It didn't help matters when the middle section broke

free in an avalanche. Rain or no rain, though, the Canadian team wanted to race. The Kamikaze Kids, as they had been dubbed, were eager to show the home folks what they could do. Like the British Columbia landscape many of them grew up in, they were, and are, brash, rugged, and a bit wild.

With this kind of build-up we thought we knew what to expect when we finally got on a plane for Vancouver: Whistler would be a hardship resort, the skier's version of a foreign legion outpost. The 70-mile drive from Vancouver to the ski area was supposed to be impossible, the snow unbelievable, the terrain as varied and complex as any three Rocky Mountain resorts put together. As usual, only some of our impressions turned out to be true.

First of all, the drive is not suicidal. The road is narrow but manageable, and along the way it caresses the edge of a spectacular blue fjord. The scenery rivals the drive from Reno to Mammoth or Santa Fe to Taos for extravagant doses of alpine inspiration. The ski area itself does present the raw, rugged, and rather primitive facilities of legend. At

Head over heels at Whistler. That's Blackcomb Mountain in the background. (Photo: © Greg Griffith)

second glance, though, the whole place seems to be under construction. Whistler is the beneficiary of large doses of money from the Canadian government and private investors (most notably the Aspen Ski Corp.). As a result it is about to become a world-class destination resort. Blackcomb Mountain, the peak that adjoins Whistler, has been stitched with ski runs and chair lifts, and an entire village is being installed in the valley between the two mountains. Whistler is already an awesome ski mountain even without Blackcomb, and the completed combination, which is open for business even as it grows and expands, will present an array of skiing challenges unmatched in the world. Imagine Aspen Highlands with Squaw Valley sitting right next to it and Keystone in between and you'll begin to get the idea. Blackcomb alone has a vertical drop of 4,000 feet, and there are plans to run a lift up another 1,200 feet into Horstman Glacier for a mind-boggling total drop of 5,200 feet. The runs that are already in place on Blackcomb are consistently pitched, giant slalom freeways that tumble straight down an endless fall line. They dodge around and through little islands of trees, then go on forever. After a mile or so you switch on the autopilot and fall into a looser swinging rhythm, an almost hypnotic, bop-till-you-drop free fall down the mountain.

Even with all of these intermediate highways, Blackcomb pales in comparison to Whistler, the main event across the valley. Whistler is everything Blackcomb isn't. There are bowls, steep trails with double fall lines, plus at least one bump run, Chunkie's, that compares favorably with Limelight at Sun Valley or Highline and Blue Ox at Vail. Whistler is a capricious mountain. The trails dogleg, change pitch, narrow, expand, grow bumps, become catwalks. They go on forever, too, but are so unpredictable you seldom get a sense of the whole place, just a series of moments.

Early in the season when the sun is low, they park a jeep with its headlights on near the lift lines so that early birds can find their way to the gondola or the Olive Chair. We met one guy who couldn't wait for that. He camped out at the top of the mountain, sleeping overnight in a snow cave so he could have the first run down the mountain in the morning. No one thought he was crazy. Such extreme behavior seems perfectly logical and acceptable when you have a mountain that offers this much.

At the very top of the mountain is a series of enormous bowls, one of which has Whistler Glacier nestled inside it. We were willing to make the climb and have powder shots up there to ourselves. You can hike to the summit and ski the Elevator Shaft or a series of steep drops called the V.D. Chutes. Most people who do so stop for a picnic on top and drink in the view of the surrounding peaks and glaciers. One day we skied with a guide who led us past Harmony Bowl and Whistler Glacier and over a ridge into Whistler Bowl, which is technically out of bounds. We were completely alone, sheltered by the cliffs, with our laughter echoing off the rock walls. We cut figure eights, then dropped through a forest of pine and fir and cedar and hemlock, eventually reaching a marked trail far below. We could not hear the sound of a lift anywhere. It was wilderness, pure and simple. Canada has a relaxed attitude about ski area boundaries; they're also relaxed about the risks you can take on a mountain if you really want to. You can go anywhere you want, but don't expect the ski patrol to baby-sit if you need a Band-Aid out beyond the area boundaries. You can hang it out anywhere you want, but you sure as hell had better be prepared to reel yourself back in, because Big Daddy won't be there to help.

One day we caught a glimpse of another acceptable use of the property as we were skiing across Whistler Glacier. This vast tidal wave of powder had been etched with the usual linked-turn graffiti, but right in the middle of the coils of tracks were three or four skiers packing down a run that was straight as a plumb bob. What rational skiers had taken in forty turns they were going to schuss. We skied over and watched these young kids wearing helmets and 223-centimeter downhill racing skis hurtle by at 60 miles an hour or so. "We do it to get used to going fast," they told us. "If you're going to race downhill you've got to get comfortable at this speed. Then you can learn the subtleties, like how to turn." The next generation of Kamikaze Kids. They asked us if we wanted to try a run. One of us (Petersen) strapped on long skis and a helmet, and crashed and burned at a highly inflationary rate of speed. In the ski patrol shack they applied a few bandages and the patrolman filled out a form. "How old?" he asked. "Thirty-two" was the answer. The young Canadians just stared. "How can someone that old be that crazy?" one of them asked. The patrolman corrected him. "How can someone that crazy have gotten to be that old?"

Below the vast, open bowls where Petersen nearly ended a career in journalism, Whistler becomes a series of long beginner and intermediate cruises through the evergreens. One trail, Franz's Run, is 5 miles long, a scenic ramble that seems to be finding its way down the mountain for the first time. It finally emerges from the forest and heads for the main base and gondola station near the main road. Another trail, Olympic, is even longer than Franz's, 7 miles of intermediate ecstasy down the other side of the mountain to the valley that is being developed into the new Town Centre (three new lifts from the village side have eliminated the need to ride the shuttle bus back to the gondola). This run is marked beginner, but the Canadians seem to take for granted a level of skills that would surprise Americans used to the gently tilted fairways of Colorado and Vermont. One result seems to be that Whistler skiers have staying power. You can spot them because they are the ones who don't get tired halfway down the mountain. If you can take Whistler in stride, 4,280 feet at one gulp, you end up with thighs that can eat most other mountains alive. At Whistler it is not unusual to ski 35,000 vertical feet in a day.

The bottom of Olympic trail and the new Town Centre are about 4 miles up the road from the older main base at Whistler. In between is a scattering of cabins and older lodges. Until the Centre takes over as the focal point of nighttime action, things will probably continue to be fairly low key here.

There is some lively night life at Whistler on the weekends when hordes from Vancouver descend. One place features strippers on Monday nights so the locals can remember what the female form looks like without ski boots and down jackets. There seem to be two groups around, the hard-core skiers who fall asleep in their beer after skiing and the partygoers who drown in their soup at lunch the next day.

It is hard to say what Whistler will be like once the place is built out to its full plan. With Aspen Ski Corp. having a piece of the action, it is tempting to say that Whistler will become another Aspen, but no one really knows. Certainly the Vancouverites will flock here as they already do. More Japanese will certainly come over on charter flights. People from the Midwest may discover that it costs no more to fly to Vancouver than to Denver, and that Yankee dollars go far in Canada. And there will be two American writers dropping in as often as possible.

BEST BETS

LODGING

The development of the new Town Centre is changing the housing scene at Whistler very rapidly, so it is best to check with the Whistler Resort Association (604-932-4222) for the latest openings. As matters now stand, the *Blackcomb Lodge* and three condominiums, *Tantalus*, *Hearthstone*, and *Clocktower*, are open in the Centre. Down the road, and located just across from the gondola, is the very attractive new *Whistler Creek Lodge*.

One good turn deserves another: cruising on Blackcomb, with Whistler behind. (Photo: © Greg Griffith)

Name it and claim it: If you are willing to climb, Whistler is all yours. (Photo: © Greg Griffith)

About a quarter mile from the gondola base is the *Whistler Resort and Club,* which used to be the Whistler Inn and has now been completely renovated. The *Highland Lodge* is a bit older but still a good choice, with a popular dining room on the premises.

DINING

As with lodging, the food situation is ever changing, mostly for the better as new restaurants and bars open in the valley. The *Creek House* and the *Cut Above* are worth-

while new spots, both in the Whistler Creek Lodge. *Russell's* and *Stoney's* are up in the Town Centre, the latter being a French Provincial outpost with a Canadian flavor (which seems to mean more beef on the menu). Locals have great expectations for the new *Umberto's* Italian restaurant since it's a branch of the well-known operation in Vancouver. Older, tried and true favorites strung out along the road between the gondola station and the Centre include the very popular *Keg,* a steakhouse, and *JB's,* a more expensive place with a French menu, located in the Whistler Resort and Club. *Beau's* at the Rainbow is also nice, as is *La Vallée Blanche*, which is located north of the Town Centre about a mile or so.

TRANSPORTATION

Vancouver is the gateway to Whistler, and it's two hours due north by car. You can also drive up from Seattle in about five hours. If you rent, try to secure a "Snow Special" in Vancouver that comes with a ski rack and tire chains. There are now at least three car rental outfits in Whistler itself if you'd rather take the train from Vancouver and only drive locally. Budget Rent-A-Car is the biggest of them, and it is possible to rent a four-wheel drive vehicle if you book far in advance. The train from Vancouver is good if you want to stick close to the Town Centre. Buses are also available very frequently, and the local shuttle bus, the Snow Goose, runs during the day betwen the gondola and the Town Centre.

RANDOM NOTES

Whistler is a lively place in a loose, casual sort of way. On weekends the place is packed with Vancouverites who gather at *L'Après* for drinks when the gondola shuts down.

Later at night L'Après and the *Mountainside Cabaret* have dancing. The lounge at *JB's* is also very popular, and *Tapley's*, a new English pub, has rapidly gained a local following for its meat pies and draft beer. If you really want some local color, drop by the *Ski Boot Inn* on Monday night when strippers (male and female—check the schedule) compete for attention with live bands. If you want to ski both Whistler and Blackcomb the same day, you can buy an interchangeable ticket for a three-dollar premium. There is a similar arrangement with five-day tickets that also includes a surcharge, but not as much. B.C. Powder Guides offer some amazing helicopter skiing by the day or week into the surrounding peaks and glaciers. Another fact to keep in mind is that the weather varies enormously between the base and the peak of both mountains. The annual snowfall is 450 inches at the Whistler summit but only 180 inches at the base. Both areas now offer free guided tours every day, a good idea especially at vast Whistler Mountain. *Whistler News* is a very handy local paper to have. Finally, Whistler has adopted the admirable habit practiced at Sun Valley of having a few small tools handy at the top of the lifts for on-slope repairs, plus the "sniffle stations," covered boxes with tissues inside. All ski areas should follow suit.

Base elevation	2,120 ft.
Vertical drop	4,280 ft.
Number of lifts	13
Skiable acres	NA
Average skiers per day	2,620
Average snowfall	450 in.
Number of trails	NA
Trail breakdown	10% beginner
	65% intermediate
	25% expert

THE EXPERIENCES

26
CRUISING: THE INITIATION

The skiers ride the chair, rising into a sky so blue, it seems alive, yielding perceptibly to their ascent. Somewhere in the vicinity of the sun, an impossibly white sailplane hangs motionless, suspended on the invisible, changing edges, catching currents, rising, falling, dancing in space. Man's ancient dream of flight realized. The skiers abandon the chair and slide across a field of white that is as weightless as the sky above. They cruise, change edges, catch currents, dance in space. . . .

Cruising is the first wonderment, the first taste of the ultimate in skiing. There comes a moment when everything is warm, loose, working. The skier feels the pure joy of getting it right, of surrendering to what John Jerome calls the haunting power of rhythmic activity. He described the feeling in his remarkable book *The Sweet Spot in Time*: "We have all experienced that moment of physical perfection when the ball sings off the racquet, when the putt rolls inexorably toward the cup, when the dive knifes into the water. But how do these miracles occur?"

In skiing, the miracle is easy to explain. To quote Scooter LaCouter, an Aspen ski in-

structor, "All you have to do is turn the mothers." The authors of *Inner Skiing*, *Centered Skiing*, and *Skiing from the Head Down* celebrate the unique sensual pleasure that comes from connected turns: "Enjoying the process. Floating in the experience of the moment. Skiing out of your mind. Letting it happen. Fascination. Forgetting each turn in time for the next. Surrender."

Or, as one beginning skier said: "Jesus Christ, what a rush."

A few years ago, *Playboy* asked Morten Lund to reflect on twenty-five years of skiing and to select the ultimate downhill runs. Under the category of cruisers, he wrote:

Each great ski run has a creative thrust to it, a fantasy to it, a rhythmical quality that defies imitation. A trail should be like a musical score, composed with one effect in mind—joy—yet subject to differing interpretations. It should improve with each playing. A candidate should combine surprise, contour, variety, challenge and charm. A trail should have enough pitch to make you ski, enough scenery to make

Trouble on Paradise: A band of marauders plunder the powder at Sugarbush.(Photo: Clyde Smith)

you stop and enough quick shifts to keep you in delightful tension (or attention). A run should use trees and terrain to vary the score, to create the sensation of entering and leaving different zones. It has to produce that satisfying feeling that comes from a well made trail cut with a skier's eye, a trail whose banks and turns coalesce in a fine sweeping descent, the exact shape of the next stretch half hidden, half revealed, fully unraveled only at the instant of execution, sanctioned by the grace of performance, demanded in subtle shifts of technique.

The great cruise runs are usually marked intermediate, but that is nothing to be ashamed of. Zen masters attain satori by doing the mundane perfectly. There are many paths to enlightenment. Choose one, find the groove, and cut it deep. Synchronize Astraltunes and try formation flying: Buddy's Run at Steamboat. Ruthie's at Aspen. The Big Burn and Naked Lady at Snowmass. The Gros Ventre at Jackson. Warm Springs, Olympic, or College at Sun Valley. Rimeline and Wanderer at Stratton. National at Stowe. Olympic at Whistler. Schoolmarm at Keystone. Riva, Simba, and International at Vail. Ridge Run and Canyon on the California side of Heavenly, Little Dipper and Olympic on the Nevada side. Antelope at Mad River. Payday at Park City. Valley Run at Waterville. Timberline at Killington. Every ski resort in America has a main vein, a cruiser's delight.

We cut our teeth on a trail at Taos called Porcupine. It's the run skiers warm up on, where they meet their friends at the end of the week to take the mountain top to bottom.

Smoking at Whistler: Cruising means pointing 'em downhill and lighting up.
(Photo: © Greg Griffith)

When you challenge the big ones in the Bugaboos, the bottom can drop out any-time. (Photo: Peter Wingle)

On Porcupine skiers come off the chair and gather at the top of a glade the size of a small pond, surrounded by dark green trees. They count heads, then push off, angling right, threading a narrow trail through close-packed trees. Suddenly the trail opens up to receive them. The trees move to the side, like dancers yielding the floor to the best couple. The upper half of Porcupine is a country road. But then the mountain rises, the skiers find themselves on an exposed ridge, alone on the crest of a breaking wave. The sky seems astonishingly close, the mountains across the valley an eyelash away. Then the trail narrows, dives around a corner, and the skiers have a chance to practice catwalk technique. As quickly as it's begun, the clattering subsides. The skiers swoop to the right into a broad gulley, the lower portion of White

Feather. A swift cut through a shadowy glade of trees, another cat track, and the skiers are caught in a crossfire of sunlight. Another right turn and the village becomes visible over the tops of trees. The skiers take the last few hundred feet of vertical—a field of moguls—with immaculate style. They pause. One person kneels to kiss the mountain. They are intimates.

Cruising is one way skiers experience grace. The dictionary defines grace as: "Un-merited divine assistance given man for his regeneration or sanctification. A virtue coming from God. Approval. Acceptance. Attractiveness. Beauty. Fitness of proportion of line or expression. A musical trill." Gee whiz. All that and a good time. Is it any wonder people get hooked on cruising?

27
POWDER: THE GIFT

We don't particularly care for powder. Look at it this way: Why spend $300 on skis, $240 on boots, and another couple of hundred on quilted gaiters and stretch pants, just to have them buried alive beneath a layer of freshly fallen snow? If you believe that, then you'll love our next book: *Ultimate Bowling*.

Powder is the second revelation, the next step in the skier's curriculum. After mastering cruising, the relationship of ski to terrain, the pilgrim begins to acquire a taste for the varieties of snow—what the resorts refer to as conditions. There is fresh, untracked snow. There is antique snow with character lines. There is used, one-owner, low-mileage snow. There is engine-rebuilt snow. There is boilerplate, bulletproof, insolent, unyielding ayatollah snow. There is blackboard-jungle snow. Death crud. A mountain can be as hard as whaletooth, with tracks as finely carved as scrimshaw. A mountain can be soft, forgiving, every track a brushstroke.

Powder is king, the gold standard by which we judge all other ski experiences. It is a blank check from nature. Sign your name on the dotted line, or anywhere you like. You are in it, not on it. Powder is one of the few conditions where the mountain seems to take notice of a skier's passing. The snow kicks up in a wake that is slow to settle. Cold smoke. Where there's smoke, there's a fire burning in the skier's thighs. Each turn ignites the snow, sending up an incandescent flare of crystals, as fine as flame.

Skiing powder is like sailing at night, when the ocean and sky merge, dark and indistinguishable. The sailor guides his boat by feel, adjusting to the tensions of water and wind. The skier is suspended in the center of the turn, balancing the tension of ski and snow. Powder is consistent. Do something once, and if it works, do it a hundred times. There is no hurry. Skiing powder causes one to savor the world in slow motion. The skier cannot rush the turn, cannot get by with a quick heel thrust or sideslip. Powder rewards grace and pulls down pretenders. There is nothing quite so exhilarating as falling in powder. There is nothing quite so exhausting as trying to get up from a fall in powder.

Once a skier gets a taste of powder, he or she will settle for nothing less. Study the

Bull's-eye: Steve Baugh gets a perfect powder hit into the deep at Targhee. (Photo: Ron Adlington)

Helicopter guide Reudi Gertsch plunders powder on a first run in the Monashees. (Photo: Peter Wingle)

statistics at the end of each of the resort chapters. The legendary powder halls are obvious: Alta, Snowbird, Park City, Targhee, Jackson Hole, Arapahoe Basin, Mammoth, Sunshine, Telluride Outer Limits at Crested Butte, Taos, the Bugaboos, the Cariboos. Take your pick. Hope for the best.

We worked on this book for two years, skied every kind of snow known to man or Eskimo. We never had a bad day, but without doubt, the days that stand out are powder days. We remember an afternoon in Jackson: The guide from High Mountain Helicopter Skiing had brought us to the top of a tree-lined alley for the last run of the day. The snow was set up, glistening. We were silent, and then he said, quietly, "This one has your name on it." We pushed off, one behind the other, locking into a rhythm. We synchronized turns, cutting into the snow, causing the whiteness to disappear—just like that—as sudden and precise as the exit of a golf ball from a tee. We stopped, breathless, at the bottom, and turned to gaze upon our handiwork. The tracks formed a powder eight, a double spiral as basic to skiing as the double helix is to DNA. Even if this book failed to sell a single copy, that day would have made this enterprise worthwhile.

There are other moments. Putting on a snorkel and skiing blind through snow that broke over our heads, down a steep chute toward the sound of someone's voice, a friend shouting "Go, go, go." We recall watching a friend come down a ridge on Westward Ho at Alta, into a pocket of powder that exploded into what the ski magazines call a face shot. Her first. She stopped in amazement and, knowing we couldn't see the smile on her face, feigned a swoon. We recall a day at Park City, a day at Stowe, a day at Stratton, a weekend at Snowbird. Powder can happen anywhere, anytime, even when you don't deserve it.

Surface! Surface! Breck O'Neil comes up for air at Jackson Hole. (Photo: Bob Woodall)

Westward Ho! Phil Davis of the Bear Valley Powder Bears hibernates at Alta. (Photo: © 1980 Robert Chamberlain)

28
MOGULS: THE TRIAL

If cruising is the initiation, and powder the reward, then moguls are the trial, the test of faith, the third level in the education of a skier. Just when the skier thinks he is getting good, he has to run the gauntlet. Moguls are inevitable. One writer called them the detritus of modern skiing, the litter. Bumps are sculptures formed by human erosion. Some are benign giants, as large as humpbacked whales, formed by skiers making wide giant slalom turns on long skis. Some are vicious, as quick and unpredictable as piranha, the result of nervous skiers on short skis. Sometimes there is a rhythm to the slope. Sometimes there is chaos.

Most of us ski to experience grace. Jeannie Ramseier, a skier who prefers the quiet of the trees at Steamboat, summed up our frustration with bumps: "Moguls are not a religious experience." They are the stuff of spectacle. Freestylers cater to the same morbid obsession that draws people to bullfights and demolition derbies. Let's watch this guy die. Elsewhere in this book, we have noted that skiing is remarkably similar to the martial arts. It seems like a form of combat, but once

you master the discipline, it is a path to something that can only be called spiritual. Bumps provide the cheap thrills and action shots. Skiing moguls is not unlike the karate experts who bash concrete block with their foreheads. Nevertheless, you have to deal with them, one way or another.

Watching skiers advance through a mogul field brings to mind two images, one from literature, one from the movies. In *The Empire Strikes Back*, Hans Solo takes the Millennium Falcon into a field of asteroids, on manual control. C3PO points out that the maneuver is likely to be fatal. Solo replies: "Don't ever tell me the odds."

In the preface to one of his books, Kurt Vonnegut warns, "You are what you pretend to be, so we better be goddamn careful what we pretend to be."

Bumps can call your bluff faster than any other situation in skiing. The ultimate bump runs are as notorious as Hollywood villains. Al's at Taos. The Plunge and the Spiral Stairs at Telluride. Stein's at Sugarbush. The Goat or Starr at Stowe. Outer Limits at Killington. Gunbarrel at Heavenly. KT-22 at Squaw.

Low-down but not dirty: Motivating through the bumps at Vail is a work of art. (Photo: 1979 Peter Runyon)

The Ridge of Bell at Aspen. Exhibition and Limelight at Sun Valley. Two Much at Copper. Psychopath at Breckenridge. Pallavicini at Arapahoe. Highline, Blue Ox, and Roger's at Vail. Chunkies at Whistler. Higher Rustler at Alta. The bottom of Primrose and Silver Fox at Snowbird. Boom Auger, Wedge, and Bubble Cuffer at Sugarloaf.

When you take on one of these runs, no one asks if you had a good time. It is enough that you survived. Perched on the edge of a field of bumps, the adrenaline kicks in. The body goes into a state of heightened awareness, or primeval readiness. Flight or fight. To bump or not to bump. Time slows, as it does in any emergency. The skier experiences each action in instant replay, slow motion, stop action. The intensity of concentration, the quickness of the tiny acts, will later filter down to other forms of skiing. What was compressed in the colliding descent through the mogul storm will become an object of contemplation, a center of confidence in calmer waters. Once a skier learns just how quickly he can change edges, he finds that he has all the time in the world.

It is an education to stand at the bottom of a field of bumps and to watch how assorted skiers come to grips with the unavoidable. They take what they've learned, and try their best to cope.

A skinny teenager who learned to ski on a 500-foot hill somewhere in the Midwest waggles his way through the bumps, waving his short skis like a saber. You can almost hear him shout, "On guard!" He lunges. The slope parries. His "no-guts-no-glory" bravado culminates in a high-speed equipment redistribution. His friends inquire about his health from the safety of the catwalk. Is he okay? "I ain't seen no one in front of me yet," he yells.

A local kid wearing noodle-soft bump skis puts his quarter down. He's a pinball wizard; he could do this stuff blind. He ricochets off moguls like a steel ball off bumpers. Some flash ten points, some light up and flash a hundred. Suddenly there is too much energy on the board. The skier tenses, and the whole world tilts. No sweat. He picks himself up, pulls the plunger, and releases himself again. He's going for bonus points, a free game.

The next in line is a heavyweight, your basic "I could of been a contender" skier. He is a barroom brawler who blasts straight down the fall line, in search of punishment. His skiing is based on reaction, recovery, brute strength. Thunder thighs. We are reminded of something our football coach once said: "Running through rows of old tires doesn't mean that you are a great broken field runner. It just means that you are good at running through rows of old tires."

An older skier appears on the field. An elastic brace surrounds one knee. He considers the slope, then moves. Each turn is an instant replay of the one before. He avoids the ice in the troughs, the sudden shocks of the dropoffs. His skis caress the flanks of the moguls, soaking up the changes in contour. He seems to forget each obstacle in time for the next, relaxed, imposing a line on the random configuration of bumps. The strategy, the intelligence behind each act, is evident. Like a sports car driver, the skier brakes before the turn, seeking smooth deceleration, controlled descent. He avoids the abrupt. With each turn, each pole plant, there is an energy, an exhilaration. We recall a snatch of melody, a line from a Paul Simon song: "He makes it look so easy / he looks so clean / he moves like God's own immaculate machine / he makes me think about all these extra moves I make, and all this herky jerky motion / and the bag of tricks it takes / to get me through my working day."*

* © 1979, 1980 Paul Simon. Used by permission.

No local stops: This steep, narrow bump run at Killington is express all the way.
(Photo: Bob Perry)

29
GETTING AIR: THE ESCAPE

A few months ago we spent the night watching a film called *Gizmo*. It was a tribute to the mad scientist, the inventor, the dreamer. For an hour we watched jerky black-and-white newsreels of would-be flyers toppling off cliffs, out of barn lofts, from the branches of trees. We thought to ourselves: If only they had gotten rid of the bamboo and linen and gone directly to skis.

Most skiers get their first taste of air by accident, as a direct result of a close encounter with a mogul. We won't say they lose control. They probably didn't have it to begin with. The skier sees what's coming, tenses, trying to put as much distance as possible between himself and the inevitable. Tries to leave the scene of the accident before it happens, subsequently is launched. Sometimes the survivor is grateful for the free ride. It's one way to get down a slope. The only good mogul is the one you don't have to ski.

Instructors tend to discourage lighter-than-air skiing. The reason is simple. As long as the skier has an edge on the ground, he has a chance of control. He can avoid an obstacle.

The minute he leaves the ground, he becomes artillery, an unguided missile with what Tom Wolfe called the glide angle of a bunch of car keys. If the trajectory intersects an immovable object, tough luck.

How can we account for the popularity of suborbital skiing? Getting air is a fundamental obsession of free-doggers, the barn-storming skiers who gather at regular intervals to launch themselves off specially constructed ramps so that they can perform complicated maneuvers in the ozone. These are the same fellows who actually take pride in their ability to knock themselves senseless in the bumps.

Or maybe it's the sensation of free fall, the dream of flight realized. Getting air provides the sensation of hanging, lost in space, taking an extravehicular walk in one of the lower layers of the stratosphere. The skier is weightless, free of the earth. It feels like forever, but as soon as his skis touch earth, he knows that it wasn't long enough.

Getting air presents the same challenge as gymnastics or diving. The skier must come to terms with a more subtle friction: air. He

Look out below: The bottom falls out on this British Columbia skier. (Photo: Eric Sanford Jr.)

must achieve balance without the firm hand of Mother Earth. What goes up must come down. What happens in the middle is the stuff of dreams. The skier relaxes, assumes a position, and as gracefully as possible, touches down. All day he has played by gravity's rule, followed its lead in every turn. For one breathtaking, heart-stopping moment, he breaks the connection. He is out there, defying gravity. There is nothing quite like it.

When you are ready to solo, when you ski from the center of your body outward, rather than from the feet up, the possibilities are endless. At Jackson Hole we watched a skier glide down through the trees off Gros Ventre. Without skipping a beat, he sailed off a snow-covered rock into a backscratcher, landed in an explosion of powder, rebounded, took a ledge full tilt into a daffy, then 100 yards later celebrated his return to the main trail with a 360. The run was a continuous event, punctuated by aerial exclamation marks, as awesome as the leaps of a virtuoso dancer or ice skating champion. At other resorts we watched cornice kamikazes hurtle off 20-foot cliffs, without a second thought, to land effortlessly 20 or 30 feet below. Maybe they never learned to ski the steeps, or just chose to avoid the sections they couldn't handle. We watched skiers drop 15 feet into Corbett's Couloir—an exercise in the aerodynamics of dead weight.

There are areas that are famous for air. You won't always see the flight paths listed on the trail map, but aficionados talk of the cornice at Squaw and Mammoth, the falls at Vail. Sugarbush has a trail called Organ-grinder that goes by the unofficial name of Grinder-Air-Grinder, in respect for the series of ledges, catwalks, and cliffs that allow skiers to hang it out and haul it back.

You can indulge in this experience at any resort, wherever there is a sudden change in terrain. Just remember the words to that old Quaker hymn: "It's a gift to be simple, it's a gift to be free. It's a gift to come down, where you want to be."

Beauty and the beast: riding the ridge above Pallavicini at Arapahoe Basin. (Photo: Keystone)

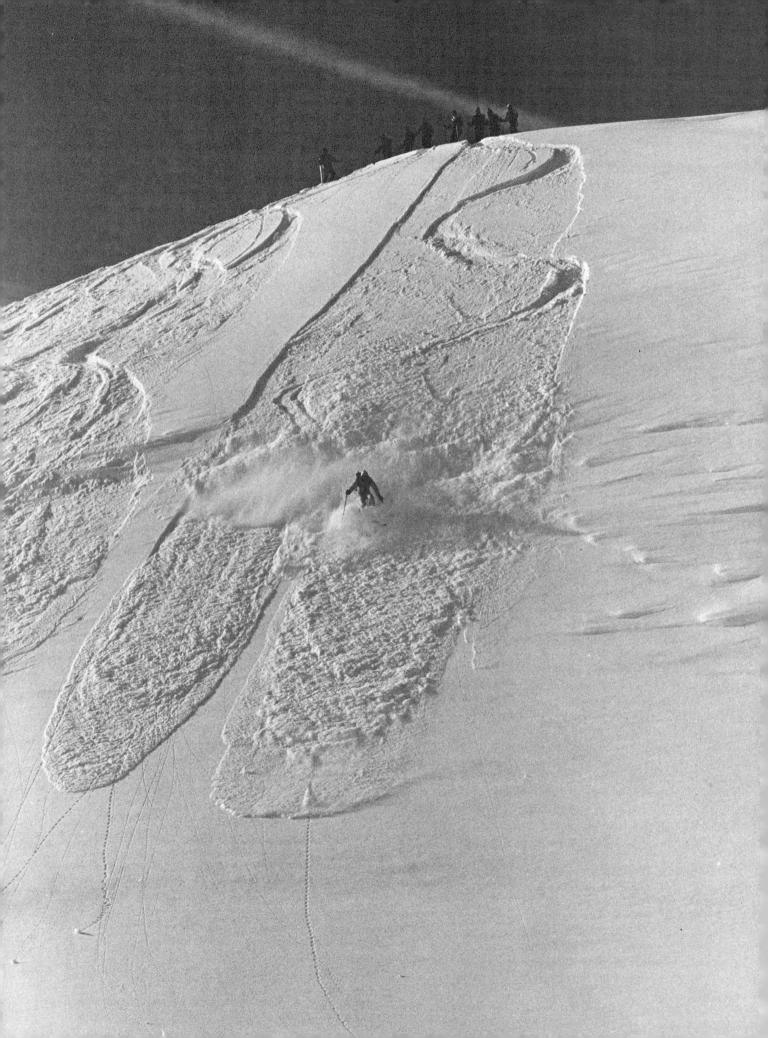

30
TREES: THE ADVENTURE OF GETTING WOOD

Tree skiing is a rite of passage. It belongs to the skillful, the deserving. Trees weed out the amateurs, the timid. They are natural hazards that raise the level of the game, that reveal the pleasures of assumed-risk skiing. When a skier knows what his skis can do, when he can turn the mothers when and where he wants to, he is ready for the experience we call getting wood. Bushwhacking.

It is a natural evolution. At first skiers tend to ski the trail map—the green, blue, and black highways that cut through the dark green, uncharted, unnamed, forbidden areas. When the skier realizes that he is capable of negotiating the trees, whole sections of the mountain extend an open invitation. The skier begins to establish a serious intimacy with the mountain. A few feet off the trail he encounters the forest primeval. The ungroomed mountain. The trees close ranks behind. The Go-for-It Air Force, the out-of-control bombers are left behind.

Every mountain is different. The forests are the unique product of the environment. Heavenly Valley has massive ponderosa pines that form a quiet cathedral for the ad-

venturous skier. The Douglas firs on Walkyrie at Taos are sentinels, watching the brave do battle with the elements. The thin silver aspens on Ajax are like the brushstrokes of a Japanese painting, tighter in the area known as Difficult Creek. The ghost trees of Twilight and Shadows at Steamboat —aspens and pines covered with hoarfrost— are spectral beings from another world. There are Jeffries, lodge poles, cedars, birch, Douglas, aspens, firs, and ponderosa. Take your pick. The Glades at Mad River. Paradise at Sugarbush. Sunnyside at Crystal. The North Face of Crested Butte. Red Dog, Broken Arrow, and Blow Your Mind at Squaw. The Echo Woods at Killington (or either side of Boomerang and Pipeline). The glades off Nosedive at Stowe. The vast terrain between Casper and Après Vous at Jackson. The massive trees off Chair 6 at Telluride. Riva Glade at Vail.

When a skier leaves the trail map, he encounters the mountain without makeup, the way it was before the hand of man touched it. There are secrets to skiing the trees. A golfer once told us that when he hits a drive, he

The problem with the steeps is that sometimes you play tag with the snow. (Photo: Peter Wingle)

Getting wood at Steamboat: Doug Muller on Twilight in late January. (Photo: Ron Dahlquist)

visualizes the path of the ball through the air. The trajectory is complete in his mind before he begins. Similarly, Zen archers do not *shoot* an arrow *at* a target. They envision the arrow, the shot, the target, and the hit as a single event. Something like this applies to getting wood. An instructor at Steamboat told us that the secret to skiing trees is this: Don't ski the trees; ski the spaces between the trees. Also, don't be afraid to bail out. When you blow it, it is better to fall down than to have carnal knowledge with a ponderosa pine. Trees array themselves according to a logic of nature—sunlight and water —that the skier understands almost intuitively. He can sense the openings. It is not

unlike broken field running, only with tree skiing, you don't have blocking ahead of you. The trees brush your peripheral vision, then disappear. The eroticism of the close call. A miss is as good as a smile.

The rewards are obvious. Trees are the guardians of secret powder preserves. The skier is far from the madding crowd, floating through snow that is light, feathery, well preserved by the shadows. In the silence, the skier may find himself providing his own soundtrack, making swooshing noises as he links one turn after another. It brings to mind the paradox we learned in college. If a skier moves through a forest when there's no one around, does he make a sound?

Getting wood, take two: rating some executive timber off Shadows at Steamboat.
(Photo: Ron Dahlquist)

31
STEEPS: THE POWER

Gravity comes in many shapes. There are steep, smooth bowls that go on forever. Headwalls that cause the bottom to drop out of your stomach. Narrow cuts through trees, under chair lifts. Cliffs. Cornices. Avalanche chutes. Couloirs. Creekbeds.

Gravity is the thrust, the horsepower, the driving force, the hidden source of energy for this elegant dance we call skiing. Denise Mc-Cluggage has described this sport as "essentially a fall, a long controlled fall from mountain top to mountain base." Skiers take the instinctive terror of heights, of vertical feet, and turn it into a game of challenge and calculated risk. They cajole, argue, go along for the ride, gambling on their ability to decipher the knotted shape of gravity. As their skills develop, skiers seek to experience the full power, the maximum energy a mountain has to offer.

Novices ski trails with a 25 percent grade or less. The trail falls 25 feet for every 100 feet of horizontal travel. Intermediates ski trails that range from 20 percent grades to 40 percent grades. Experts ski everything else— slopes that range from 40 percent grades to

absolute vertical. We have been told that a slope that has a grade higher than 55 percent will not hold snow. There is a gentlemen's agreement between gravity, snow, and mountain. It is nature's way of telling skiers to calm down.

When a skier makes a mistake on an intermediate trail, little happens. He may pick up speed, but there is plenty of room (and time) to recover. When a skier makes a mistake in an avalanche chute, there is no cushion. The acceleration is immediate and quickly becomes terminal. One break in concentration, a moment of hesitation, and the mountain takes over. The skier goes from controlled descent to free fall. He does not pass Go. On the steeps, every act is crucial. The skier doesn't just fall; he plummets, out of control. He hits bottom, or worse.

By the time a skier is ready to tackle the steeps, he has more than a casual understanding of gravity. He has a confidence in technique, the mechanics of cruising. Most of the books of ski instruction do not have separate chapters on skiing the steeps. Essentially, the technique is the same. It's the

Dodge City: An adventurous tree skier at Park City risks going out on a limb. (Photo: Pat McDowell)

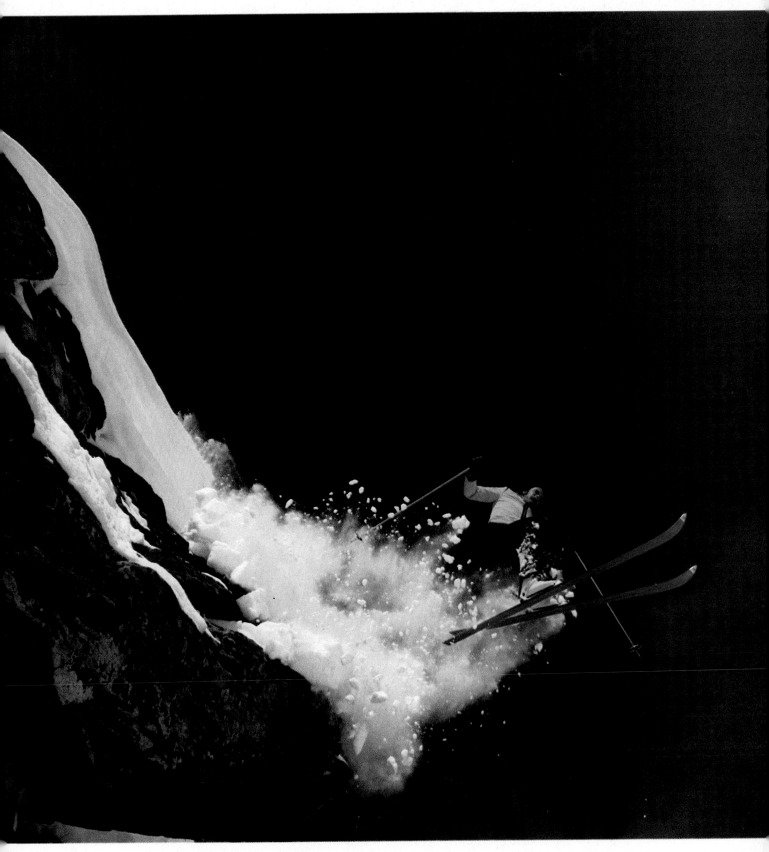

Been down so long it looks like up to me: more air at Jackson. (Photo: Bruce Morley)

The shadow knows: A High Mountains Helicopter client gets air near Jackson.
(Photo: © 1979 Bob Woodall)

confidence, the attitude, that is different.

The steepest runs in America comprise the major leagues of skiing. At Alta, there is High Rustler, the slopes off the Yellow Trail, the Baldy Chutes. At Jackson, the Hobacks, the Alta chutes, and Lander Bowl. At Telluride, the Plunge and Spiral Stairs. At Arapahoe, Pallavicini. At Sun Valley, Christmas Bowl. At Snowbird, Pipeline, Mach Schnell, and Wilbere Chute. At Stowe, Starr and Goat. At Mammoth, Climax and Hangman's. At Park City, all of Jupiter Bowl. At Heavenly, Milky Way Bowl. At Taos, Al's Run, Upper Kachina, and the Stauffenberg Chutes. At Squaw, all of KT-22, and Upper Sun Bowl. At Killington, Outer Limits. Tuckerman's Ravine on Mount Washington.

Skiing the steeps unleashes a surge of adrenaline. It is unavoidable, the body's way of preparing itself for disaster. There is good reason to be scared silly when the bottom is about to fall out. And yet, skiers who seek the steeps do not do it for the adrenaline rush. They do it for the calm in the eye of the storm. Jean Meyer, head of the Taos ski school, says that a skier who tackles the steep is trying to keep a promise he has made to himself. It has to do with concentration, will power, the ability to project an image of the completed turn that leaves no room for error, fear, or failure. "Skiing the chutes isn't so much letting the adrenaline flow as staying very quiet and concentrated as you begin your turn. No, it's quietly putting it all together."

The skier standing at the top of a cornice clicks on a silent movie of the perfect carved turn, an image that will command and coordinate all the separate physical acts that add up to the completed turn. If he can handle the first turn, he's got it made, regardless of the slope. He has climbed to the top of something called the Funnel. Behind him, there is a mountain. In front of him, there isn't. He is acutely aware of his edges, the thin sliver of metal that holds him in place. If he leans too far into the hill, the edges will cease to hold. He will plummet, down the fall line, in a cloud of dust, with a hearty Hi-Yo-Holy Shit. Too little edge and he will wash out, with the same results. He watches as, one by one, his companions drop out of sight, to reappear as tiny figures at the wrong end of a telescope, down where the funnel empties into a bowl.

At the back of his mind, the skier recalls a newscast that described the ultimate roller coaster. The ride at Great America begins with a descent—down a 55 percent grade. The energy from that drop powers the rest of the ride. The skier is looking over the crest of the ultimate roller coaster. He pushes off. Nothing fancy. Now is not the time to change technique. If he can find the edge, he can go along for the ride, letting the ski do what it was designed to do. The first few moments of free fall are chaotic. Impulses flood the brain, like cars piling into the first turn at Indy. The skier races his skis down the slope, trying to keep his weight over the center. Gravity pulls him down into the core of the turn, the sweet spot of the ski. He sucks the tails up as he changes edges. He connects the arcs of the turn into a series of wide, swooping giant slalom turns. A cloud of crystalline snow, backlit by the sun, chases him down the slope. He finds the groove and makes it deeper. The adrenaline, generated by fear, blossoms into joy.

There is air and there is air. Just follow the bounding skier at Sugarbush. (Photo: Chan Weller)

32
ABOVE AND BEYOND:
THE OUTER LIMITS

Once you have gazed upon the throne room of the mountain gods, a trail map seems impertinent, a presumption of scale in the face of the immeasurable. Somehow the notion that the raw energy of the mountain can be subdivided, channeled, made safe for the masses, seems a mockery. At most resorts, anyone capable of climbing onto a chair lift can go right to the top, turn around, and ski down a trail deemed safe for his or her ability. The mountain as amusement park. Buy your ticket, stand in line, sit back, enjoy the ride. For all they care, the slopes could be made of prefab concrete.

Our favorite mountains are those with something left over—with 1,000 feet of untamed rock thrusting above the highest chair lift. Places where the management dared not route skiers. The following come to mind: Jackson Hole, with a massive tower of stone rising above the Gros Ventre. Mount Baldy at Alta. Squaw Peak. The top of Whistler— all of the bowls and chutes above the T-bar. Delirium Drop at Sunshine. Outer Limits at Crested Butte. The summit of Mount Mansfield. The snowfields at Sugarloaf. Kachina

Peak at Taos. Pipeline at Snowbird. The back side of Arapahoe. Such abundance does not intimidate. To paraphrase Andrea Mead Lawrence, these mountains do not dwarf the spirit, but rather put it into proportion. You are a guest on something greater than you can imagine. Still, one veteran has described the above and beyond in simple terms: "Extreme skiing has one characteristic. If you fall, you die."

More often than not, the impulse to explore the outer limits of a mountain is the result of a tendency to avoid crowds. Climbing opens up whole parts of the mountain, private preserves of powder, virgin slopes, the supersteep. The skier learns to work for his pleasure. He has as much fun going up as coming down. The climb and descent become a single event, a more intimate appreciation of vertical. When altitude is hard earned, one does not squander the energy with a few careless turns. What was exertion in one direction becomes exhilaration in the other. The stretch of the bow, the release of the arrow, Grasshopper.

Climbing, exploring the above and be-

Ain't no mountain high enough: At Crested Butte skiers hike for the top. (Photo: Russell/Kelly)

yond, is a quest for private satisfaction, personal discovery. There are no witnesses; the skier doesn't need any. He finds unrepeatable moments—porcupine tracks in the snow, the abandoned ore cart outside a mine entrance. If he turned these moments into table talk, he would be labeled a naturalist, a purist, or worse. The skier who ventures above and beyond has to be in condition, skilled, comfortable with any kind of snow.

A hostess volunteers to show the skier the top of a steep bowl called Sunspot at Squaw Valley. They begin by sidestepping up an icy ridge that's barely wider than their skis are long. On one side is a 100-foot cliff. Two inches in front of their skis is an equally steep precipice that ends in a tumbled mass of jagged rock. The skier becomes totally involved in the miracle of edging, concentrating on the tiny acts that will keep him from sliding to an unfortunate and untidy demise. His life wants to flash in front of his eyes, but the film is jammed in the projector. The ridge terminates at the base of a cliff. The skier and the hostess take off their skis, balance them on one shoulder, and with a free hand, begin to climb an orange ladder, which they assume is fastened securely to the rock. The ladder gives way to a cable stretched taut across a sheet of ice. They pull themselves to the summit. When they are able to, they check out the scenery. The Sierras go on for miles. The sunlight ricochets off the waters of Lake Tahoe, doing something that they have never seen light do before.

The skier wonders if he can call a taxi. The only way down is on the other side of a cornice. He can almost hear the gun click behind his back. The hostess slips over the edge. Her job description says that it is her duty to show newcomers the easiest way down. The skier slips over the edge, at an angle to the headwall. As carefully as he can, he establishes contact with the slope, planting his pole, pulling himself into the center of the turn. The first turn is cautious. He over-edges. Gradually, he lets the skis slide, stroking the mountain as he would calm an animal (down, boy). He focuses on completing each turn. The price of freedom is eternal vigilance.

At the bottom of the slope, the skier is giddy with adrenaline. This is a take, a silent movie that will last for the rest of his life. He recalls the details: the lichen on the face of the cliff, the layers of rock, the orange flecks of paint, the sheen of the ice, the exact size of the mark in the snow made by the toe of his boot. He will never be less than the person who did this.

Out to launch: Brian O'Keefe in suborbital flight at Mount Bachelor. (Photo: Mike Epstein)

33
CROSS COUNTRY: THE FINAL FREEDOM

A skier is laboriously moving along a high traverse at Alta. He is lifting his skis clumsily over rocks, climbing toward a notch that will take him to a slope of untracked powder. As he labors past a stand of twisted trees, he stops to catch his breath and drink in the view. The rocks around him seem to glow in the sun. He feels he is moving along the edge of Creation. He looks around him and discovers he is sharing his perch with a hawk and a three-legged coyote, both of whom are there without a lift ticket. Suddenly, silently, three people on cross-country skis glide by, effortlessly cresting the ridge, claiming the powder pocket.

Once a skier discovers the wonder of going beyond the bounds of the lifts, it is only a matter of time before he takes to cross-country skis, declares his complete independence. When the lift lines resemble small towns and the trails look like freeways at rush hour, the time has come. When the resort becomes a city, he goes cold turkey on the convenient and makes his own way. Cross-country offers an escape route. The skier can go as far as he wants in any direc-

tion. Endurance is the only limit. The skier sacrifices the thrill of speed and downhill descents for the slow, patient effort of the explorer. Going above and beyond offers a taste of mountaineering. Cross-country completes the process.

Alta and Crested Butte were the first ski areas where we encountered people who had forsaken the high-topped plastic boots and space-age accouterments of modern alpine skiing. Instead, they descended the mountain on three-pins, skinny skis, making graceful Telemark turns or trying their best. Norpine, going downhill on cross-country skis, is the skiing equivalent of ballroom dancing, a slow, graceful ballet. One skier explained his shift of loyalties: "Cross-country skis put more demand on the person. They require a greater arsenal of techniques, a more intense concentration, a higher level of involvement. In contrast, alpine skiing seems like chauffeur-driven transport." As we moved through the Rockies and, later, New England, we found cults devoted to exploring the limits of minimal equipment, maximum man.

As one skier explained: "Isn't it amazing

The double helix: Two cross-country skiers find bliss and the perfect telemarks. (Photo: Russell/Kelly)

Going home: kick and glide, angel ride. A skier heads for Beaver Creek. (Photo: Ron Dahlquist)

the examples of extreme behavior that can be traced directly to boredom? After you've done everything there is to do on downhill skis, the only thrill comes from playing with the primitive, the antique."

At Keystone, we rented skinny skis, grabbed a touring map, and headed for the trailhead at the end of the road. We parked our car near a collection of buildings that was half ghost town, half snowmobile garage. We entered the woods and climbed for an hour, through a dark forest, past a frozen lake, into a wide-open, sunlit bowl. We discovered an abandoned mine, complete with rusted ore carts and broken-down shacks. We were a hundred years back in time, a million miles from nowhere. We had forgotten our names and what we did for a living. We reached into our packs and pulled out apricots, chocolate bars, gorp, cider, cheese, and bread. As we feasted in solitude, we wondered if any of the skiers we had left behind at Keystone, standing in line at the base lodge cafeteria, were having as good a time. One thing for sure, cross-country teaches you the meaning of smug.

Cross-country gives the skier complete freedom. The Forest Service has put a limit on new resorts. The destinations that are available to the downhill skier are the first mountains that the pioneers of the Tenth Mountain Division found. Vail. Aspen. Arap-

ahoe. Once a skier takes to three-pins, he finds his own mountain, his private playground. He can explore Yellowstone in private, go one on one with Old Faithful. He can trek over Pearl Pass from Crested Butte to Aspen, the ultimate way to arrive at the last resort. He can kick and glide, over secret trails outside of Sun Valley, Mammoth, or Park City, to soak in a hot spring with friends. Nature's own Jacuzzi. He can don a coal miner's lamp and pole his way across rolling meadows in the middle of the night to the Pine Creek Cookhouse, outside of Aspen. He can spend a week in Jackson, New Hampshire, the Vail of cross-country skiing, without exhausting the 191 kilometers of maintained trails. He can drop over the backside of Lake Louise and follow a trail to a lodge that has welcomed cross-country skiers since 1930. He can set out on a 200-mile Haute Route around Lake Tahoe. He can sign up with Canadian Mountain Holidays for a five-day trek through the Cariboos, sleeping in isolated cabins and snow caves. He can ski to work, along the edge of Lake Michigan, the day after a blizzard has paralyzed the city of Chicago. He can make his own way, choose his own hours.

As it was in the beginning, so shall it be now and forever. By returning to the basics, cross-country skiers have reinvented the sport. The good old days are now.

Not only do three-pin skiers find peace and quiet, but there are also no lift lines. (Photo: © 1978 Bob Woodall)

34
SPRING SKIING: THERE IS A SEASON, TURN, TURN, TURN

At each of the twenty-five resorts we visited, we asked locals to describe the best day they had ever had on the mountain. Inevitably, they cited a day in the spring. The Easter storm that dumped 2 feet of Colorado powder on Squaw by mistake. The day at Snowbird when twenty skiers did human trail-grooming on a field of soft moguls, bashing their brains out, detonating each bump with complete abandon. The day at Sugarloaf when there was a foot of new snow on Good Friday. The day that Shirley and Jenny took off their tops at Alta. Time after time we heard tales of unexpected snowfalls, empty mountains, picnics, friends, fun, odd contests, crash and burn parties.

Most American skiers are immune to the pleasures of spring skiing. Maybe it's because of the IRS. When April comes around, skiers bury themselves in 1040 forms. By the time they surface, their neighbors are into golf clubs and tennis racquets. They are missing the time of their lives. One of the authors has vowed never to go skiing before March 15. He cites certain obscure statistics. At Alta, the average snowfall in April is about 100 inches, second only to the snowfall in March. You can ski powder up to your shorts. The same for Squaw and Arapahoe. In addition, most areas offer late-season discounts, so you get to indulge your obsession at bargain rates.

The truly advanced skier has no regard for the calendar. He seeks the endless winter. If there is snow, he will ski it. Mammoth is open until July. Arapahoe has had 3 feet in June. Mount Batchelor in Oregon is open all year round. Killington strip-mines its base of man-made snow and spreads it around until the cows come home. According to one late-season skier at Killington, if you closed your eyes, you could almost believe that Vermont was Colorado.

When spring rolls around, everyone in ski country acquires an altered state of consciousness. The grins become four feet wide. The snow still falls, the sun still shines, but the tourists are long gone. People have been known to indulge in controlled substances or reasonable facsimiles thereof. We heard one story that we think describes the skiing subculture perfectly. We promised not to name

Yes, we have no bananas: Doug Mayor captures spring craziness at Snowbird. (Photo: Snowbird)

Ah, spring. When the sap starts flowing and anything can happen on the slopes. (Photo: Greg Griffith)

the resort, but the story has been verified. It seems that some degenerate phoned in a bomb threat to a ski area. A search uncovered several sticks of dynamite in a locker in the base lodge. The management was faced with the problem of clearing the cafeteria without panic until the bomb squad arrived. They sent the scruffiest character they could find through the line at the cafeteria. As he moved past the French fries and hot chocolate, he whispered, "It's a bust." Within five minutes, the base lodge was empty.

Even without drugs, the attitude readjustment in the spring is worth noting. At Squaw, the lift attendants set up a charcoal grill and serve barbecued chicken to those most deserving—i.e., anyone having a good time. At Banff, the locals celebrate a religious holiday in honor of Saint Domini—the namesake of a popular jug wine—by consuming large quantities of same. At Mammoth, there are picnics, costume parties, and bikini parades. Amen. At Vail, the management sponsors something called Mountain Madness. The locals dress up in gorilla suits, banana suits, Tinkerbelle suits, etc., and take to the mountain. At Snowmass, skiers construct a jump near one of the swimming pools at the base. At the end of the day, they cruise down, hit the ramp, and launch themselves into the pool—boots, skis, and bota bags. At every mountain that is still open, skiers strip down to T-shirts and bikini tops to catch some rays.

At Jackson, the bowls beyond the Hobacks are finally open to skiers. Cody is kept clear for the annual powder-eight contest, but the energetic can trek out to Rock Springs or Green River for some fine back-country skiing.

In New England, the faithful make the annual pilgrimage to Tuckerman's Ravine, to scare themselves silly on the Headwall.

At Keystone, a chalkboard near one of the lifts sums up the feeling: "Smile. Everyone will wonder what you are up to."

35
HELICOPTER SKIING: THE FINAL CHAPTER

In this section of the book, we have tried to outline a skier's curriculum, a pilgrim's progress through the ultimate ski experiences. Cruising offers the thrill of speed, powder the variety of snow conditions, steeps the many faces of gravity. Getting wood, above and beyond, and cross-country introduce the skier to the terrain: He emerges with a respect for the undiscovered, the raw, ungroomed mountain. If a skier advances this far, he is ready for the final challenge. Heli-skiing.

Ever since Hans Gmoser started flying skiers into the Bugaboos in 1968, heli-skiing has signified the ultimate in skiing. It is expensive. It is for experts only, thank you. If you are good enough, and can afford it, you get to make first tracks, all day, every day. To the victor belongs the unspoiled. In a single week, a skier may encounter winter's entire repertoire: powder, corn, death crud, mashed potatoes, windpack, crust. He may descend glaciers, steeps, trees, bowls, meadows, entire mountains. He may gambol in the sight of mountain goats, carve turns in the scrutiny of eagles. On the other hand, he

may run into a week of fog and not ski at all. It is a gamble, for very high stakes. But by every account, it is worth the expense.

Here's what it feels like: A nylon web belt encircles the skier's waist, pulling him down, holding him in place in the cramped cabin of a helicopter. The noise from the engine behind his back is deafening. The helicopter ascends alongside a cliff, then hovers over a landing area the size of a dining table. The rotors kick up a cloud of snow that obscures an orange-tipped stake just outside the window. The pilot sets the craft down. The skiers unbuckle, climb out the door, and crouch in the maelstrom, trying to shield their eyes. The guide pulls skis out of a basket attached to the side of the helicopter. He signals the pilot, and the helicopter lifts off. Suddenly there is complete silence. The skier looks at his companions. They are alone on the crest of an unnamed peak, in an ocean of mountains in the middle of nowhere. There is only one way down.

The skiers brush snow off their skis, then step into their bindings. The solid click of equipment is reassuring. The guide leads

them to the edge of a bowl. He instructs everyone to wait while he tests the slope for avalanche danger. He pushes off, moving down the fall line through 2 feet of powder with a style that is as methodical and efficient as touch typing. The guide is as regular as clockwork, balanced, fluid, economical. He skis a quarter-million vertical feet a year, more than most people ski in a lifetime. He is wise, weathered, totally unhurried. The group is spellbound. This is how it should be done. Next?

The group sets off, one after another. Their tracks look like a patrol wandered into a minefield. But soon enough they learn the secret of endless powder. The tracks come together. The turns become tighter, just like that. There is instant feedback. It is the perfect classroom.

On the second run of the day, the group stops on the flank of an adjacent mountain and looks across the valley at the tracks of their first run, shining in the sun. The tracks are a neon scrawl across the snowfield— a snowfield that shimmers with a surface tension of its own. They can almost see it inching down the side of the mountain. Avalanche. For the first time, the skiers realize that the mountain has a life of its own. The snowfield changes, moves in its sleep, kicks the blanket aside in its dreams. The snow ripples, flows, pulled by gravity. They have merely scratched the surface. A cloud of white billows and rolls down the face of a cliff. The sound reaches the group a few seconds later.

One knows the war stories. Nine people lost in an avalanche. Three people killed in a crash. One does not go heli-skiing to satisfy a death wish. One skis to satisfy a life wish, to meet a mountain on its own terms, as an equal.

At the end of the first day, our group voted to follow the guide back to the office, for an impromptu lecture on the history of a winter. Heli-skiing operator Mike Wiegele's guides keep a detailed record of the weather. They take samples of the snowpack. Something

that happened three months ago can lie in wait, hidden beneath a tempting layer of powder, to trap and destroy the unwary skier. Wiegele charts water content, the volume and direction of the wind during a storm, some seventeen factors in all. Anything that might signal avalanche danger. In addition he charts atmospheric tides: when the sky breathes, mountains move. We looked at the fine notations on the graph paper, the record of slides, snowfalls, temperature, conditions. We had to relate to the entire winter. We were not skiing mountains, we were skiing time.

It is hard work. The people who sign up for a week of heli-skiing are not looking for night life. They are interested in vertical feet: 125,000 feet a week, minimum. We heard of one group that was grounded for three days by bad weather. They took to skiing the roof of the lodge and each night entered the accumulated vertical on a chart that hung next to the bar. Heli-skiing offers honest exhaustion, a rare commodity these days. The base lodges are on the spartan side. Wiegele houses his skiers in the Blue River Hotel. At night, they sit on the porch and listen to the owner's son tell knock-knock jokes. They watch the town dog relieve himself on the town fire hydrant. One of the skiers in our group, a lawyer from Georgia, announced that he was going to the post office to purchase stamps. He promised to lick them real slow. It was the high point of the week. This is not life in the fast lane as we know it. We suppose that someone could dress up in furs and take esoteric drugs and listen to knock-knock jokes, but British Columbia will never be mistaken for Aspen.

Still, there are exceptions. The folks at the Cariboo Lodge (part of Gmoser's Canadian Mountain Holidays) tell of an English girl who danced topless in the bar every night for a week. Avalanche Thompson, the ski tuner with Wiegele's outfit, told us about a group from Venice, California, who ended their stay by taking off their clothes and dancing naked at a disco party in the ski shop. Pic-

Over, under, sideways, down: Only a helicopter can give peak experiences like this. (Photo: Gary Brettnacher)

Two skiers on Vowell Glacier, heading for the Snowpatch Spire, Bugaboos. (Photo: Peter Wingle)

Signing a blank check, issued by Mother Nature. This one's cashed in the Monashees. (Photo: Mike Epstein)

tures of the event are kept in a shrine in the main office. The terminally horny can pay a quarter, pull a curtain aside, and gaze upon the decadence of the outside world. What we are trying to say is this: If you shell out $2,000 for a week of skiing, you get a week of skiing. You don't get Aspen, parties, or après ski.

Canadian Mountain Holidays (Box 1660, Banff, Alberta, Canada, 403-762-4531) offers the widest range of heli-ski experiences, with five base lodges serving separate mountain ranges. Skiers who sign up for the Bugaboos or Cariboos stay in well-designed, isolated lodges. No telephones, no television, no contact with the outside world. Folks who ski the Bobbie Burns in the Monashees stay in trailers, but it doesn't seem to matter. Veterans claim that there are slight differences between the areas. The Cariboos are the least intimidating: A strong intermediate can get by. The Bugaboos are for the greedy: Skiers rack up incredible amounts of vertical. The Monashees are for savage ego skiers who are into the steep, the deep, and trees. The Selkirks are no sweat. A word of warning: Canadian Mountain Holidays groups tend to be less than patient with individuals who find themselves over their heads. Skiers have been known to offer to refund someone's total bill, just to get rid of a person who holds the group back. In contrast, Wiegele (P.O. Box 1824, Banff, Alberta, Canada, 403-762-4171) is more forgiving. His guides take the time to teach newcomers the basics of powder skiing. If you are at all unsure of your ability, start here.

Better yet, try one of the heli-ski outfits in the United States. Several mountains offer heli-skiing as an alternative to the feeding frenzy that hits a resort on a powder day. High Mountains Helicopter Skiing (Box 2217, Jackson, Wyoming, 307-733-3274) is our personal favorite, servicing four ranges near the Tetons. Utah Powder Guides (Park City Utah, 801-649-9730) operates out of Park City, dropping skiers into the Uintas and Wasatch mountains. At Snowbird, the Wasatch Powderbird Guides (Box 57, Snowbird, Utah, 801-742-2800) take skiers to the lightest, driest powder in the United States. In California, the Sierra Guide Service (P.O. Box 697, Bridgeport, California, 714-932-7778) takes skiers from Mammoth to less crowded mountains. In western Canada, Whistler Heli-Ski, Ltd. (Box 258, Whistler, British Columbia, Canada, 804-932-5331), provides an alternative for skiers who tire of the Whistler-Blackcomb combination—if that is possible. Most of these outfits offer one-day rides—you don't have to sign up for a week in Canada or mortgage your house.

Heli-skiing is expensive (up to $2,000 a week), but it is worth every penny. We recall a day in the Cariboos when we stopped at the bottom of a run and looked back up the slope at our track. We unpacked our camera to record the evidence—a scrawl as unique and unmistakable as our handwriting. For better or worse, this is how we ski. The print hangs over our desk, a reminder of the day we performed without a net. More often than we care to admit, we study the track, scrutinize the finer points, the sequence of pole plants, the spray of snow marking an edge change. It is ours, and it is all right, thank you. This is the true appeal of heli-skiing: a week of memories that will last forever.

Morning Glory run in the Cariboos. Who could concentrate on skiing? (Photo: Peter Wingle)

Son of Steep Mother: another angle on our cover shot, a real Canadian Mountain holiday. (Photo: Peter Wingle)

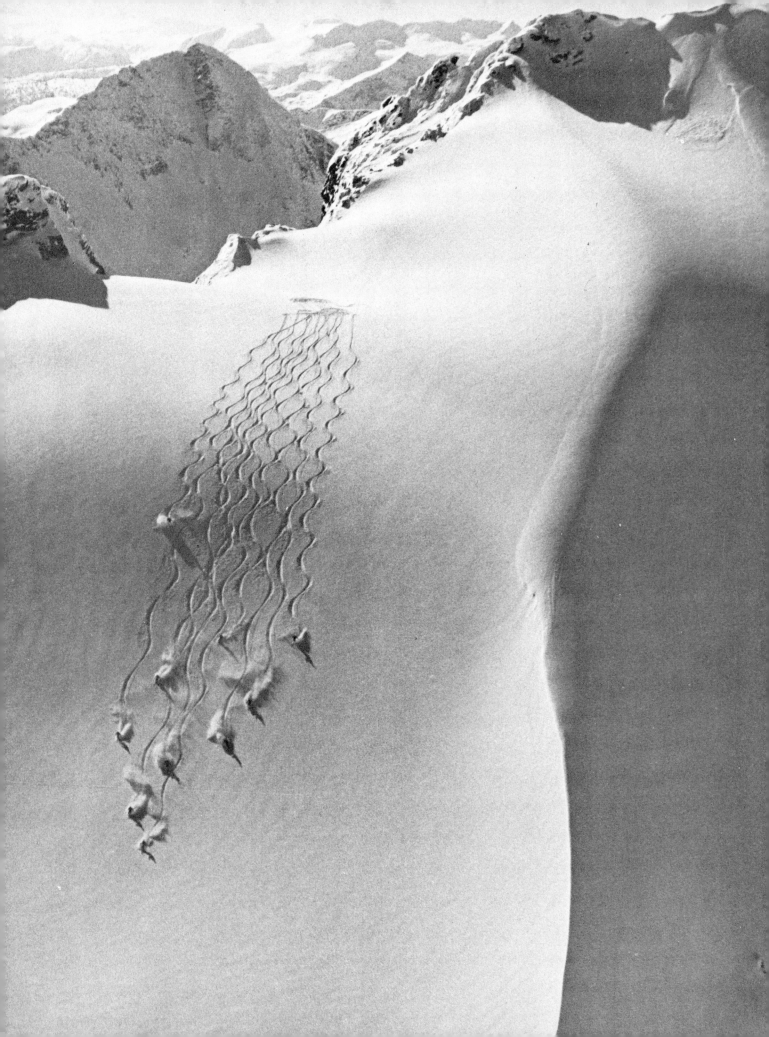

Entering the throne room of the mountain gods. (Photo: Peter Wingle)